Alter-Globalization

Alter-Globalization
Becoming Actors in
the Global Age

Geoffrey Pleyers

polity

First published in 2010 by Polity Press

Polity Press
65 Bridge Street
Cambridge CB2 1UR, UK

Polity Press
350 Main Street
Malden, MA 02148, USA

ISBN-13: 978-0-7456-4675-6
ISBN-13: 978-0-7456-4676-3(pb)

A catalogue record for this book is available from the British Library.

Typeset in 11 on 13 pt Sabon
by Toppan Best-set Premedia Limited
Printed and bound in Great Britain by the MPG Books Group

The publisher has used its best endeavours to ensure that the URLs for external websites referred to in this book are correct and active at the time of going to press. However, the publisher has no responsibility for the websites and can make no guarantee that a site will remain live or that the content is or will remain appropriate.

For further information on Polity, visit our website: www.politybooks.com
This book has been published with the support of the FNRS-FRS.

*To my parents, Marie-Louise and Joseph Pleyers-Siebertz,
for their devotion and their example.*

Contents

Foreword by Alain Touraine

Globalization – not only of the economy, but of numerous areas of social and cultural life – has, over the past decades, been the most visible and disquieting aspect of the evolution of a capitalism which was and still is primarily led by the United States. This globalization called forth and arouses a global social movement, founded on a critique of globalization as well as the defence of diverse sectors – women, ethnic minorities, and all who are subject to authoritarian or totalitarian regimes – which have nothing in common but apparently being subject to capitalism in its most brutal and intractable forms.

The response was immediate; the globalization of capital corresponded to a broad movement, present in most areas of the world. Although it assumed different names in various countries, notably in the United States, the movement rapidly positioned itself as 'alter-globalization' rather than 'anti-globalization' – the latter being susceptible to many misunderstandings. A general consensus emerged that a globalization which could also have positive dimensions should not be rejected and analysis and action should be focused on proposals and strategies to fight the negative form of capitalism.

As well as a great many mass actions, this movement spawned analyses, interpretations and proposals from all parts of the world. To consider Geoffrey Pleyers' the best one does not deny the quality of others; well-documented and relying on the most in-depth analyses, above all it presents a movement both truly global and adapted to the economic context of each country and region.

Geoffrey Pleyers is a Belgian citizen who was born in a village at the junction of three borders: of the Netherlands, Germany and Belgium itself. It is an extraordinary region which, having lost all the industries on which its wealth was based (mining, iron and steel, textiles), was able, in a matter of years, to attain a better and more dynamic situation than many parts of Belgium. Like many others in this region, Geoffrey Pleyers attributes this rapid and remarkable recovery to the region's openness to the outside world, both necessitated and made possible in the first place by the quasi-coexistence of several cultures and networks of exchange. Thus Geoffrey Pleyers' origins may have contributed to shaping the perspectives of a man who not only possesses a deep knowledge of Western Europe and Mexico, but who has criss-crossed the globe for a decade, studying almost all national and international forums on-site, and who was able to grasp from the outset that the diversity of forms of action in the movement was not simply a product of the internal diversity of the movement.

The main contribution of Geoffrey Pleyers, and what makes this book an indispensable tool, is that he clearly exposes the mixed strengths and weaknesses of a movement which was, and remains, a grassroots movement in which activists from poor countries occupy a place observed in no other movement. This remarkable fact forces one to acknowledge from the start the strength, originality and dynamism of a movement which, starting in the south of Brazil, has organized gatherings and forums on all continents. It is impossible to shake off this impression. Briefly, without losing sight of the different forms of action in each country and in each stage of its development, it is a solid and incontrovertible fact that the contemporary world has never known a movement as large and dynamic, in all parts of the world, as the alter-globalization movement.

This first observation rapidly leads to a second. This movement was not only a response to the impact and apparent triumph of capitalist globalization. Not only has it contributed greatly to the feminist cause and the defence of minority rights, but above and beyond this – and here lies the most important observation – this movement has not sought its legitimacy in the crisis of an economic, political or cultural system. The movement has not only been critical. In fact, it was and is the first large social movement to have been founded less on rejection than on the assertion of the rights of a large majority of the population. While, at its most extreme, the globalization of capitalism created a distance and even a rupture between the very rich and the others, the alter-globalization movement, because it brought together all dimensions of criticism and claims, managed to oppose the most powerful economic forces. Beyond all specific demands, it asserted itself first and foremost as the defender of the rights of human beings, ransacked in so many fields and places by the very fact of the global, hegemonic nature of an extreme capitalism, so irrational that those whom the alter-globalization movement fought must soon collapse under the weight of their own irrationality.

Rather than attacking different forms of domination, or seeking the reasons for the formation of social movements in the 'laws' of capitalist economy, the alter-globalization movement accorded first rank to the rights of those for whom and in whose name it fought, rather than to the nature of that which it fought. The alter-globalization movement was the first movement to assert a concept of human rights, freedom and justice within globalization, recalling the great moments and texts at the end of the eighteenth century in France and the United States, while, over the past half-century, positive discourses were weakened to the point of being reduced to an increasingly feeble economism, incapable of explaining the importance of new movements – new because of their location, and new because of the nature of the groups they defended through recourse to fundamental human rights. This is why these powerful movements were not aimed at the revolutionary goal of taking the power of the state by force.

But this discovery of the specific characteristics of the alter-globalization movement leads to an understanding of the weaknesses of this movement – weaknesses which are continually recognized and do not justify a purely critical judgement of these actors, who have so widely awakened struggles against injustice. The globalized economy is a system of production which provides a particularly large amount of power to centres of economic decision-making, which are almost always situated at the heart of the most powerful national economies, and specifically the

United States. But can the alter-globalization movement directly confront a political power? I have already provided the obvious response: simultaneously, a social, cultural and political movement, the alter-globalization movement, which has given rise to so much activism, could not directly and victoriously attack the globalized capitalism's economic and political centres of power. Some believe that it is possible and even necessary to focus action on a direct offensive against the United States and its allies. This approach has gained greatest influence in France (largely due to the impact of *Le Monde Diplomatique*), where it led the ATTAC movement to adopt a properly political programme, at least until the 2007 change in leadership. However, as much as the movement could be strong at the base, strength at the top was impossible because national and local powers, as well as cultural contexts in each country, prevented the fusion of all the components of the movement into a force and political or military action capable of overturning global capitalism. While some collective actions, from Seattle to Genoa, demonstrated that confrontation with adversaries could quickly become violent, the political action of the movement at the international level remained weak. The movement cannot be blamed for this weakness, since for several years the attention of the entire world was captured far more by the alter-globalization movement than by the Davos summits, which were clearly linked to economic and political elites of the most powerful countries and didn't attract a comparable interest. For a certain period, it even seemed that the Davos Club sought to imitate the alter-globalization movement in some ways. In fact, as history was soon to show, this global capitalism even escaped the control of those who led it. But the absence of political results fragmented and divided the movement. While the French increasingly prioritized political action, in the Jacobin tradition of their country, in most other regions this approach was rejected, both because it divided the movement and because, in a more general way, it was impossible to force a political concept on a movement which had always been stronger and more creative at the base than at the top. The declining leadership of the French movement by ATTAC activists represented the end of a trend which in reality was never in the majority internationally.

But what weakened the movement the most was the collapse of the economic system it fought. A series of 'bubbles' bursting and the emergence of several financial scandals heralded a major crisis which, starting in 2007, became visible to everyone, spreading from the subprime crisis (that is, mortgage credit) to the entire financial system. Because neither the economy nor collective social action could fight the crisis, which risked becoming more serious than that of 1929, it became necessary, in a movement made possible by improved economic understanding, for States, led by the United States and large European countries – while the European Union itself did not play a major role – to pour trillions of dollars into the paralysed economy, stimulating motion and liquidities without which the economy would have exploded.

It would be bad faith to condemn the powerlessness of the alter-globalization movement here, because the banking sector and billionaire businesses had no greater success in acting on the financial system until the States, and no longer the bankers, took charge of a situation which teetered daily on the verge of catastrophe, a run on the banks.

This brings us back to the conclusion which I alluded to at the beginning of this foreword. The global nature of capitalism, the great autonomy of financial capital from 'the real economy' (a separation which is obviously never complete) and the alter-globalization movement are different aspects of a more global crisis that we could consider to be the end of a thirty-year period during which the neoliberals, beginning with President Reagan and Prime Minister Thatcher, held nearly complete sway over the global economy and, consequently, over the lives of most people in the world. The alter-globalization movement grasped this transformation best: the end of the blind, unlimited belief in the rationality of the market; the reappearance in economic thought of the indispensable role of the state; and the reappearance in thought of the equally indispensable role of a vision of human beings which does not reduce them – either individually or collectively – to the caricature of *Homo economicus*, which had thought to achieve the triumph of rationality by trusting in economic conduct deemed rational, with all other conduct considered irrational.

One cannot expect that, after several years or decades of crises, more or less serious, global economic life will return to the way it was before 2008. What this movement made clearest was the urgent necessity of reconstructing ways of thinking and acting capable of mobilizing all dimensions of human action, in order to resume wilful control over economic activities which had succeeded in escaping all bounds and all the regulatory forces indispensable to the functioning of such an economic system. The contemporary economy cannot be reduced to the movement by which leading economic actors cast off all forms of control. That is only the first aspect of this economic system. The second is the re-establishment of mechanisms and institutions capable of regulating and controlling the economic world in order to ensure the redistribution of wealth and a decrease in inequality. The alter-globalization movement asserted the necessity of breaking with the Washington Consensus and seeking the equivalent of what was, after the Second World War, an alliance between a strong state and social movements, sufficiently powerful to push the state to subject the economy once again to the demands of justice. There is thus no better introduction to what must very quickly become a new political way of thinking than knowledge of the alter-globalization movement. The work of Geoffrey Pleyers offers an indispensable analysis in this regard.

Alain Touraine

Acknowledgements

This book is the result of an adventure that has taken me to various regions of the world over the last ten years. At every stage of the journey, I have had the privilege of counting upon the stimulating insights and the support of four exceptional professors: Michel Wieviorka, Alain Touraine, Martin Albrow and Jean De Munck. This book is the opportunity to express my gratitude to them all.

I am also greatly indebted to David Held, Mary Kaldor, Iavor Rangelov, Hakan Seckinelgin, Sabine Selchow, Dominika Spyratou and Fiona Holland who were all so welcoming at the LSE-Global Governance centre; to Kevin McDonald, Philippe Bataille, François Dubet, Yvon Le Bot, Luis Lopez and Alexandra Poli at the CADIS (EHESS-Paris); to Marc Poncelet, Marc Jacquemain and Jean Gadisseur at the University of Liège; to François Houtart and my colleagues of the CriDIS at the University of Louvain; to Ilán Bizberg and Sergio Zermeño in Mexico City; to James Jasper and Jeff Goodwin in New York and Jean-Louis Laville in Paris with whom I hope to carry on this debate. A special thanks to my fellow research-travellers and exceptional friends Nicole Doerr, Jeff Juris, Razmig Keucheyan, Giuseppe Caruso and Emanuele Toscano. This research gave me the opportunity to spend time with amazing people. I would especially like to thank Fabrice Collignon, Jean-Marie Roberti and Jai Sen.

Mary Foster did a great job in translating most of this book. I would also like to thank Sarah Lambert and Neil de Cort, at Polity Press, for their support. The Belgian Foundation for Scientific Research (FNRS) and the University of Louvain have provided me with excellent research facilities and a freedom that is seldom available to young scholars. May they find in this book a just reward for their trust.

To Rebeca, I would like to say how grateful I am for her faithful support in spite of the time and travels I dedicated to this research, and how privileged I feel to share with her the happiness of daily life. It has also been a privilege to join the Ornelas-Bernal family and to spend time with them at both sides of the ocean. To Gordy, Julie, Shirley, Benoit, Arnaud and Thierry, I would like to say how much I value their affection and the time we have spent together. I am running out of words to express all I owe to the unwavering support of my parents, Marie-Louise and Joseph Pleyers, who gave me both love and freedom.

Part 1

Alter-Globalization – Becoming Actors in the Global Age

Introduction

Bangalore, India, 2 October 1993

Half a million Indian farmers march against proposals included in negotiations of the General Agreement on Tariffs and Trade (GATT), the precursor to the World Trade Organization (WTO). The farmers claim that the GATT will have devastating effects on their livelihoods and particularly on their control over seeds. In May, the global network of small and medium-sized farmers, Via Campesina, is constituted. It soon gathers over 100 national and local farmers' organizations, totalling more than 100 million members in fifty-six countries. It promotes 'social justice in fair economic relations; the preservation of land, water, seeds and other natural resources; food sovereignty; sustainable agricultural production based on small and medium-sized producers'. Via Campesina also seeks to put into practice viable and sustainable alternatives grounded in the idea of food sovereignty. The farmers' network is prominently involved in many demonstrations against the WTO as well as in most World Social Forums and alter-globalization networks.

San Cristóbal de las Casas, Chiapas, Mexico,
1 January 1994, 0:10 a.m.

On the day the Free Trade Agreement between Mexico, the United States and Canada enters into force, an army of indigenous people assume control of seven towns in Chiapas, one of the poorest states in Mexico. The movement does not seek secession, but demands 'a Mexico in which indigenous people have their place'. The struggle is also for democratization of the country and against neoliberalism and domination by the market. Rejecting a system based on profit, they demand a world which 'puts people at the heart of its concerns' and which respects differences. After a few days of fighting, hostilities cease and the word becomes the only weapon of the Zapatistas. In 1996, they convened the first Inter-galactic Gathering, bringing together hundreds of supporters from all continents. This was the beginning of the international People's Global Action network and one of the principal antecedents of the World Social Forums.

Birmingham, UK, 16 May 1998

Here, 70,000 people form a human chain around the Conference Centre where the G-8 summit is taking place. On the initiative of the international campaign Jubilee 2000, they are calling for the cancellation of third world debt. Among the participants are many 'ordinary citizens'; belonging to no particular political organization, they are simply concerned with world affairs. In the morning, scholar–activists hold several workshops to explain the implications of the debt issue. Somewhat later in the same city, the international activist network 'Reclaim the Streets' launched its first Global Street Party, closing roads to all but pedestrians and cyclists. This action will be replicated around the world and its festive nature will be encountered at innumerable actions against international summits over the years to follow.

Paris, France, 27 October 1998

Following mobilizations by a coalition of more than eighty organizations, Prime Minister Lionel Jospin announces to Parliament that France is withdrawing from negotiations of the Multilateral Agreement on Investment (MAI). The decision terminates a long series of negotiations aimed at liberalizing trade, services and international investment. In June of the same year, following an editorial by Ignacio Ramonet in *Le Monde Diplomatique*, ATTAC[1] is born. Its members will eventually number 27,000 in France alone, and it will have local chapters in over forty countries.

Seattle, Washington, United States of America, 1 December 1999, 6.00 a.m.

Here, 50,000 protesters block access to the conference centre. The failure of the WTO negotiations will catapult this young movement into world news. All elements due to make the alter-globalization movement a success are already present in the Seattle mobilization: network-based organizations and affinity groups; use of the internet and new communication technologies; a festive and carnivalesque atmosphere; images of broken windows; workshops where scholar–activists break down the discourse of WTO experts; and a broad convergence of civil society actors, including labour, black blocs, NGOs, green activists, experts and artists. Many other counter-summits and protests will follow, unfolding according to the same model, although without achieving the same success as Seattle: Washington DC, Prague, Sydney, Nice, Brussels, Quebec, Seville, Evian, Cancún, Mar del Plata, Hong Kong, Gleneagles, Heiligendamm, Pittsburgh and many more. Every time the 'masters of the planet' meet, tens of thousands of alter-globalization activists will converge.

Porto Alegre, Rio Grande do Sul, Brazil, 25 January 2001

In this city in southern Brazil, the first World Social Forum convenes, simultaneously with – and in opposition to – the thirty-first World Economic Forum in Davos. After the counter-summits, alter-globalization activists want to 'move from opposition, to the construction of alternatives'. Between 12,000 and 15,000 activists from around 100 countries come together to insist that 'another world is possible': a fairer world, with greater solidarity, and greater respect for differences.

As the first global protest movement since the fall of the Berlin Wall, alter-globalization came to public attention through a series of global events which erupted into the world news. Far from opposing globalization, its activists strive to contribute to the emergence of an international public space to solve the major problems of our era (Kaldor, Anheier & Glasius, 2001–3; Held, 2007), be it climate change or financial transactions. Alter-globalization activists aim to 'contribute to the development, in each citizen, of the international disposition which is the precondition for all effective resistance strategies today' (Bourdieu, 2001: 20). International mobilizations and the World Social Forums in particular have allowed thousands of activists to live a global experience and encounter people from all continents on the basis of common issues and struggles. Participation in such events strengthens the 'global consciousness' of each participant and a sense of her own globality (Albrow, 1996): 'When I participated in this forum for the first time, I felt that I was of this world for the first time' (African activist, WSF 2003); 'As an individual, I felt that I took part in the life of this world far more after having participated in the forum. There was a really different feeling than the one I had at other international gatherings' (Indian activist, WSF 2005).

The term 'anti-globalization', bestowed on the movement at its inception, was quickly recognized as inappropriate for a movement which endeavoured to 'globalize the struggle and globalize hope', to borrow the slogan of Via Campesina. However, it wasn't until 27 December 2001 that the neologism 'alter-globalization' appeared for the first time, in the context of an interview with A. Zacharie, a young man from Liège (Belgium), published in *La Libre Belgique*. He argued that the prefix 'alter' conveys both the idea of '*another* globalization' and the importance of constructing *alter*natives (interview, 2003). This term rapidly became widespread in francophone circles. Diverse variations then began to be employed in Latin America in 2003;[2] while the term 'alter-global' gained currency in Italy. In the English-speaking world, the movement was first qualified as 'anti-globalization', then 'anti-corporate globalization' and eventually 'the global justice movement'. A significant number of scholars and activists have, however, come to adopt what had already become the most current terminology worldwide: 'alter-global' or 'alter-globalization' – which appeared in Wikipedia in March 2009 – terms already adopted by Korean, Brazilian and German activists and analysts.

From the first uprisings to the global crisis

Three major periods can be distinguished in the short history of the alter-globalization movement.

The first is marked by the formation of the movement out of diverse mobilizations against neoliberal policies in all regions of the world. The globality of the movement became increasingly apparent, particularly during mobilizations around global events, the most commented on in the press being the Seattle protests. The alter-globalization movement was thus organized around expert meetings and counter-summits which launched the movement internationally, but also around movements which, like Zapatism, understood themselves as helping to challenge the dominant global ideology at the local level.

During this first phase, engaged intellectuals played an important role in attracting public attention to the issue of globalization and in challenging neoliberalism, at the time the uncontested hegemonic ideology. These intellectuals also initiated numerous civil society organizations and networks – which remained a feature of the alter-globalization movement until the end of the second phase – such as ATTAC, Global Trade Watch, and Focus on the Global South.

The first World Social Forum, held in Porto Alegre in January 2001, marked the beginning of the second phase, which was dominated by social forums, gatherings oriented less towards resistance than to bringing together alter-globalization activists from different parts of the world and, in some cases, elaborating alternatives. Although many columnists proclaimed the movement dead in the aftermath of 11 September 2001, maintaining that the 'war against terrorism' had replaced economic globalization as the central issue,[3] this period can in many ways be considered the golden age of the alter-globalization movement. It was then recognized as a new global actor.

From 2000 to 2005, the movement grew rapidly on every continent. There were 50,000 protesters in Seattle in 1999. A year and a half later, 300,000 marched against the G-8 in Genoa in July 2001; the same number in Barcelona in March 2002 at a European summit; a million in Florence in November 2002 at the closing of the first European Social Forum (ESF); and 12 million worldwide against the war in Iraq on 15 February 2003, a global day of action initiated by alter-globalization networks. The number of participants in the yearly World Social Forum climbed from 12,000 in 2001 to 50,000, 100,000, 120,000 and 170,000 successively until 2005. After its success in Brazil, the World Social Forum moved to India in 2004, and the Social Forum evolved to spawn many hundreds of forums at the local, national and continental levels.

The alter-globalization movement emerged at the pinnacle of globalization in the second half of the 1990s, in a context dominated by economic issues, international trade liberalization and the rapid spread of new information and communication technologies (Castells, 1996–8). However, the global context changed at the beginning of the new millennium. Before the first World Social Forum took place, George W. Bush replaced Bill Clinton in the White House and the WTO had been subjected to its first failure in Seattle at the end of 1999. The internet speculative bubble burst in the spring of 2001, throwing into question the euphoria of economic and financial globalization. At the same time, fraud and the collapse of major global companies, such as Enron and Worldcom, tarnished the image of the financial sector. The Bush administration started wars against Afghanistan and then Iraq. Opposition to war was integrated as a major theme at the 2003 and 2004 Social Forums, but subsequently declined in importance. The 2005 WSF was focused chiefly on global governance and economic issues: third world debt, fiscal justice, reform of international institutions and global regulations, etc. After a slow-down between 2001 and 2003, international trade resumed, with markets regaining their vigour post-2003 and enjoying a period of exceptional growth until mid-2007. China's entry into the WTO in 2002 and its rising power represented a new advance for economic globalization and trade liberalization.

The alter-globalization movement managed to win over a large part of public opinion in several countries. In 2001, a survey was published showing that 63 per cent of the French population agreed with 'civil society organizations which demonstrate against neoliberal globalization during global summits' (*Le Monde*, 19 July 2001). From 2002 to 2005, even right-wing politicians and representatives of the World Bank wanted to take part in the WSF. The 2002 European Social Forum in Florence and the 2005 World Social Forum in Porto Alegre marked two high points of this period of alter-globalization – remarkable for their size (respectively 50,000 and 170,000 participants), their openness to very diverse political cultures, and the active involvement of grassroots activists in their organization and in the discussions which took place.

Between 2002 and 2004, the war in Iraq became a major concern among the alter-globalization activists. During this period of the movement, several anti-imperialist thinkers rose in popularity as they did in the 1970s. Their conception of war as the 'ultimate stage of neoliberal globalization' (Ceceña[4] & Sader, 2003; Chomsky, 2003) was widely popular among the activists: 'The militarization of globalization is now the sole means of imposing neoliberalism' (a panel at the WSF 2002, see also Klein, 2007). The alter-globalization movement globally tried to mobilize against war the same strategies and tactics they had developed to confront international institutions. As they had done against the Washington Consensus, activists strove to break the consensus in the US administration, media and most of the population, and to cast the political decisions into debate. But in the face of fundamentalists and war-mongers, their denunciation of the irrationality of the war in Iraq as a risk management strategy appeared to have no echo until the end of 2006, long after the strong mobilizations against the war in 2003.

After an impressive ascendant phase from 1995 to 2005 – though not without its setbacks and retreats – the international movement experienced several less than successful events and entered an irresolute phase. However, the decline of some of the major European alter-globalization organizations and networks does not diminish the fact that the movement achieved fundamental success on two levels: geographic expansion and the end of the Washington Consensus. The WTO trade liberalization process was hit by a series of setbacks and the Washington Consensus was massively discredited. The 2008–9 global financial crisis vindicated much alter-globalization analysis, demonstrating that it had been correct on many points. The global crisis was taken to confirm many alter-globalization analyses and some of the movement's ideas were even adopted by heads of state. The right-wing French President Nicolas Sarkozy didn't hesitate to appropriate alter-globalization slogans – 'the ideology of the dictatorship of the market and public powerlessness has died with the financial crisis'[5] – and the British Prime Minister Gordon Brown became a defender of a taxation on financial transactions.[6]

Paradoxically, many actors of the alter-globalization movements appeared to have a difficult time adapting to a new ideological context it had helped to bring about. However, chapter 10 will show that, in this third phase, this does not reflect a decline in the movement so much as a reconfiguration at three levels. The movement became more oriented towards obtaining concrete outcomes which its activists hope will emerge out of the crisis of neoliberalism. It is increasingly structured around networks and individualized commitments rather than rooted in activist organizations. Moreover, its geography has evolved considerably. The movement has declined in some of the former strongholds in Western European countries while the social forum dynamic has been reinforced in regions which are symbolically or strategically important (North America, the Maghreb, Africa). Besides, the infatuation with alter-globalization's ideas and with its forums has not diminished in Latin America, as the adoption of anti-neoliberal policies by several heads of state in the region and the participation of 130,000 activists at the WSF in Bélem, Brazil, in January 2009 can attest.

A global movement

From Porto Alegre to Mumbai and Dakar, from Seattle to Genoa, Hong Kong and Pittsburgh, a long series of mobilizations have been conceptualized and lived as steps in the same movement. On what basis can one refer to a single, integrated movement, unifying events and actors as heterogeneous as retired scholars, rebel students, US trade unionists, Indian dalits, self-organized neighbourhoods in Argentina, indigenous communities, Korean and Brazilian farmers, artistic happenings in Italian cultural centres, Whitechapel squatters, actions against transgenic cornfields, and workshops in which retired people become familiar with macroeconomics?

First of all, the unity of the movement should not be confused with the existence of a single organization encompassing its various components. On the contrary, the existence of such a structure would risk paralysing the movement. The unity of the movement relies rather on social meanings[7] shared by the actors who embody them (Touraine, 1978; Melucci, 1996) and on the major challenge they face – asserting the importance of social agency in the face of global challenges and against the neoliberal ideology: 'Citizens and social movements can have an impact on the way our common global future is shaped.' This has been the central message of demonstrations around the world carried out under the banners of this movement, which has declared that 'another world is possible'. This central meaning is the starting point of the unity among alter-globalization actors and events on all continents, though neither individuals nor organizations are identical.

From this perspective, the unity of the movement is not in the least incompatible with a heterogeneity of its actors. A. Touraine (1978: 124) reminds that 'we sometimes forget, in speaking about *the* workers' movement, that it is embodied by unions, parties, cooperatives and mutual aid organizations'. Similarly, the alter-globalization movement is embodied by diverse and relatively autonomous actors and events: advocacy networks, citizens' networks like ATTAC or Global Trade Watch, Social Forums, trade unions, youth activists, indigenous peoples, human rights networks, green activists, third world solidarity networks, etc. From this perspective, the present book aims at analysing alter-globalization as a historical actor which has a coherence of meanings. While a series of experiences, speeches, gatherings and demands can be associated with this historical actor, none of these precisely or completely corresponds with the historical subject of alter-globalization (Dubet & Wieviorka, 1995: 9). However, it is at this level that the unity and coherence[8] of the practices, events and actors of alter-globalization can be grasped.

Two paths to becoming an actor in the global age

Identifying alter-globalization as a historical subject that affirms and strengthens citizens' ability to act within a global context immediately leads to other questions: How to become an actor in this global age? How to have an impact on the world's affairs when even elected politicians are bypassed by decisions taken by transnational companies or by experts at international institutions? How to oppose the Washington Consensus agenda efficiently?

Data from field research show that alter-globalization activists do not provide one common answer, but elaborate two distinct ways of becoming actors in the global age. One focuses on subjectivity and creativity, the other on reason and rationality. Each one has its own logic, its core values, its approach to social change and its ways of organizing the movement.

On one side, alter-globalization activists struggle to defend their subjectivity, their creativity and the specificity of their lived experience against the hold of a global, consumer culture and the hyper-utilitarianism of global markets. Their concept of social change is clearly bottom-up: rather than seeking to change the agendas of policy makers, these activists want to implement their values and alternatives in their experience of daily life, in local communities and in the networks and organizations of the movement. They claim to create autonomous spaces 'delivered from power relations' where they experiment with horizontal networks, alternative consumption and participatory processes. In part 2, three case studies will be used to illustrate this particular concept of social change: the autonomous process which indigenous Zapatista communities in south Mexico have experimented with; an alternative social and cultural centre in Belgium; and networks of young 'alter-activists' who are both strongly individualized and highly cosmopolitan.

On the other side, alter-globalization *citizens* have emerged as actors in the global world relying on knowledge and *expertise*. Part 3 will show how these activists offer alternative policies to the Washington Consensus, producing expert reports that show that current policies are not only socially unfair but also irrational according to economic and scientific criteria. In this way, thousands of activists believe that building a more active citizenry and a fairer world requires citizens to become familiar with scientific knowledge and debates, especially in the field of public economics. They consider the major challenge to be the bounds between the economy, operating at a global level, and social, cultural, environmental and political standards, which are still largely reliant on national policies. These activists thus highlight the urgent necessity of stronger and more democratic international institutions and of efficient measures capable of controlling the global economy and instituting redistribution and participation at the global level. Their approach to social change is institutionalized and rather top-down, focusing on global standards and policies, global institutions and strongly structured civil society actors able to put their issues on the agendas of national and global policy makers. Correspondingly, their organizing modalities are also often top-down and hierarchically structured. Because the movement assigns a key role to its experts and its cosmopolitan, engaged intellectuals, a major risk is that a few intellectuals assume strong leadership of the movement. Case studies of ATTAC-France and of the WSF International Council reveal that many organizations associated with this alter-globalization track have shown little concern for internal democracy. While they promote a more participatory society, many of these organizations have been reluctant to implement participatory organization internally.

This book proposes these two paths of globalization as a framework for understanding the structural tensions in a movement which is diversely embodied by specific actors. We will seek to understand these two political cultures (Escobar, 1992), each of which constitutes a coherent logic of action, defined as sets of normative orientations, practices and ways of organizing the movement (Dubet, 1994), as well as ways of relating to an adversary and approaches to social change. The aim of the present volume is less to give a panorama of the organizations, networks and social movements that embody the alter-globalization movement than to develop an analytical perspective of their main logics of action, taken as 'heuristic devices which order a field of inquiry and identify the primary areas of consensus as well as contention' (Held & McGrew, 2002: 3; cf. Weber, 1995 [1922]).

This requires adopting a comprehensive approach, seeking to understand the movement from the inside and to grasp the projects and values which guide the actors, the way they built movements, organizations and networks, and their approach to social change. This 'system of meanings is not generally clearly provided in the discourse of the actor but ... directs the orientations of the action' (Touraine, 2000: 271). Actors' discourses must hence not be taken at face value. Through analysis, we will seek to uncover the impossible in their aims, specifically investigating the limits of these projects, the structural contradictions, the distance between the achievements and espoused values of the movement, and how these actors differentiate and distance themselves from, or even pervert (cf. Wieviorka, 2003), the founding meanings of the alter-globalization movement.

Beyond alter-globalization, this book focuses on the approaches to change developed by the two paths of the alter-globalization movement as they help us to understand the conditions under which social actors can have an impact on social change in the global age. The progressive transition to a global age represents a profound historical transformation (Albrow, 1996; Castells, 1996–8; Held et al., 1999), involving fundamental changes in political and social spheres. In today's 'global society', the possibility for activists and citizens to take action is not necessarily lessened, but the modalities for effective action have shifted profoundly. This is notably the case because the context of action is no longer national society, and the state is no longer the central actor in a political and social system. Reformulating the possibilities for action in this global world constitutes a major challenge for our time and the central issue of alter-globalization. This book proposes to discuss it starting from concrete experimentations by social actors which have developed two distinct, and in some ways complementary, political cultures.

To accomplish this, we will have recourse to field data obtained in a wide range of contexts, from western countries and from the global south, pertaining to globalized actors and to those resolutely anchored in the local.[9] In a first phase, we will rely on observation and analysis of those actors who have most strongly embodied these currents in regions where alter-globalization was at is pinnacle. In parts 2 and 3, our approach will consist initially of isolating in a heuristic manner the two paths of alter-globalization in order to draw out, beyond the specificity and particularities of each actor, the meanings and coherence which underpin the actions of the different currents. Within this approach, we will first of all isolate the two main logics of action assumed by alter-globalization activists (chapters 2 and 5). These logics will then be illustrated by empirical case studies, beyond ideal-type models (chapters 3 and 6). We will then focus on their concept of social change as well as the stakes and values of their struggle against the neoliberal ideology (chapters 4 and 7).

The encounters, interactions and tensions between these two paths of alter-globalization will be examined in the fourth part of the book. We will first (chapter 8) describe and illustrate three modalities of encounter between the two paths (dichotomization, assimilation and cross-fertilization). Then, in chapter 9, we will examine the main debates to which most of the tensions between the two paths of alter-globalization can be traced: privileged level of action, organization of the movement, and approach to change. Finally, chapter 10 will analyse the ways in which the core tendencies of the movement have been reconfigured since 2005, in a period that is no longer characterized by the hegemony of neoliberal globalization but by its crisis.

First of all, chapter 1 will pose the basis of the argumentation by discussing the assertion of social agency as the central meaning of alter-globalization, emphasize the main dimensions of a questioning and renewal of political citizenship and activism that marked the movement, and make explicit the methodological and field research choices on which this work relies.

1

The Will to Become an Actor

An actor against neoliberal ideology

A constitutive relationship with neoliberal ideology

The 1990s were marked by the expansion of markets in former communist countries, strong economic growth in the United States and United Kingdom, and a period of trade liberalization. Such, at any rate, was the dominant meaning attributed to globalization at this time. This inevitable and 'happy globalization' (Minc, 1997) was celebrated by some, while its detractors often adopted a demagogic discourse in which globalization became the root of all evil, transformed into a general explanation which dispensed with all analysis.[1] Alter-globalization activists adopted a different position. Their criticisms were levelled not at globalization per se, but at the consequences of economic liberalization and market supremacy. R. Passet, president of the Scientific Committee of ATTAC France, emphasized that 'it is not a matter of denying that the opening of borders has greatly contributed to an increase in the global product these past years' (Grain de Sable[2] 415, 8 April 2003). Alter-globalization activists do not oppose globalization but an ideology: neoliberalism. Hegemonic throughout the 1990s, the neoliberal ideology managed to control the direction and meaning of globalization, tying the progressive transition to a global society to the image of a self-regulated global economy, beyond intervention by policy makers.

The origin of neoliberalism can be traced to the end of the 1940s, when a handful of intellectuals met at Mont Pélerin, Switzerland. With F. Hayek as their central thinker, they opposed the then dominant Keynesian policies and the expansion of the social state, which they believed constituted impediments to economic development. From the beginning of the 1980s, neoliberalism assumed a dominant role. This was symbolized by Mrs Thatcher taking office in Britain in 1979 and R. Reagan in the United States in 1980,[3] with their emphasis on 'free capital movements, monetarism and a minimal state that does not accept the responsibility for correcting income inequalities or managing serious externalities' (Held & McGrew, 2007: 188). With the fall of the Berlin Wall, neoliberal ideology became hegemonic. The dominant, quasi-uncontested, interpretation of the events of 1989 was that they represented a total and definitive victory for market democracy. Journalists and opponents of this ideology referred to the package of principles promoted by the IMF, the World Bank and the American Treasury as the *Washington Consensus agenda* (Williamson, 1990). Focused on the elimination of barriers to free markets, the neoliberal agenda encouraged countries to privatize public services and companies, drastically reduce the economic role of the state, limit public spending, liberalize international trade, services and investments, open to foreign direct investment, decrease public expenditure on well-directed social targets and secure property rights (Held & McGrew, 2007: 187–9; Anderson, 1999).

Driving these policies was the will to promote a purely economic rationality, liberated from all obstacles stemming from regulations designed to moderate the economic system. After the fall of the Berlin Wall, neoliberal ideology and free trade were presented as the sole and inevitable path of modernization and transition to a global society: 'There is no alternative,' as Mrs Thatcher stated. Increased unemployment or poverty rates were presented, 'as inevitable fluctuations, beneficial in the long run, or as the result of systemic constraints' (Boltanski & Chiapello, 2005[1999]: 28; D. Cohen, 2004). Placing the market at the centre of the organization of social life and international relations, the neoliberal ideology makes actors disappear in favour of a global system ruled by markets, in which governments are relieved of their capacity for intervention: a world without actors and alternatives.

This is precisely what alter-globalization activists oppose. The World Social Forum slogan 'Another world is possible' was intended to reject the 'End of History' (Fukuyama, 1992), to denounce the notion that 'the future is no longer produced by the unfolding of a humanist project, as conscious as possible of potentials and pitfalls. It is produced by blind forces imposed like a power external to humanity: the "laws of the market"' (Amin, 2001). The first challenge for the alter-globalization movement was to throw into question this concept of globalization, which dominated, almost without debate, in the mid-1990s. Their objective was to 'change minds, a necessary detoxification after two decades of neoliberal brainwashing' (ATTAC, 2000b: 14); 'People should know that markets are not self-regulated' (A. Zacharie, interview, 2003). The 2008 and 2009 global economic and financial crisis showed they were right in much of their analysis.

This conflictual relationship with the neoliberal ideology is constitutive of the alter-globalization movement. It is within a conflictual relationship with an adversary that a social movement constructs itself (Touraine, 1978). Unlike a radical rupture between two *enemies* who seek to destroy each other, two movements in conflict (rather than at war) struggle over *shared* cultural values, issues and orientations. The workers' movement shared the values of industrial society (progress, the importance of industrial production, etc.) with the capitalists of the era. Globalization, individuation of activists' commitment as much as executive careers (Boltanski & Chiapello, 2005[1999]), networked organization (Juris, 2004; Pleyers, 2009), the importance of communication and the culture of the event, are all features of this reflexive (Beck, Giddens & Lash, 1996; Dubet, 1994), information society (Castells, 1996–8), inhabited by both alter-globalization activists and their neoliberal adversaries.

The myth of Seattle

The mobilizations against the WTO ministerial summit in Seattle, December 1999, highly dramatized the opposition to the political fatalism of the market and the assertion of the possibility of acting: citizens managed to block the WTO trade liberalization process. However, an objective analysis of the battle of Seattle soon reveals the mythical and constructed character of this alter-globalization victory. The failure of the Millennium Round of the WTO owed much more to the tensions between the United States, the European Union and certain countries of the global south (E. Cohen,[4] 2001) than to the 50,000 protesters outside, ten times less numerous than those at the G-8 summit in Genoa. Nevertheless, the failure of the Seattle negotiations was attributed by the press, public opinion and even WTO officials[5] to the protesters. One could also note that the issues at stake in Seattle were hardly more important than those addressed at previous summits. In 1994, the summit held in Marrakesh gave birth to the WTO, but attracted only limited popular opposition. Moreover, the alter-globalization movement did not originate in Seattle. Its mobilizations owed much of their impact and their very existence to the dynamism of already well-established alter-globalization networks, such as Global Trade Watch, the International Forum on Globalization, and ATTAC, which had already raised popular awareness about the questions at issue.

Whatever their real impact, however, the events of Seattle were invested with major significance: through mobilizing, 'ordinary citizens' and civil society organizations can have an impact on decisions taken at the highest level, even by international organizations which had previously appeared to be inaccessible. That the failure of the negotiations objectively owes more to disagreements among WTO members than to protesters changes nothing. The historian E. P. Thompson (1963) has demonstrated the great importance of myths and heroic acts in the construction of collective consciousness, just as W. I. and E. S. Thomas (1928: 572) maintained 'if men define situations as real, they are real in their consequences' (see Merton, 1995). In this way, attributing the failure of the WTO to the alter-globalization movement validated the appearance of a new actor and inaugurated a period of strong growth. Seattle became the model for counter-summits, the very symbol of resistance to the Washington Consensus and the expression of the will of thousands of people around the world to 'reclaim the power of initiative and decision-making' (activist from ATTAC-Liège, December 1999). The failure of the Multilateral

Agreement on Investment in 1997, then of the Millennium Round of the WTO in Seattle, came to show that the current model of development allowed room for political choices, and was not a matter of 'inevitable historical necessity' as the neoliberals had claimed. What was shouted, sung and danced at the Social Forums was a refusal of the ineluctable nature of neoliberal policies and an assertion of the possibility of 'another world': the will to participate in decisions affecting world future.

Two high-profile activists, which the following chapters show belong to two quite distinct trends of alter-globalization, can be quoted in this regard. The French-Spanish intellectual I. Ramonet, author of the *Monde Diplomatique* editorial which gave birth to ATTAC, proclaimed that 'the suffering in this world is not inevitable. To rectify it, thirty billion dollars per year would be sufficient. It would be sufficient to levy 4% tax on the 225 biggest fortunes in the world! Thirty billion dollars per year, that's what the Europeans and Americans spend on perfume. There is nothing impossible about it' (ATTAC at Le Zénith, 19 January 2002).

Embodying a new generation of activists, Naomi Klein conveyed a similar message at the second WSF in Porto Alegre, Brazil:

> We grew up with messages of impossibility. It was impossible to confront poverty, impossible to have a foreign policy independent of the United States. . . . Everything was impossible. But today, the world has changed. There is a new generation and now, it is possible. It is possible that people participate in choices as in Porto Alegre. It is possible to have independent media. . . . We are constructing an alternative to a culture which says that no other society is possible.

Thus, while the omnipotence of the market and of economic globalization was proclaimed everywhere, with the corollary that states and, *a fortiori*, citizens had limited capacity to act, this protest movement insisted that globalization had not vitiated social agency. Young and not so young, 'ordinary citizens' and long-standing activists sought to 'reappropriate the future of the world together', 're-conquer the spaces lost by democracy to the financial sector'[6] (a text of ATTAC-Liège, 2000), and *participate* in decisions on which their destiny depended. This will to become an actor is omnipresent in interviews with alter-globalization activists encountered in different countries: 'Either we choose to be a cockleshell adrift in the sea, or we say, "I want to row" . . . , to say, "No, I want to struggle, I want to have an impact, I want to try to influence decisions, even in a small way"' (interview, 2000).

Two paths of a movement

Along with other actors, alter-globalization has contributed to a profound shift in dominant approaches to political economy and to the transition to a global society. In a context where policy makers, structured political participation and representative democracy have shown their limitations in the face of global challenges, how did this global but heterogeneous movement manage to become an actor in the global age and against neoliberal ideology? How did this 'will to become an actor' translate in concrete terms? Responses drawn from empirical observation yielded paradoxical results. Here are four examples:

1. In the course of our research on alter-globalization youth, our interest was essentially focused on particular groups, observed in London, Paris and Mexico, as well as at the World Social Forums and numerous international mobilizations. The similarities in their discourse and practice were striking, though no formal link existed between them. These networks of urban youth, with an innovative and very individualized political commitment, all claimed a strong Zapatista inspiration. How to explain the appeal of an indigenous, rural movement, engaged in a struggle to defend communities, to very individualized, urban youth?

2. Another permanent paradox of alter-globalization resides in the co-existence, within the same movement and sometimes the same location, of very different practices. Can the street parties in Birmingham, samba parades in Porto Alegre, concerts, festive and playful actions really be part of the same movement as the summer universities, conferences and Social Forums' workshops, which bring together hundreds of activists to sit through eight hours of lectures a day on 'extremely boring' themes, to borrow the term of the president of a local chapter of ATTAC?

3. The third example is drawn from the mobilization against the WTO in Cancún. Hundreds of NGOs and advocacy networks had worked for months in order to be accredited by the WTO and thereby gain access to the negotiation centre, in the hopes of having their arguments heard by government delegates. A mile from the Cancún congress centre, an Italian alter-globalization activist argued, 'I am not here to try to influence the ongoing negotiations. I'm not interested in that.' Why then did he travel 12,000 kilometres to take part in the mobilizations at Cancún? A response was suggested by one of his fellow countrymen in the ensuing discussion: 'We don't want to enter into negotiations or influence governments. . . . We want to create something different: alternative spaces that don't follow the rules dictated by the WTO and the G-8.'

4. Finally, in discussing a thirty-year-old Belgian alter-globalization leader, two activists of the same age offered sharply divergent opinions:

> At ATTAC, many people said that Benjamin was starting to take up too much space. But he's the one with the expertise. He works hard. He has written seven books! I don't even want to know the hours he keeps. I don't mind if someone who works so hard is put in front.
>
> ATTAC, they are the people who speak on behalf of others. Benjamin, we know each other, but it really pisses me off when he speaks for me. I don't have an intellectual problem, no problem with articulation, none with expressing myself which would prevent me from doing a TV interview. . . . Really, it is robbing others of their speech; he is out to lunch when he says that their points of view are better founded than mine.

These four examples constitute enigmas which are particularly intriguing because they resurfaced, in multiple variations, in each country where this research was conducted. Their repetition in very distinct contexts indicates they should be considered not as insignificant incoherences of a disparate movement, but as the result of structural characteristics of the alter-globalization movement. These paradoxes become intelligible once we conceive of alter-globalization not as a homogeneous movement but as an *uneasy convergence of two tendencies, one centred on subjectivity, the other on reason, and both asserting the will to be an actor within and in the face of globalization and against neoliberalism.* The first tendency is based on experience and subjectivity and primarily assumes the shape of an expressive movement. The second is centred on expertise and can be considered more of a movement focused on instrumental aims, rational arguments and a modernization purpose. Each of these paths constitutes a coherent whole of normative orientations and logics of action (Dubet, 1994). Each in turn will form the subject of the next two parts of this book. Before that, the second half of this chapter will introduce the major aspects of the alter-globalization movement as a call for a renewal of political activism and its relations with other civil society actors. It will conclude by listing the main field research and materials from which this study is drawn, explaining their selection on epistemological considerations concerning a global, multi-sited and multilayered actor.

Social agency in the global age

Rethinking social change and social movements

Alter-globalization embodies a call for the *renewal of political citizenship and activism.* One of the major challenges facing alter-globalization lies in the reconfiguration of the political imaginary and, in particular, the conceptualization of social change. This means bypassing the classical idea of revolution as well as complementing representative democracy, which remains anchored in the nation-state (Held, 1995). The two paths of the alter-globalization movement constitute two concrete experimentations in this perspective. They establish practices through which citizens, social movements and civil society attempt to have an impact on the course of things. In this context, the alter-globalization movement is inscribed in the continuation of reflections and recent experiences, notably those of the actors of emerging global civil society (Kaldor et al., 2001–3, 2004–9; Della Porta & Tarrow, 2005; Keck & Sikkink, 1998) and those of new social movements which marked the first decades of post-industrial society (Touraine et al., 1980), notably the green and feminists movements, as well as democratization movements in

East Europe and Latin America (Kaldor, 2003; Touraine et al., 1983).

Although it carries over some of the issues raised by previous protest actors (Agrikoliansky, Fillieule & Mayer, 2005), alter-globalization also questions these and tries going beyond certain limits. In the wake of changes wrought by successive waves of new social movements since 1968, the alter-globalization movement challenges the forms of activism and the concepts of change associated with the large movements of industrial society (Wieviorka, 2005). This is the case, for example, with trade unions, which often find themselves helpless in meeting the threat of offshore relocation. Alter-globalization represents an attempt to relocate the struggle and the defence of workers in a global arena (Waterman & Timms, 2004; Carlsen, Wise & Salazar, 2003). While 'claims for the recognition of group difference [had] become intensely salient in recent periods, at times eclipsing claims for social equality' (Fraser, 1997: 2), neoliberalism and economic globalization in the 1990s raised inequalities to levels that hadn't been seen since 1945. To the new generation of activists, for whom Naomi Klein (2002a: 25) has become a spokesperson, 'the promise of increased cultural choice was betrayed by other forces'.[7] Some post-materialist values (Inglehart, 1977; in particular, respect for diversity, personal development and recognition) remain central to the alter-globalization movement, but they are now combined with a renewed interest in economic inequality and social justice.

Alter-globalization also represents a response to the profound transformations in the field of third world aid and international solidarity NGOs. Since the 1990s, the World Bank and the IMF have relied on what they considered to be a 'comparative advantage' of NGOs in terms of efficiency, cost and output, mobilizing them in private–public partnerships (Kaldor, 2003; Pirotte, 2007). Numerous NGOs were then solicited by international institutions to take up social services abandoned by states. Between 1990 and 2000, the percentage of NGOs stating that their objective was to provide social, medical and educational services grew by 79 per cent, 50 per cent and 24 per cent respectively (Kaldor, Anheier & Glasius, 2003: 15–16). Far from their utopian beginnings, many NGO activists regretted being reduced to bandaging wounds resulting from the application of the Washington Consensus, while struggling within a particularly competitive NGO market (McLaughlin, Osborne & Ferlie, 2002). Moreover, some activists became convinced by the idea that 'improving the situation of the South [would occur] mostly through a change in policy and ideology in the North and in international institutions'.[8] Many of these converted into actors and often founders of the alter-globalization movement,[9] transitioning from development aid to shared struggles against neoliberal policies and global institutions. Classical models of development cooperation and international solidarity rested largely on the transfer of resources, knowledge and a model of development from the north to the global south. Holding the World Social Forums in cities of the global south became a symbol of the will of alter-globalization activists to base their movement on mutual exchanges of experience, analysis and knowledge, flowing both from north to south and from south to north.

Alter-globalization activists also want to establish a distance from traditional political parties and 'traditional politics'. Qualifying their political involvement as 'citizen' or 'activist', activists insist that it is 'non-politician'. The ambiguity of the relationship of alter-globalization activists to political parties stems from the will of the movement to *combine public activism with a rejection of some aspects of traditional political engagement.* This didn't prevent many activists from placing their hopes in the electoral victories of progressive leaders in Latin America, at the risk of sometimes becoming disenchanted (Alternatives Sud, 2005). Nor do actors of traditional politics and those of the alter-globalization movement live in two separate worlds: some activists moved from one sphere to the other, while others sought to instrumentalize the movement for electoral gain. Various leftist parties also actively supported the alter-globalization approach while respecting its autonomy and its own logic. Moreover, many parties have 'one foot in civil society, and another in the state. While they represent collective aspirations and organize society by creating strong identities on one side, on the other, they adopt the rules of electoral power struggles and the restrictions imposed by political expediency in terms of leadership and vertical relations over their membership' (Olvera, 2003: 35).

The valorization of diversity

The renewal of political culture proposed by alter-globalization is also founded on a strong valorization of diversity, promoted as one of the constitutive values of the movement in various dimensions: *identity, model of convergence, relationship with the adversary* (opposition to homogenization wrought by transnational corporations) and *models of alternative societies* ('a world in which many worlds fit').

Classic models in the study of social movements consider internal diversity as a feature of a preliminary stage of a movement's formation, during which the movement must 'draw one unified challenge from disparate and changing coalitions' (Tilly, 1986: 546). Through increased meetings and common activities, diversity should gradually give way to stronger group unity. From this perspective, the coexistence of many variations within a movement is only temporary; it will soon be overtaken by greater conformity, as the movement matures, or by a dispersion of its various components.

On the contrary, alter-globalization activists proclaim: 'We have absolutely no intention of making ourselves homogeneous' (a leader of the Italian Social Forum, in Antentas, Egirun & Romero, 2003: 88). Rather than attempting to eliminate difference, they actually insist that it is 'necessary to preserve these differences within the movement' (Susan George, Paris, December 2000). 'Unity in diversity' and 'Our differences are our strength' have become watchwords for many speeches and texts presenting diversity as a positive feature rather than a flaw.

Many social and national movements of the nineteenth and twentieth centuries, whether nationalist or working-class, regarded growing internal uniformity as necessary to their development. Alter-globalization activists refuse to pay the price of uniformity: a limitation of heterodoxy and plurality. This is a major rupture with the movements of industrial society: 'When we demonstrate that the new century and the new millennium are those of differences, we mark a fundamental rupture with what the 20th century was about: the great struggle of hegemonies' (Subcomandante Marcos, interview in Michel & Escárzaga, 2001: 140). While a unified movement implies the existence of a central power, the internal preservation of diversity relies on multiple, intersecting networks. Therefore, on a local and global level, a growing number of activists feel the need not 'for some kind of central organizational committee calling from above for mobilization, but for a network, for communication purposes above all, that allows us to interconnect and make the important points of the movement known' (R. Bolini, in Antentas et al., 2003: 84).

In their statement from the 2002 WSF, one of the most successful texts resulting from the Social Forums, several hundred delegates of grassroots organizations and civil society networks proclaimed that 'each population, culture and identity is the heritage of humankind for current and future generations'. This valorization of diversity was advanced primarily by four important components of alter-globalization. Latin American indigenous peoples demanded 'recognition of the fact that there are many different worlds, that there are distinct cultures that must be respected on all social, cultural and economic levels'.[10] Diversity is also a particularly important theme for alter-globalization activists in India. During the WSF in Mumbai in 2004, many activities aimed to 'celebrate diversity', whether that of sexuality, of culture or of religion. Similarly, the Charter of the World March of Women, approved in over 100 countries around the world in 2004, proclaimed, 'We are building a world where diversity is considered an asset and individuality a source of richness' (Women's Global Charter for Humanity, 2000). Finally, youth 'alter-activists' also highly value diversity, whether it concerns culture, sexual orientations or each activist's individual specificities. Diversity is performed in their demonstrations and carnivalesque parades, where the strength of the collective arises from the individuals' differences and initiatives (see part 2). This valorization of diversity also constitutes a recurring argument evoked by alter-globalization activists to distinguish themselves from, and to oppose, communalism, fundamentalism or nationalism as well as neoliberalism: 'In the face of market and quantitative homogenization of the world, in the face of false capitalist universalisms, we want to reaffirm the richness represented by cultural diversity and the unique contribution of each people, each culture, each individual';[11] 'We are fighting against hegemonic thinking (*pensée unique*). It is therefore out of the question for us to create a new form of hegemonic thinking. It is through our multiplicity that we will be able to make things change' (a Parisian protester, 2002).

In taking on this challenge, activists have gradually formed a new ideal and idealized[12] model of convergence, based on the articulation of differences rather than homogenization: the Social Forums (Pleyers, 2004). It is based on the creation of 'open spaces' (Sen & Keraghel, 2004) and on a broad culture of dialogue and discussion (Whitaker, 2006). Alter-globalization's management of its own diversity is also based on networking, consensus building and tools like Babels, the global volunteer translators' network which has played a fundamental role in most continental and World Social Forums since 2004.

The open-minded politics and practices it promotes create a real challenge to hegemonic thinking as well as to the habits of activists with more traditional methods of convergence and organization (Sen, 2004: 212). The Zapatista dream of 'a world in which many worlds fit' leads to a different concept of democracy and decision-making processes, based more on consensus and participation than majority rule. Consensus allows very different social actors to come directly together, from trade unions' or Via Campesina's delegates who represent millions to small self-help local groups or youth alter-activists' ephemeral networks. However, this form of decision-making process poses numerous concrete problems. While it avoids the 'tyranny of the majority', consensus is characterized by the absence of explicit rules and can allow an individual or a group to exercise unchecked influence in an assembly.[13] In addition, discussion within a very heterogeneous movement relying on a multiform, reticulated structure is often long and complex. Frequently, the decisions which result 'do not go beyond the least common denominator', unhappily for those actors more heavily invested in alter-globalization or more radical. Finally, the decentralized, reticulated structure of this movement is not always efficient: each decision demands lengthy discussions.

Beyond the nation-state: a multi-layered actor

Typically, when people talk about alter-globalization, they refer to Porto Alegre, Genoa or another city that has hosted a global event. The global has indeed become an increasingly prominent level of action and imagination within the movement. Nevertheless, 'a net increase in globality does not necessarily mean an equivalent decline of locality' (Albrow, 1996: 10) – both because globality takes shape in local territories and national contexts (Sassen, 2007, 2008) and because global struggles may become a focus for local action. Thus, the fact that the alter-globalization movement may be a global actor does not mean it is 'de-territorialized' and disconnected from local realities and specificities: the Boston Social Forum doesn't look like Manchester's or Sheffield's. As C. Tilly (2004: 90) stated, the globalization of the movement has produced both common elements – shared culture, practices and action models, such as Social Forums – and diversity, 'because each region's organizers found ways of integrating social movement strategies into local conditions'.

Much empirical evidence indicates that the national level should not be underestimated. It remains deeply influential on the organization of global movements (Smith & Wiest, 2005; Tarrow, 2005) and on the way claims are framed (Della Porta & Tarrow, 2005). The nation-state also remains the main context in which democracy is organized (Held, 1995): its institutions as well as its debates. In this framework, citizens share a language, a specific political and social landscape, and national political actors they try to pressure. Even the EU Treaty aimed at instituting the European Constitution was put to referendum and essentially debated in the national frameworks. A good number of organizations which fed into the alter-globalization movement between 1997 and 2005 in fact emerged at this national level (Pleyers, 2007: 139–7): ATTAC-France often mobilizes on national issues and adopted a structure different from those of ATTAC-Belgium and ATTAC-Germany. With the increase in international alter-globalization gatherings, the issues, dynamics and transnational connections all contributed to decreasing the importance of the national context as international networks and the continental level assumed a mounting significance in the movement.

Between the perspective of I. Wallerstein (1999: 19), who believes that, 'in the current transition, it is useful to work at both the local and global levels, but of relatively little value to work at the level of the nation-state', and those of social scientists whose analysis of alter-globalization is drawn entirely from the national context (Agrikoliansky, Fillieule & Mayer, 2005), our empirical observations lead us to view the national as indispensable to understanding the movement, though analysis should not be limited to that level. The national scale must thus be inscribed within an articulation of other levels.

Therefore, the alter-globalization movement can be reduced neither to its global expressions nor to a juxtaposition of its local and national variations. Research needs therefore to be not only multi-sited (Gille, 2001) but also *multi-layered*. Field research for this book has been conducted in a significant variety of contexts, observing activists at local, national and international gatherings. Besides the World Social Forums and global mobilizations, the main field research was conducted in France, Belgium and Mexico. Shorter research stays took place in Spain, England, Nicaragua and Argentina. Studying the alter-globalization movement at the global level is indispensable, both to understand the broad nature of and challenges facing this actor and to grasp the subjective experience of the global by its activists. The seven World Social Forums (in Porto Alegre (2001, 2002, 2003 and 2005), Mumbai (2004), Bamako (2006) and Nairobi (2008)) as well as several global and continental events – like the anti-G8 and anti-WTO mobilizations in Genoa 2001, Evian 2003, Cancún 2003 and Heiligendamm 2007, and the mobilizations around the London G-20 in 2009 – represented opportunities to grasp the specifically global dimension of this movement.[14] The three European Social Forums (Paris 2003, London 2004, Malmö 2008), European mobilizations (Nice 2000, Liège 2001, Ghent 2001, Brussels 2001 and 2005, Seville 2002) and a dozen continental meetings, including the important 'European Preparatory Assemblies', showed the growing importance of this level within the movement.

At the same time, empirical research on a global movement remains strongly situated and its analysis depends in part on the author's field research. While news analysis and interviews with leaders have emphasized the dimensions of the movement (e.g., Fougier, 2008), ethnographic field research has led social scientists to emphasize the energy and creativity of these activists, suggesting the emergence of a distinct culture of activism rather than the lack of maturity or strength of a social movement (e.g. McDonald, 2006; Juris & Pleyers, 2009; Osterweil, 2004; Ponniah, 2006). The ethnographic approach indeed allows emphasis to be placed on emerging elements that have been largely ignored by other methods. Through its lengthy time commitment, it allows 'adjustment between hypothesis and evidence, especially in the form of interrogating activists about what they think they are doing' (Jasper, 2007a: 97; see also Cefaï, 2007). Moreover, Martin Albrow (2007) has shown that ethnography remains a particularly appropriate method for studying global actors.

The development of our general approach and the choice of field research were adapted to take into account three central characteristics of the movement: its multi-layered and multi-situated nature; the distinct repertoires (Tilly, 1986) and logics of action of its two main trends; and the evolution of the movement towards a more reticulated structure, less centred on social movement organizations. Beginning in October 1999, research material was collected in some 250 activist meetings, over 800 lectures and numerous actions; 152 semi-directed interviews followed a similar path. Informal exchanges and debates with hundreds of activists have been among the most precious materials. Activist tracts, books and documents have also been useful for understanding the expert and intellectual components of alter-globalization.

Part 2

The Way of Subjectivity

It is above all the pursuit of experience that matters: reason always follows, its phosphorescent blindfold over the eyes. (André Breton, *Surrealism and Painting*, 1928)

2

The Experience of
Another World

Resisting through subjectivity

Fifteen hours into the gathering in the village of Juan Diego, Chiapas, which played host to the Meeting of the Zapatista *comandantes* with youth and NGOs in August 2005, speakers continued, one after the other, to take their turn at the stand and exchange local experiences. At three in the morning, it is Tito's turn, a youth from a suburb of Mexico City: 'I don't know how to speak well in public. Actually, there are only two things that I know how to do well: graffiti and hip hop. So I am going to sing one of my songs; a rebel, a Zapatista song.' The atmosphere rose a notch and soon people were on their feet. The young singer took the opportunity to launch into a second song, 'dedicated to Subcomandante Marcos', and then a third. Despite the lateness of the hour, the fifteen or so Zapatista *comandantes* all remained to listen to this teenager, who expressed in his own way the difficulties of life in the poor suburbs, his disappointed hopes and his desire for a better world.

Instead of theoretical arguments or economic calculations, activists of the way of subjectivity strive to resist neoliberal globalization and to construct themselves as actors through performances and lived experience. Against the commodification of culture, pleasure and experience by global corporations, they assert their creativity and their subjectivity, understood as the affects, emotions and thoughts raised by or created by the will to think and to act by oneself, to develop and express one's own creativity, to construct one's own existence. These activists believe that 'That which is oppressed and resists is . . . not only particular groups of people who are oppressed but also (and perhaps especially) particular aspects of the personality of all of us: our self-confidence, our sexuality, our playfulness, our creativity' (Holloway,[1] 2002: 157). Lived experience, the assertion of subjectivity, identity and creativity are set up against the triumph of market utilitarianism. They are placed at the heart of these expressive movements, which resist the domination of every sphere of life by the rules of the market, against 'those who would like to rationalize the art of living' (an actress during 'ATTAC at Le Zénith', 19 January 2002).

This subjectivity and creativity are expressed through the many actions taken, from the subversion of advertising ('ad-busting') to festive carnivalesque parades and companies of clowns during blockades of international summits. Everywhere, it is a matter of 'posing against the misery of power, the joy of being' (Hardt & Negri, 2000: 496). Such theatrics aim to make events attractive and media-worthy, to invite the audience to engage with an issue or simply to have fun and enjoy themselves while protesting. In these experiences of resistance, the actor's entire person is involved in the action; her thought, of course, but also her body (McDonald, 2006) and emotions (Goodwin, Jasper & Polletta, 2001). For most *direct action* strategies, it is the body which is put into play to defend the occupation of a building or block access to international summits. Movement repression and police violence against alter-globalization demonstrators (Della Porta, Peterson & Reiter, 2006) are read by activists as a growing will to limit their freedom and to control of subjectivity.

In the three chapters dedicated to the *way of subjectivity*, we will rely on observations and interviews in five case studies of actors embodying different modalities of this logic of action. Starting in 1994, the indigenous Zapatista movement has implemented the autonomy of rural communities in Chiapas, Mexico. For its part, the autonomous social and cultural centre Barricade is established in a working-class neighbourhood of Liège, Belgium. It hosts diverse activities, all of which aim to create new sociability and practical alternatives to consumer society and to passive leisure activities. Young alter-activists offer a very individualized form of political engagement, in which creativity and the autonomy of activists hold a central place. The Argentinian *piqueteros* are activists in the unemployed movements which emerged following the consequences of strong neoliberal policies adopted in the 1990s. They were frontline actors in the mobilizations of 2001 and 2002, which led to the resignation of two Argentinian presidents in ten days. During our visit to Buenos Aires in February 2003, we were particularly interested in the 'autonomous' fringe of the *piqueteros* who were characterized by a very critical attitude towards government, the will to self-organize and efforts geared towards reorganizing neighbourhood life. The social policies of N. Kirchner and the decision of many *piqueteros* leaders to join the 'officialist' camp marginalized this autonomous tendency in the following years (Svampa, 2005). Finally, the 'Intersiderale' fluid network brings together some twenty very creative alter-activists in Belgium. They participated in the mobilizations against the G-8 at Genoa, Evian and Rostock, but for the most part are active at the local level. In 2003, they occupied a former school for several days, turning it into the 'School of the Cybermandais' with workshops and concerts. They later became involved in the parades of the 'EuroMayDay' network and initiated a defence movement for vulnerable workers.

Spaces of experience

To experiment and to experience

Achieving a political impact is not the first aim for these activists. They are constructed around two aspects of experience: *to experiment* and *to feel* (Dubet, 1994: 92; McDonald, 2006). On the one hand, these activists want to defend the autonomy of their *lived experience* in the face of the domination of all aspects of life by global cultural industries and economic powers (Illich, 1973; Habermas, 1984). They are rebelling against the manipulation of needs and information. Their movements represent a call for personal freedom against the logics of power and of production, consumption and mass media. However, as A. Touraine (2002: 391) explains, 'We cannot oppose this invasion with universal principles but with the resistance of our unique experiences.' Moreover, for the alter-globalization activists, political engagement is *lived* rather than calculated: 'It is very important to me to *live* an alternative experience like this, to show that we can *live* differently, and that it works';[2] 'I *lived* [the European Social Forums of] Florence and Paris, but I have not yet *experienced* the World Forums.'[3]

On the other hand, alter-globalization activists refuse all preconceived models and plans to create this *other world*, and privilege learning by experience, by trial and error, in the process of experimenting. Activists consider the struggle as a *process of creative experimentation* in which the values of 'another world' are put into practice within organizations, in the Social Forums (Grubacic, 2003) or in daily life. They understand 'building another world' from the starting point of their concrete, alternative practices and experiences: alternative consumption, horizontal and participative organization of activists' networks and communities. As the introduction to the alter-activist space parallel to the 2003 European Social Forum in Paris explained, 'We don't dissociate our practices and our objectives. We choose a horizontal, anti-sexist, self- and eco-organizational way of working, starting with affinity groups.' In this 'prefigurative' activism (Epstein, 1991; Graeber, 2002; Juris, 2008a), the objective does not precede action, but is concomitant. Like Gandhi, activists of this way of subjectivity believe that 'We must be the change we want to see in the world.' Activists of the way of subjectivity have seized upon and developed this idea: 'It's not tomorrow that there will be changes; they are visible today in the movement.'[4]

Subjectivity and experience being at the heart of the engagement, it does not only play out against an external adversary or system. It is also within the personality of each individual and in each actor of the movement: 'The struggle is just as strong against oneself as against the enemy. We must be conscious of and recognize the tendencies to pride and opportunism that we all have, since we are all steeped in this system' (young Argentinian activist). Activists' subjectivity is immersed in the movement, giving not only their time but their emotions and their very being. It is consequently also a matter of transforming the self, one's relations to others and to oneself – particularly since the goal is 'escaping the spirit of competition and consumerism promoted by neoliberalism' (an activist during the 'Beyond the ESF' gathering, London, 2004). In the same way, the main thrust of Zapatism lies in the transformation of social relations within communities themselves – whether relations of production, political decision-making, gender relations, or the assertion of dignity as recovered self-esteem.

Confronted with the invasion of life by the logic of the global market, these actors seek to build *spaces of experience*: *places sufficiently autonomous and distanced from capitalist society which permit actors to live according to their own principles*,[5] to knit different social relations and to express their subjectivity. In this way, daily life, a social centre, or alter-globalization gatherings become *spaces* where alternative practices are tried out and lived. They are simultaneously places of struggle and the 'antechambers of a new world' (Ornelas, 2007). They allow each individual and each collectivity to construct themselves as subjects, to become an actor in their own lives and defend their right to be different.

The forms and duration of these spaces of experience vary greatly. Some allow participants to entirely (re-)construct their lives, such as the Zapatista communities[6] and their *Caracoles* (Good Government Councils); some *piqueteros* neighbourhoods in Buenos Aires; new rural communities (Mésini, 2003); alternative squats;[7] and the settlements ('asentamentos') of the Brazilian movement of landless peasants (MST, cf. Wright & Wolford, 2003). The group of landless peasants we visited in 2002 in the south of Brazil had established not only small individual farms on the land they had appropriated but also collective organic fields, a school applying Freirean pedagogy and a health centre which practised natural, traditional and alternative methods. Some of these actors have developed logics of utopian communities, which seek to embody alternative values in their practice and in the organization of their movement (P. Starr, 1979: 246).

Other *spaces of experience* are more ephemeral: border camps, alternative camps at G-8 summits and some occupations last only a matter of days. From 1 to 4 May 2003, for example, a group of 'disobedient' and self-organized activists occupied an abandoned school in Liège. They organized discussion workshops, an independent radio, concerts and parties, building a community life that sought to escape the 'practices and values promoted by capitalism'. More transient still are the 'occupations' and 'reap-propriations' of the streets which generally only last a couple of hours. This type of action was highly valued by the Reclaim the Streets network at the end of the 1990s: 'Whether we were reclaiming the road from cars, reclaiming buildings for squatters, reclaiming surplus food for the homeless, reclaiming campuses as a place for protest and theatre, reclaiming our voices from the deep dark depths of corporate media, or reclaiming our visual environment from billboards, we were always reclaiming.'[8] Less peacefully, 'autonomous anti-capitalist zones' are created by black bloc radical fringes, notably during mass protests against the G-8. They seek to destroy all symbols of capitalism and consumer society (bank machines, bank logos, advertisements, luxury car brands, etc.) in a given area (Bey, 2003 [1991]). With the notable exception of policemen, they target wealth and never people.

Everyday spaces and social relations

Actors of the way of subjectivity insist on the local roots of their political engagement. The Italian social centres lend a deep local embeddedness to the dynamics of the Italian alter-globalization movement (Montagna, 2006). In the same way, though they challenge macro-economic policies and participate in national and international alter-globalization gatherings, the most innovative of the Argentinian *piqueteros* networks were primarily active at the neighbourhood level, whether organizing the distribution of medicine, a children's canteen, the rehabilitation of urban zones, or approaches to local authorities. As D. Merklen explains (2009:149), the neighbourhood is often 'the privileged location for the organization of solidarity efforts and cooperative initiatives, base for collective action and source of identification'. They are also spaces in which alternative practices can be experienced and the value of the conviviality of social relations re-established. Neighbourhood, city and community hence represent *spaces of experience*: places to experiment with new relationships and where alternatives are put into practice. At the local level, activists establish alternatives which may appear limited in scope, but which embody some of the central values of alter-globalization: 'They said, "You are utopian . . ." and I replied, "Yes, we are utopian. I embrace it. But everything we've said up to now, we've done . . ." ' (a Barricade activist quoted by Louviaux, 2003: 150).

Under the influence of local movements, some neighbourhoods have become, 'terrains of subjectivization: over the past years, a process of production of social relations has been at work in the territory of the neighbourhood. This subjective operation has transformed the physiognomy of urban neighbourhoods; progressing from a passive mode of occupation to active, multiple modalities of inhabitation' (Colectivo situaciones, 2002: 169). Activists want to change the world starting locally, with their neighbourhood assemblies in Buenos Aires and their communities in Chiapas. From this perspective, the goal of organizations is not to increase the number of their activists, to grow in order to attain a national, or even international, reach, but to build for the long term and remain locally anchored. Zapatism was able to rebound after its failures over legal reform on the national political stage thanks to its roots in local reality and communities. Likewise, although it seemed utopian in 1996, the Barricade cultural centre has not ceased developing diverse activities while remaining tied to its neighbourhood.

When alter-globalization activists close to the subjective pole meet during international gatherings, they exchange experiences of struggle as local activists. Though they are inscribed within a movement of global significance, alter-globalization youth close to this way of subjectivity anchor their political engagement in the local: 'We have an international goal and it is essential to articulate ourselves in the global movement; but, at the same time, we must act locally. There is lots of work to do at this level; for example, occupations of buildings in the fight against real estate speculation' (young Catalan activist, WSF 2002). In the same way, the results of a large quantitative and qualitative study of German youth highlighted that 'politics, for the younger generation, is not a question of waiting for an opportunity to open up in the parliamentary-governmental realm, but of conditions of daily life, in the neighbourhood, school or municipality' (Hurrelmann & Albert, 2002: 14).

Rather than in global utopias or heroic acts of revolutionaries, the resistance to neoliberalism emerges and the movement expresses itself in 'small acts of daily life of each and every one'. The separation between daily life and activism disappears as

everyday activities and life itself become the fields and issues at
stake in social conflicts. Barricade's Collective Purchasing Group
launches its discussions about agriculture and food policies
from the starting point of the daily meal. In past decades, revolutionaries abandoned their women and children in order to
devote themselves fully to the advent of a revolution that would
transform the world. Today, such attitudes run against the grain
of a movement whose objective is to transform social relations
and everyday life.

For these activists, the world is changed, above all, through
the construction of new forms of sociability. In response to the
question, 'What has your involvement in this movement changed
for you?', a former manager, currently unemployed and active in
a *piqueteros* movement in a suburb of Buenos Aires (MTD
Quilmes), stated, 'Before, I didn't know my neighbours. I left for
work in the morning, I returned at night and I spent the evening
in front of the television. Now, neighbourhood life is very important for me. We neighbours help each other a lot. And because I
am a delegate, I must go and discuss with many people.' In opposition to mass media, which they accuse of having 'atomized the
society in front of TV sets' (activist from Intersiderale), activists
have created local and community radio stations[9] to strengthen
social fabric in their neighbourhood.

In the face of widespread social disaffiliation (Castel, 2003
[1995]), activists (re-)create convivial relations in neighbourhoods
and organizations, thereby linking their personal quest for a more
convivial life to a struggle against the 'anonymous relationship'
on which contemporary society is based and which they consider
to emerge from 'the capitalist and individualistic ideology': 'The
greater the spread of capitalist networks, the more isolated individuals become. In other words, in order to contribute to the
progress of globalization, they must recognize themselves as
atomized objects, they must de-subjectify themselves' (Ceceña,
1997). Against 'capitalism which subjects all our relationships to
money' (interview with J. Holloway, 2003), these activists seek
to establish 'alternative solutions, like collective purchasing
groups, where people will meet and discuss with each other . . . It's
essential!' (an activist from Barricade, 2003).

Whether their objective is organizing cultural activities in a
neighbourhood, promoting the use of bicycles in the city, or

organizing an alternative consumers' network, the creation of 'spaces of experience' and reinforcement of social links are core issues in these groups. These local movements create a local collective and community spirit. This is not far removed from what Alexis de Tocqueville (2000) considered to be the roots of democracy in America. It is also the core of 'social capital' in which R. Putnam (1993, 2000) sees the roots of democracy and individual and social well-being.[10] Far from a nostalgic communitarianism, this means strengthening, on a collective basis, the 'capacities' to choose one's own life, which Amartya Sen (1999) takes as one of the principles of a just society (De Munck & Zimmerman, 2008).

Behind the promotion of cultural activities or of the bicycle as a means of transportation lies an important social project: 'turning from productivity to conviviality is to replace technical value with ethical value; materialized value with realised value' (Illich, 1973: 28). Convivial social relations are the core of activist commitment. Activists locate the roots of their conflicts at the heart of contemporary society, contesting some of its central values. Against the cult of global brands and the anonymity of (super-)market relations, they oppose the authenticity of direct local relationships through which consumers will meet the small, local producers. They call themselves 'objectors to growth and speed', and question the monopoly of economists over the determination of well-being on the basis of economic growth and the GDP.

Social movement organizations as spaces of experience

The organizations of the movement constitute other *spaces of experience* which must allow individuals to realize themselves and experiment concretely with practical alternatives. The way of organizing the movement thus assumes a crucial importance, 'because it also projects what could be another society'.[11] It must consequently reflect the alternative values of the way of subjectivity: horizontal organization, strong participation, limited delegation, rotation of tasks, respect for diversity, etc. Alter-globalization youth are particularly sensitive to these issues: 'Our way of working must reflect the values we defend in our resistance' (a

Wombles activist, London, 2004); 'For us, it is very important to have a horizontal organization, without a leader, in order to respect all participants' (Mexican youth activist, 2003). In this way, the alter-activist camps and autonomous spaces on the margins of the Social Forums, the assemblies of alter-activist youth networks or the Wombles space parallel to the 2004 London ESF were all characterized by a democratic management and the participation of almost all people present in the discussion, and the distribution of tasks among a broad group.

Because lived experience can't be *delegated*, activists are careful to avoid mediation and strictly limit the practice of representation: 'You can't delegate your words and feelings – otherwise, you are giving yourself over to someone who will speak in the name of your singularity, your specificity, your desires and what you need as your rights' (activist from the Intersiderale network). Similarly, rather than a few Zapatista leaders, hundreds of indigenous Zapatistas shared their concrete and specific experience of the movement during the three Zapatista 'Encounters with the Peoples of the world' held in 2007.

This set of concerns also leads to the rotation of organizing tasks within a group; be it within Zapatista communities, the alter-globalization youth camps, or numerous collective purchasing groups. The main goal of this rotation of tasks and the refusal of leadership is to limit the distinction between 'project organizers' and other activists who assume the role of 'passive consumers'. All participants should be the active subject of their own engagement rather than 'sheep who always follow' (a Malian activist at the youth camp, Bamako, WSF 2006). However, in many networks, the rotation of tasks remains an ideal that groups strive for, but rarely fully achieve. Despite the will and enthusiasm for these participatory forms of organization, reality is otherwise in numerous forums: 'In this Forum, there are actually a few leaders and a lot of sheep' (the same young Malian activist). This problem notably arises in short-term gatherings which are open to all, such as the autonomous spaces around Social Forums, or the alternative camps at international summits.

Concretely, some activists become far more involved than others and acquire greater influence. In fact, the limited formalization of these spaces in no way protects them from the play of power (Crozier & Friedberg, 1980; cf. Foucault, 1984). The proclaimed will to equality can also be undermined by the emergence of certain charismatic or media leaders. The Mexican press, for example, never ceased seeking leaders of the 1999 student strike, even to the point of creating them (Rochín Virues, 2002). Around the world, media have generally contributed to the emergence of certain figureheads of alter-globalization who have proven to be particularly effective communicators, such as Subcomandante Marcos or José Bové. For many small local leaders, maintaining non-hierarchical relations hence requires a constant vigilance:

> I initiate things, but that doesn't mean that I know most about them. For example, for the bookstore or the cybercentre, it is not up to me to talk about that, because I am no longer carrying the project. But people want me to talk about it! They always ask for a representative. I propose that several of us go; but no, they want just one. And by doing that all the time, the others dump on you also. When I ask who wants to go represent Barricade, they say, 'Pierre, you go!' . . . There is also the pleasure of representation; the pleasure of hearing people say, 'What you are doing is great.' You have to take care not to keep it all for yourself! (Barricade social centre, Liège, 2003)

These more horizontal and participatory forms of political engagement demand a serious commitment from each activist and a long collective learning process in order to acquire the necessary skills to accomplish the different tasks, as well as to develop a sense of self-organization. This political culture, heavily emphasizing broad participation, is inscribed within an opposition to the dominant political logic, in which efficiency is the central criterion (de Sousa Santos, 2004: 187). In structuring Social Forums, for example, choices are made which run counter to immediate efficiency: 'It is essential to give each person the right to speak, even if this slows the process and the discussion. This of course reduces efficiency but, in the long term, it is the only way to structure a *true social forum*.'[12] However, once adopted by all participants together, such plans prove to be more stable and efficient than those organized in a traditional way, because their implementation no longer depends on a single leader, and because each activist has a better grasp of the plan and what is at stake.

Nevertheless, the time and investment these practices demand are considerable. Each group eventually grapples with the dilemma of maintaining the participation of all and a strong internal democracy on the one hand, and the need for some efficiency on the other. Consequently, principles of self-organization are generally applied with a certain flexibility. This prevents them from developing into a rigid dogma and recognizes the reality that not all members will be involved in the project with the same intensity and that a certain delegation is, at times, indispensable. The point is to encourage a more active involvement and avoid excessive delegation.

Autonomy and personal experience

This *way of subjectivity* is also an appeal to personal and collective freedom against the logics of power and production; to a desire for autonomy in the face of the domination exercised over different aspects of life. In the face of a system and of a domination which colonizes all aspects of life (Habermas, 1989), the will to control and preserve the autonomy of one's own experience against economic powers and the manipulations of needs and of information occupies a central place:

> Most important for our political engagement is having more autonomy in our capacities to act, our ways of being, our autonomy of production, our life: to be able, yourself, to articulate your life, your work, outside a total dictatorship that tells you what to do, how to do it, when to do it. For me it didn't seem possible to live like that. (An activist from the Intersiderale network, 2 May 2003)

This struggle for the autonomy of experience takes different forms in multiple fields of battle. By asserting their culture, their difference and their values, numerous indigenous movements express, 'A blanket rejection of the domination of the market and its bureaucracy, reclaiming autonomy over ways of thinking, life and communication, which is articulated and combines with other ways of thinking, life and communication' (Hocquenghem & Lapierre, 2002: 11). Such community – and non-communalist

– movements combine autonomy and openness, emphasizing interdependence rather than independence or dependencies. The next chapter will return to the Zapatista case to examine community expressions of these forms of political engagement.

Similar struggles are also expressed at the individual level by activists who defend the autonomy of their experience in the face of consumerism and the culture of mass society. The resistance to the domination and manipulation of subjectivities by media and advertising hype is a major dimension of their activism. Cyber-activists try to protect the internet space against commercial influence (Naughton, 2001) and believe they have achieved a certain success in this: 'Despite all the attempts to turn the Net into a giant shopping mall, the default ethos still seems to be anti-shopping' (Klein, 2002b: 99).

The negation of subjects to serve a commercial logic was expressed in a particularly crude way by the executive director of the first French television channel (TF1):

> There are many ways of talking about television. But from a 'business' perspective, let's be realistic: at its core, the business of TF1 is to help Coca-Cola, for example, sell its product. . . . In order for an advertising message to be taken in, the brain of the viewer must be available. The mission of our TV programmes is to make it available; that is, to divert and relax it in preparation between two messages. *What we sell to Coca-Cola is time of available human brain.*[13]

Activists of the way of subjectivity rose up against 'this society in which there is constant formating! It isn't an exaggeration to say that when you walk out of your house, you are submerged in advertising. You turn on your TV or your radio and you receive many injunctions, particularly through the media' (Intersiderale activist).

Some activists believe that 'organizing one's own life and one's time' may only be achieved through the renunciation of their professional careers[14] in order to disengage radically from the imperatives and manipulations of the production–consumption society: 'I used to earn a lot. But I had no time and my job was pointless. Today I no longer buy twenty CDs each month as I used to do, but I live far better. . . . Giving up my professional career was no sacrifice. On the contrary, I was "sacrificing" myself before. Now, I can do what I have always wanted to do' (a 'free electron' of the alter-globalization movement, Brussels, 2004); 'My paid job was uninteresting. It was no life! I was doing nothing at all for myself, except earning money because you spend money on stuff that doesn't really interest you' (Intersiderale activist, 2003).

The quest for autonomy is not restricted to the opposition to consumer society and institutions. It is also directed at *activist organizations*. The new features of political engagement are marked by greater individuation and distancing from organizations (Ion, 1997; Schumacher, 2003), and sometimes outright distrust of them. Just as with actions considered to be *direct*, many activists strive to extricate their political engagement from *mediation* – of political parties, but also of unions and activist organizations (McDonald, 2006; Pleyers, 2004; L. Bennett, 2005; Notes from nowhere, 2003). Wishing to avoid all forms of delegation and to remain in control of their own activist experience, many participate actively in the movement without belonging to any organization, as '*free electrons*' – that is, as *individuals keeping their distance from all association but reserving the right to interact as they see fit with groups and organizations which appear, temporarily, to correspond better to their ideas and the types of action they wish to take.* More than 60 per cent of the participants in the 2005 World Social Forum were registered as individuals, unaffiliated with any organization.[15] Most activists of this way of subjectivity who take part in gatherings or demonstrations do so out of commitment to their own, personal values, and not as a member of a civil society organization. These tendencies are particularly striking among alter-activist youth[16] who strongly challenge delegation and institutionalization in favour of more individual and transient practices. Each asserts herself first and foremost as an individual: 'I am an individual and I don't want to be embedded!' (Parisian student, 2002). Concerned with their personal autonomy, these youth assert an individualism which is compatible with collective engagement: 'Individualism is not a bad thing. To me it's not egoism but respect for each person in her specificity. It is fundamental that everyone be able to choose the lifestyle they want' (young activist from Liège). Individuation, understood as 'production, recognition and use of individual differences, acceptance of each person as an individual in their singularity' (Marie, 1997: 37; cf. Bajoit, 2003; Melucci, 1995), thus becomes a central demand and the basis for new forms of involvement in the alter-globalization movement. Whether in activism or consumption, individual rights, aesthetics, ethics or hedonism, 'the care of self as a central value is everywhere, in good and in bad' (Touraine & Khosrokhavar, 2000: 113; Bajoit, 2003). The orientation of this individuation constitutes the central issue in a cultural struggle which opposes alter-globalization activists to marketing and global capitalism.

Joy of experience

To be involved in these alter-globalization movements is not about self-abnegation or sacrificing part of one's life for a cause. Alter-globalization camps and direct actions are intensely lived, and activists feel joy in being together and taking part in these actions. Reflecting on the blockade of roads into Heiligendamm (Germany), where the G-8 summit was held in June 2007, a London activist emphasized, 'Under every black mask was a smile, in every stone thrown against the common enemy there was joy, in every body revolting against oppression there was desire.'[17]

Creativity, the festive aspect of political engagement and the assertion of different aspects of one's subjectivity are not only the means of engaging in a cause, they are the very heart of resistance to neoliberal globalization. Whether it is a street party in Birmingham or samba processions in the youth camps of Porto Alegre, celebration is part of political engagement. This festive aspect has been very much present in numerous direct actions. After a pre-planned traffic accident, British passers-by witnessed a crowd of youth bursting out of metro stations, surrounding the cars, turning on the music and starting to dance. Their party lasted until they were chased off the streets by the police. In this way, the Reclaim the Streets network endeavoured to challenge the place of cars in our societies. The same spirit inspired protest-ers against the WTO in Cancún. After destroying the barricades which separated them from police forces, instead of starting a confrontation, the alter-globalization activists launched into a gigantic square-dance, using a blend of Latino, North American and Korean music. 'Festive resistance' is fundamental for many activists of the way of subjectivity, though it is often misunderstood by more traditional activists and the press.

For activists of the way of subjectivity, conviviality and interpersonal exchanges are the very heart of the activist experience and the essential markers of the advent of *another* world. For the Collective Purchasing Group of Louvain-la-Neuve, the box of fresh fruit and vegetables is in the end less important than the social relations created by the activity and the sharing of ideas and emotions which flow from it. In the same way, the organization of a panel or a theatrical performance at Barricade is only a prelude to a more informal evening of discussion. Beyond the promotion of the bicycle as a means of transport, people participate in 'critical mass' also because they enjoy the conviviality of collective riding. Friendship has also come to constitute a fundamental element of political engagement in networks of alter-globalization youth: 'Friendship between activists is very important. If you are going to change the world with someone, you must have a relationship of reciprocity with a strong ethical quality' (Mexican student from the GAS9 – Global Action Septiembre 9 – collective). An activist from the nascent alter-globalization coalition in Nicaragua even sees it as a reflection of the quality of the movement in different cities: 'The base of the movement is much healthier in Matagalpa than in Managua. Here [in Matagalpa], people begin meetings by asking, "how are you?" – yourself, not your activist network? The quality of interpersonal relationships among activists is crucial' (interview, 2003).

Alter-globalization gatherings and forums thus came to represent spaces of socialization, opportunities for new experiences, possibilities for exchange and occasions to celebrate. Whether discussing logistics or debating a political or economic problem, activists insist that meetings should not end there, but stress 'the importance of knowing each other, exchanging experiences and not just exchanging emails' (Spanish activist during Zapatista meeting in Cancún, 2003). This is the heart of the World Social Forums, which aim to 'bring together citizens from the whole world who do not agree with neoliberal policies' (French activist).

The perspective of these activists is very far from the countercultural movements of the 1970s, in which resistance to the consumer society demanded self-sacrifice: 'In Berlin's alternative circles in the '70s, resisting was hard. It was not always funny, but we thought that we had to continue because we were the last ones resisting this consumer society' (interview with Berlin activist, 2003). Today it is no longer a matter of resisting whatever the cost, accepting the sacrifices which result from an oppositional attitude to society. Whether through a festive atmosphere, conviviality, new experience or self-fulfilment, pleasure is integral to political engagement. Happiness, conviviality and friendship counter the 'cold relationships' of capitalism, consumerism and mass society. Thus, as A. Hirschman (1982: 148–9) emphasizes, one cannot separate 'the fact of working for public happiness and the fact of enjoying it. These activities bring their own reward. . . . In fact, the efforts of struggle, which should count among its costs, prove to be an integral part of its benefits.'

To *learn by experience*

Refusing all preconceived plans for creating this other world, activists of this way of subjectivity privilege learning by experience and trial and error in the process of experimentation. The Zapatista expression 'learn by walking' (*aprender caminando*) captures this idea and was taken up in diverse forms in numerous interviews: 'We are learning with each step we take' (a *piquetero*).

Learning through an exchange of experiences is also central to alter-globalization meetings and travels. For example, regular visits to the producers allowed members of the Barricade Collective Purchasing Group to understand what lies behind product quality, the importance of certain demands about agricultural policies and the work of small farmers. Similarly, before beginning the Zapatista March on Mexico City in 2001, Comandantes Susana and Yolanda emphasized the importance of meeting with women from other areas of Mexico: 'We will learn something from you and you from us. In this way, we can help each other to struggle together' (*La Jornada*, 19 February 2001). Workshops organized by activists closer to the way of subjectivity focus on the exchange of lived experience among a horizontal and participatory group. Without necessarily avoiding them, activists call into question traditional structures of learning, particularly lectures in which speakers are placed on a stage in front of a passive audience. Horizontal, participatory work-shops are set up against the model of 'schools where people think they know and don't want to learn any more'.[18]

Travels and meetings with activists from abroad have also taken a central place in the sharing of experience among the alter-globalization movement, with 'alter-tourists' whose purpose is to meet local activists and to learn about their struggle and innovative practices. Trips to Porto Alegre, for example, have allowed many activists to participate in neighbourhood participatory budget assemblies. A dozen foreign observers were present during two of the three participatory budget assemblies in which we participated and the subject has quickly spawned many studies and articles (Hassoun, 2001; Fisher & Ponniah, 2003; Gret and Sintomer, 2005). Similarly, foreign volunteers came and went in Zapatista villages, intent on profiting from the experience at the same time as contributing. In 2002 and 2003, it was Argentina's turn to receive waves of international activists coming to encounter the *piqueteros*, the neighbourhood assemblies, and workers at occupied factories. Each *piqueteros* organization had its few successful models in the suburbs of Buenos Aires which, on some days, welcomed up to five groups of foreign sympathizers and intellectuals. Later Venezuela and Bolivia played host to waves of western activists who hoped to learn more about alternative experiences underway. The exchange wasn't one-way. In return, local activists often asked their foreign visitors to share the experiences lived in their countries or from the World Social Forum. The presence of alter-tourists also testifies to international support for a local experiment, providing not only a source of pride for local activists but protection against repression. The latter aspect is particularly important for Zapatista villages that constantly host 'international observers'. In Buenos Aires too, links established with international visitors and foreign media greatly contributed to the re-opening of the worker-run Bruckman factory. Sometimes the contacts established lead to actors from the global south being invited to Europe or North America to speak about their experiences. Returning home, the alter-tourists share their experiences with activists in their local networks, thus contributing to the globalization of the movement's experiences. Anchored locally, singular experiences transcend borders and are inscribed in a global movement.

Activist films, which blend images of the events and interviews with people active in past events, have become essential tools for transmitting the memory of the past struggles. For example, two activist youth produced a report on the labour strikes in Belgium at the end of the 1950s. But it is mostly the recent memory of the alter-globalization movement which the films of media-activists help construct. The Indymedia film *We Are Everywhere* (2002), for example, presents an overview of some of the high points of the alter-globalization struggle, while *The Battle of Seattle* (2008) led a younger generation to discover a romanticized version of one of the founding events of the movement. Both films provide new-comers with a perspective on the movement strongly marked by subjectivity. New information and communication technologies, and in particular the internet, are extraordinary tools in this per-spective. As we will see in chapter 3, youth activists make a very extended and efficient use of it, producing narratives and movies to share their experience of global protest and local actions.

However, these channels have proven much less efficient than unions and civil society structured organizations at transmitting memory and lessons of past experience. During a blockade action against the 2007 G-8 summit in Heiligendamm (Germany), spokes-councils emerged. The young activists lengthily discussed 'new' ways of organizing decision processes through affinity net-works, considering it an original democratic experience. Among the audience, an American scholar activist in his thirties who had much experience in counter-summits wondered whether he should tell his younger fellows that very similar decision-making pro-cesses had been set up in Seattle and then further developed in activists' camps: that the problems and initiative proposals had already taken place in countless protests before. He decided, however, not to interrupt the discussion: 'They should experience it on their own and have this great experience we had ten years ago: believing that we were re-inventing politics and activism' (interview) – exactly what his own activist generation did ten years earlier, 'inventing' 'new' activist 'autonomous, open and horizontal' practices that were actually very similar to those implemented in several social movements in the 1960s and 1970s (Lotringer & Marazzi, 2007; Polletta, 2002).

The feeling of experimenting with new and innovative prac-tices is extremely exciting. However, it limits the capitalization of past experience and leads activists to repeat mistakes that their predecessors devoted much of their energy to dealing with: 'A lot of all our experience and what we learnt from our failures has been lost.'[19] Without structured organizations able to preserve activists' experience outside and beyond individual activists and their affinity networks, the transmission of the experience, successes and failure of the generation of Seattle has often been problematic. For today's youth, Zapatista uprising seems an old story and, even in the USA, few have heard about Seattle, as many activists have experienced: 'I was teaching in [Washington] DC. When I asked to the class if they knew what happened in Seattle, only two raised their hands. . . . We are not doing a good job in sharing with the next generation.'[20] Loose networks certainly correspond to the spirit of the time (Sennett, 1998) and youth aspirations. They raise major concerns, however, about the continuity and the visibility of the movement.

Diversions[21] of experience

Actors of the way of subjectivity are highly dedicated to the movement's internal issues, and see it both as a tool to improve the world and as a space where alter-globalization practices should be implemented. They focus on their own experience sometimes to the point of neglecting their adversaries and the societal change they aimed to struggle for. The focus on the movement's own organization may, for example, lead some actors to focus all its energy on internal logic and aims or to the emergence of a closed identity. Individualized features of this activism culture may lead to hedonist actions lacking in general significance or dissipating in sporadic activism. With the ascendancy of a logic of pure experience, the hedonism of experience as a goal in itself may override the social and political stakes of the movement.

Organization at the heart of the movement

As pointed out in the previous sections of this text, Zapatistas, social centre activists, autonomous *piqueteros* and young alter-activists are highly attentive to the internal dynamic of their movement's organizations. This can extend to the point where some alter-globalization groups come to devote the best part of their energy to efforts to organize their spaces or level – sometimes ferocious – criticisms at groups more oriented towards efficiency than internal democracy. In such cases, opposition to neoliberalism and social change take second place. A. Roy, a figurehead of alter-globalization in India, warns as follows: 'The Forum needs to flee from this great risk. It absorbs our best energies, mobilizes the most generous minds only for us to start thinking, after four days, about the next meeting. In that case, it won't bother our enemies. It will keep being our own music, but it will never reach to be our struggle.'[22] Paradoxically, spaces of experience can in this way come to constitute a means of containing the zeal of protest actors; concentrating energies, for example, on the organization of life in an alternative camp rather than opposition to the G-8.

Dissolution into hedonism

Other, related types of identity diversions stem from the ascendancy of a logic of pure experience, in which the hedonism of experience as a goal in itself overrides the social stakes of the movement. Two risks can be distinguished here: a purely hedonistic approach which can degenerate into a mere pursuit of libido; and dissipation into a multiplication of experiences without coherence.

In the forms of activism adopted by those following the way of subjectivity, the celebration of experience and the festive character play an integral part in political commitment. However, does lived experience constitute a form of resistance in itself? Do experience and celebration constitute, in themselves, political protest against neoliberal globalization? In 1997, a street party organized by Reclaim the Streets brought together 20,000 people in Trafalgar Square. The organizers perceived the party as a political action, but this perception was not shared by the majority of young passers-by who joined the party, some of whom engaged in acts of hooliganism. Leaders of the movement were subsequently worried that, 'the subtle theory of "applying radical poetry to radical politics" is getting drowned out by the pounding beat and mob mentality' of parties (Klein, 2002a: 318). One of the founders of Reclaim the Streets explained, 'If people think that turning up to a street party once a year, getting out of your head and dancing your heart out on a recaptured piece of public land is enough, then we are failing to reach our potential' (quoted by Klein, 2002a: 318–19). Similarly, during a commemoration of the 1968 massacre of students in Mexico, numerous acts of vandalism, lacking all political significance, were perpetrated by some high-school students. Their actions were strongly condemned by more politicized activists: 'They passed a glazier's and broke all the panes of glass. Just as activists in Genoa did at the banks, but in this case it was simply because they were window panes. It makes no sense!' (young Mexican activist). Disconnected from a more global social project, the experience of an alter-globalization happening or an alternative party can have no greater significance than an unqualified search for pleasure, libido. The celebration of lived experience, hedonism and the festive aspect which are present in the forms of political engagement pursued in the way of subjectivity are, moreover, also at the heart of the consumerism promoted by the market and manipulated by the cultural industries (Marcuse, 1981 [1964]; Gordy Pleyers, 2006). But it is precisely such de-subjectification and manipulations that actors of the way of subjectivity are opposing.

The active involvement of each person in the alter-globalization project, minimizing the distance between 'project organizers' and 'ordinary participants', appears to be a means of avoiding these diversions; involvement reinforces an actor's consciousness of the significance and meaning of actions taken, maintaining the link between the concrete experience and the global significance attributed to it.

Fragmentation

Similarly, political engagement based solely on experience can lead to a dissipation which prevents the construction of the unity of an actor. In this case, alter-globalization events are lived by their participants as isolated events, like successive collective adventures, responding to a deep thirst for lived experience and the cult of the instantaneous. Jumping from a happening to a Social Forum, living the political engagement in the moment, the individual activist risks dispersal without constructing a unity beyond the diversity of her experiences. The risk is all the greater because, as we have seen, activists of the way of subjectivity are not guided by any pre-established programme and are often only temporarily associated with any particular organization. Continuity of the movement consequently becomes a crucial challenge.

In this context, reflexivity and a constant interrogation of one's own political engagement are the fundamental parameters by which the actor 'strives to construct her experience and give it meaning' (Dubet, 1995: 120). It is in this subjective and reflexive labour of an activist on herself that a unity and coherence is forged out of the alter-globalization engagement beyond consecutive events and the shuttling from meetings to actions, ephemeral networks to sporadic Social Forums.

3

From the Mountains of Chiapas to Urban Neighbourhoods

Having sketched the foundations of the way of subjectivity, in this third chapter we will introduce three actors who develop this logic of action in diverse ways: the Zapatista movement, inscribed in indigenous communities and a rural context; Barricade, an alternative cultural centre in Liège, which grew out of a local, city setting; and young alter-activists whose activism is particularly marked by contemporary individuation, at once global and tied to local actions.

The Zapatistas

The Zapatista Uprising

According to Mexican president Carlos Salinas de Gortari, the coming into force of the Free Trade Agreement between Mexico, the United States and Canada on 1 January 1994 formalized the 'entry of Mexico into the First World'. This was also the day chosen by indigenous rebels to start their revolt and expose a different face of neoliberalism. After ten years of preparation and intense discussions among communities (Muñoz Ramirez, 2003), the Zapatista Army of National Liberation (EZLN[1]) made headlines around the world by militarily occupying the city halls of six towns in Chiapas, a state in southern Mexico. Heavily repressed, the indigenous insurgents withdrew to their villages. Under the pressure of a large mobilization by Mexican civil society, the Mexican president declared a cease-fire after twelve days of hostilities. Abandoning the ways of previous Latin American guerrilla movements, the Zapatistas have since renounced the use of any arms except the pen and the word. But Chiapas remains in a state of war: 11,000 Mexican soldiers are stationed around the insurgent villages and incidents are frequent. The most serious of these resulted in forty-five deaths in the hamlet of Acteal in 1997. After a few quieter years, incidents have again multiplied since 2006 (Capise, 2008).

Around central values inspired by Mayan cultures, the Zapatistas have formulated demands on three levels: recognition of local autonomy by the Mexican state; a genuine democratization nationally; and an end to neoliberal policies internationally. The movement's capacity to engage at the international level relies largely on the prodigious communication skills of its spokesperson, characterized as the leader of the 'first information guerrilla' by M. Castells (1997). From the outset, the insurgent Subcomandante Marcos provided universal meaning to the movement's specific demands (EZLN, 1994: 243; Le Bot & Marcos, 1997: 209), making Zapatism one of the major reference points of the way of subjectivity in the alter-globalization movement. In addition to Subcomandante Marcos' innumerable press releases, the preferred mode of interaction with Mexican civil society was convening public assemblies in the autonomous communities of Chiapas, to hear the advice of civil society on diverse issues and to make known the opinion of Zapatista leaders. The main assemblies of this kind took place in 1994 (the National Democratic Convention), 1996 (first Intergalactic gathering), 2005 (preparatory meetings for the 'Other Campaign'), 2007 ('Meetings of the Zapatista People with the Peoples of the World') and 2008 ('Digna Rabia' Festival). Large foreign delegations participated in each international gathering called by the Zapatistas, while the presence of numerous observers in the Zapatista zones and the support committees established in European and North American cities have assured that a continuous contact with foreign supporters is maintained (Olesen, 2005; Khasnabish, 2008).[2] However, certain announcements to the contrary notwithstanding, the Zapatistas have never officially taken part in any alter-globalization event.

Dignity and autonomy as central principles of Zapatism

While echoes at the international level are one of its successes, the Zapatista movement's strength lies in the indigenous communities of Chiapas, which are 'its essence' (EZLN, 1994: 133) and the basis from which it has always bounced back since 1994. The movement has joined economic, cultural, social and political demands around two central principles: dignity and autonomy (Ornelas, 2007).

Dignity, understood as the assertion of shared humanity, is at the heart of the Zapatista movement.[3] In rising up, they asserted that 'human dignity is not only the heritage of those who have acquired the basic conditions of life; those who possess nothing materially also possess what makes us different from things and from animals: dignity' (EZLN, 1994: 71): 'What we are demanding and what we, the indigenous peoples, need is not a big or small place, but a place with dignity within our nation; to be taken into account and treated with respect' (Comandante David, quoted by Ceceña, 2001b: 162). While the Zapatista movement seeks political and legal reform to benefit indigenous communities, and while it denounces the impact of neoliberalism in Chiapas and the rest of the world, the primary reason the Zapatistas revolted was to oppose the negation of their dignity, of their specificity as indigenous communities and of their capacity to control their own destinies.

The Zapatistas assert their dignity by demanding control over their lives and over decisions which affect them and which were made by governments and transnational corporations (EZLN, 1994: 51–4). Reappropriation of their lands and natural resources thus acquires a central importance. These indigenous peoples' will to be an actor translates into demands for autonomy[4] and self-determination in which they see 'the opportunity to construct [themselves], within this country, as a different reality' (Marcos, interview quoted in Michel and Escárzaga, 2001: 139), to preserve some aspects of their community ways of life while remaining citizens of a larger nation which recognizes their right to be both equal and different. Autonomy – whether de facto or sanctioned by law – allows the construction of *spaces of experience*, 'a sort of democratic space to resolve confrontations among different political proposals' (EZLN, 1994: 97). These spaces allow experimentation with another possible world: 'It's about managing to construct the antechamber of a new world, a space with an equality of rights and of duties' (Marcos, quoted by Ornelas, 2007). The Zapatista uprising is thus asserted against 'a concentration of power which has taken control of the futures of communities, municipalities and local life; which has practically stolen all of their autonomy to govern and direct their collective life' (Zermeño, 2005: 244).

Construction of local autonomy

In 1995 and 1996, the Zapatistas participated in negotiations with a federal commission delegated by the government, eventually reaching an agreement on the status of indigenous communities and on the legal recognition of indigenous peoples (Díaz Polanco & Sanchez, 2002). Between the conclusion of these 'Agreements of San Andrés' and 2001, the Zapatistas focused extensive efforts on getting the negotiated agreement ratified by the Mexican congress. Several Zapatista delegations travelled to the capital. The last of these, the 'March of the Colour of the Earth' in the spring of 2001 gathered more than a million supporters in Mexico's central square. A Zapatista delegation was then received by the national congress, but in vain: despite exceptional popular success and strong national and international media impact, Mexican legislators refused to recognize indigenous communities as subjects of rights nor their right to some local autonomy.

A new period then opened for the Zapatista movement. The indigenous rebels decided to re-focus their energies on the construction and reinforcement of local autonomy, which their communities had in fact enjoyed since the uprising of 1994 (Marcos, 2007 [2003]). The August 2003 creation of the *Caracoles*, bodies which coordinate among several autonomous municipalities, is a particularly noteworthy development. Outside the system of political parties and Mexican institutions, autonomous municipalities organize the life of dozens of villages, hamlets and boroughs. In turn, since 2003, they have been grouped into five autonomous regions (the *caracoles*), each of which has its 'Good Government Council', composed of fifteen to twenty-five people and tasked mainly with coordinating municipalities, external relations and justice. The 'instigators' responsible for the different sectors (education, health, agro-ecology, etc.) are elected for a three-year, unpaid and non-renewable mandate. Part of the common land serves to provide their livelihood and cover expenses related to the mandate.

In this new period, meetings based on exchange of experience and practices related to local autonomy have replaced the marches to Mexico City and the huge national and international civil society gatherings. The new gatherings were not meant to influence policy makers but to reinforce the process of local autonomy now at the heart of Zapatism and to share this experience with Mexican and foreign activists. The 'Meeting of Vicam' (Hocquenghem, 2009), held in October 2007, was of particular importance as it gathered 550 delegates representing fifty-eight indigenous peoples of the Americas, following an initiative taken by the Zapatistas. The three 'Meetings of the Zapatista peoples with the peoples of the world' were more focused on the Zapatistas' experience. From 30 December 2006 to 2 January 2007, the first meeting was held at Oventic, an indigenous village in the mountains of Chiapas; 6,000 indigenous people, 232 'local Zapatista authorities' and 1,300 activists from different Mexican states and forty-seven countries listened to the testimonies of the Zapatistas about the concrete organization of their local autonomy. From 20 to 29 July 2007, a second 'Encounter with the Peoples of the World' brought several thousand supporters to three autonomous communities to listen to reports of headway made and challenges to autonomy in these regions. A few months later, from 28 December 2007 to 1 January 2008, La Garrucha hosted the third gathering, exclusively dedicated to the struggle of women.

Instead of the highly mediatized spokesperson of the movement, Subcomandante Marcos, several hundred indigenous people spoke at these gatherings to express the strength of the local processes which constitute Zapatism. While the communiqués and official speeches of the movement, most of which have been Marcos' work, have said little about the process unfolding at the local level and generally limit themselves to the national and international situation, the 'Encounters with the Peoples of the World' have specifically focused on the concrete practices of local autonomy. Each of the round-tables at these assemblies was dedicated to a specific aspect of this autonomy: local government, education, health, ecology, culture, the economy, collective work and women's struggles. The various speakers defined autonomy as a process which 'allows people to decide how to live and how to organize themselves politically and economically': 'Autonomy – it's about governing ourselves as indigenous people, saying how we want our political authorities to work, no longer being subordinate to policies coming from above.' As Comandante Brus Li stressed, 'there are no guidelines on how to become autonomous'. The Zapatistas thus construct their autonomy in daily life, with difficulty and certain contradictions, but within a dynamic that advances according to their maxim, 'learn by walking'.

Organizing communal life and local political authority in a radically different way from the caudillism which previously dominated in Chiapas is at the core of the indigenous movement. While they have chosen not to adopt traditional paths of political engagement, Zapatista communities do not limit themselves to a will to 'change the world without taking power' (Holloway, 2002). They are in the process of reorganizing local power so that delegates 'order by obeying the will of the community'. Both the rotation of tasks and the importance accorded to popular assemblies are part of the attempt to prevent a concentration of power in the hands of a few. Nevertheless, empirical studies in Zapatista municipalities show that issues of power and differences of opinion remain problematic in many villages and in the relation between the indigenous grassroots and the Zapatista Army (EZLN) commanding committee (CGRI[5]).

The EZLN remains a military organization – and thus highly vertical – while the predominance of Subcomandante Marcos in strategic domains (political and military strategy, communication with Mexican society, etc.) runs counter to the horizontal form of social organization espoused by the movement. The influence of the Indigenous Revolutionary Committee, the military command of the movement, may have diminished with the establishment of the *Caracoles*, the civil authorities coordinating several villages. However, several decisions indicate that this authority retains an important decisional power and is not always in agreement with the local bases of the movement. S. Mélenotte's (2009) empirical studies show that Zapatista authorities have not always listened to their base's opinion, particularly when groups of refugees wished to regain lands that they had held before the conflict.

There are undeniable differences between the Zapatism 'from above' – more political, notably embodied by Subcomandante Marcos, more given to denunciations of neoliberalism and quick to engage in national politics – and the Zapatism as practised in local communities, in which realizing local autonomy with limited economic means is a long process of learning, and for whom improving the difficult conditions of daily life counts for at least as much as the global struggle against neoliberalism. These 'two Zapatisms' are not disconnected. Whenever necessary, local populations have demonstrated their strong support for Marcos and the commandants through public mobilizations. But while the political Zapatism seems at times to be at an impasse or engaged in long tours around the country which risk distancing it from local realities, the less media-covered construction of local autonomy seems to move forward, despite many difficulties and the contradictions inherent to this form of engagement, based on practical experiments carried out by those who live them.

As with most organizations of the way of subjectivity, transcribing ideals into practice remains a constant challenge. The concrete implementation of local autonomy proves a long and arduous process. Managing power relations within communities, fair distribution of tasks, and discussing decisions to be taken by consensus requires a long practical and political learning process. A more difficult challenge still is found at the economic level. Without the help of any Mexican institutions, life is rough in these poor regions, with large refugee populations in certain villages. For example, in the municipality of Polho, 2,000 residents are hosting 6,000 refugees. Refusing government aid, some Zapatista villages have necessarily become dependent on aid from international organizations such as Médecins du monde, as well as sporadic aid from international support committees. But this aid has declined over the years and the basis of economic autonomy has not been fully re-established. Moreover, the entire Mexican countryside has suffered an unprecedented crisis (Bartra, 2009), in the face of which migration often seems the only way out, even for many indigenous movements' activists (Aquino, 2010; Le Bot, 2009). While the political dimension of automony is a major challenge which has empassioned researchers and activists, the economic viability of autonomous communities often constitutes their Achilles' heel. In the *asentamentos* of the Brazilian movement of landless farmers (MST), work is highly valued and the produce is sold on local markets as the income is an essential element of community sustainability. In contrast, Zapatista communities have only established few alternative distribution channels through international support committees and sell some of their production and crafts on local markets. These incomes are, however, much too scarce to ensure the communities' economic sustainability.

A *subjective and expressive movement*

The Zapatista movement is not inscribed solely in the way of subjectivity. It proposes political and legal reforms, approaches the Congress, calls on the Mexican state and negotiates with state representatives. It positions itself within socio-economic debates when it denounces the Plan Puebla-Panama, neoliberal policies and the exploitation of natural resources in Chiapas by Mexican and transnational capitalism (EZLN, 1995).

Although the Zapatista struggle is limited to a poor region of south-western Mexico and has hardly managed to transform national laws and institutions, it has radically transformed the lives and self-perception of thousands of peasants in Chiapas, who are now 'proud to be autonomous',[6] and who proclaimed during the first 'Encounter with the Peoples of the World' (2007) that 'if we aren't able to change the world, we are struggling so that the world doesn't change us' (Betto, Caracol no. 4). Within their compass, they 'seek to develop actions to transform society' (Magdalena, Caracol no. 2). The strength of the words of Zapatista *women* impressed all participants at the Zapatista gatherings. While they all recognized that some macho attitudes still exist in the communities, things have greatly changed since the Zapatista struggle made the promotion of equal relations between men and women within communities one of its central axes (EZLN, 1994: 107–10). While they were previously married by force, confined to household tasks and often beaten, indigenous women have taken a growing and increasingly visible place in the communities and the movement. Few girls had access to education before 1994. Thirteen years later, at the 'Encounters with the Peoples of the World', over 100 women spoke in Spanish to an international audience to attest progress in their struggle, while calling attention to the road that still lay ahead. With the Zapatista movement, they have gained equal rights and have an increasing influence, both in the movement's assemblies and in community life. Among their first decisions was the prohibition of alcohol in the communities, which is still in effect. Several major Zapatista figures have been women, including Comandante Ramona who had a major influence in the movement and Comandante Esther who spoke to the Mexican Congress in 2001.

The autonomous communities have also invested heavily in an alternative system of education. Fifty-two new schools have been built in the region of the *caracole* of Oventic alone, hundreds of teachers have been trained, and thousands of women have learned to read. Autonomous teaching sees itself as steadfastly opposed to 'the individualism indoctrinated in students by government schools', consequently adopting alternative pedagogy such as the Freire method and developing playful aspects, collective work, and close connections between manual and intellectual learning. The primary level is now in place throughout the autonomous municipalities, while secondary schooling is being developed and already exists in Oventic. Zapatista education doesn't correspond to national programmes and does not aim to facilitate access to higher education or universities, which are deemed to be individualizing. The Zapatistas insist on 'students bringing their skills back to the communities'. Education also represents a central element of the preservation of local cultures and languages 'through which our values are transmitted' (first Encounter with the Peoples of the World, 2007).

A long-term transformation

Despite the difficulties of concretely implementing local autonomy within a context of economic crisis and a military occupation of part of the territory, the grassroots activists and local section delegates of the Zapatista movement who took part in the

'Encounters with the Peoples of the World' testified with enthusiasm about the concrete experience of de facto autonomy; of life in communities resolutely outside neoliberalism; of practices of *another possible world*. While some have pronounced the Zapatista movement moribund since 2002, and while Marcos appears to flounder in the bogs of Mexican anti-politics, the ongoing processes at the local level testify to the vigour of an actor engaged in long-term social and cultural transformation.

Many western movements generate high energy for short periods of time. Almost three decades after the emergence of the movement, the processes unfolding locally in the Zapatista territories have proven to be long-term, as the substantial investment in alternative education confirms. The indigenous revolt has helped transform the place and perception of indigenous peoples in Mexico and abroad. Previously invisible, they have now become significant actors on the Latin American continent (Le Bot, 2009). The subjective and expressive nature of this movement and its experience-centred engagement allows the Zapatista movement to articulate identity-based and universal demands, a combination that is far more complex to achieve at the political level (Benhabib, 2002). The Zapatista movement is thus built on the collective experience of resistance rather than theoretical reasoning or only an assessment of historical experiences (Ornelas, 2007). By asserting their culture, their difference and their values, indigenous movements express their rejection of a homogenized society under the rule of global markets. They build local structures that give their inhabitants an access to active citizenship and that call for a fundamental change in the relationship between the local and the global scales.

Rooted in local communities, the Zapatista movement combines autonomy and openness, emphasizing interdependence rather than independence or dependencies. It shows that identities and communities can then become resources for subjective resistance to markets and neoliberal globalization (Ceceña, 1997; Castells, 1996–8), without leading to local enclosure and communalist withdrawal. Similarly, several Latin American indigenous peoples' movements articulate their specific identities with universal meaning (Le Bot, 2009; Varese, 1996). They demand 'recognition of the fact that many worlds exist, that there are distinct cultures which must be respected in their social, cultural and economic integrity' (a CONAIE delegate, WSF 2002). These movements have thus managed to raise key questions for the alter-globalization movement, particularly on the issue of identity.

From the very beginning, the alter-globalization movement brought indigenous struggles together with struggles against neo-liberal globalization in the north. The convergence of indigenous struggles with those of the western world shaped alter-globalization from the beginning, particularly in the Americas. However, indigenous movements only found their place at the Social Forums by degrees. The Forum of the Americas in Quito in 2004 and the pan-Amazonian Social Forums of 2003, 2004 and 2005 constituted important steps in this process. While in 2003 and 2005, they were considered 'little heard' in the forums, indigenous peoples' movements were the main actors at the 2009 WSF – less by their rather limited presence at the event's main podiums than by the impact of their ideas on participants.

Beyond shared adversaries (neoliberal policies, proposed Free Trade Agreements, and natural resource extraction by transnational companies), the cultures, values and practices of indigenous movements have been a major source of inspiration for activists of the way of subjectivity around the world. In return, alter-globalization activists and their forums have provided indigenous movements with an unprecedented audience. As we will see in chapter 10, their traditional and spiritual relation with nature and 'Mother Earth' has placed indigenous people at the forefront of the struggle against climate change.

Barricade social and cultural centre

Social centres

Since the 1970s, squats and occupied buildings have been part of the alternative social landscape of many cities of North America and Europe, particularly Germany, Denmark, Italy and England. Some of these were primarily occupied for housing, while others have become social and cultural centres. These activist spaces became high points of sociability, political engagement, convivial social relations and (counter-)cultural creativity, stigmatizing the surplus of the 'consumer/waste society'.

In the 1990s, social centres became a major component of Italian civil society and alter-globalization. There they developed a creative, locally rooted activism which attempted to differentiate itself from the violent excesses of the Italian extreme left of the 1970s (Lotringer & Marazzi, 2007) as well as the politics of the traditional left. At the heart of the different political and cultural projects developed in these occupied buildings and spaces are the convivial relations woven among the activists, the practices of self-organizing the space, and experimentation with alternatives in everyday life. Local roots in the neighbourhood are also a key element of Italian social centres (Toscano, 2011; Montagna, 2006). Some of these alternative social centres have played a very active role in the alter-globalization movement. They have brought to the movement a subjective engagement which had hitherto occupied a very secondary place in organizations which dominated alter-globalization in many regions. In London, squats and social centres were heavily involved in 'Beyond the ESF', an autonomous and particularly creative space held in parallel to the London European Social Forum (ESF) in 2004. In Malmo (Sweden), another squat hosted a wide range of meetings and discussions as well as a vegan canteen during the 2008 ESF. In Liège, Barricade, a social and cultural centre, has been at the heart of local alter-globalization confluence from 2001 to 2004. Although it developed autonomously, with barely no international networks, the practices implemented in this centre come particularly close to the way of subjectivity of the alter-globalization movement, as the next pages will show.

A space of experience in Liège

A Belgian French-speaking town with some 180,000 residents, Liège has been deeply affected by the industrial decline. It was in this city that Belgium's most vibrant alter-globalization network developed, particularly between 1998 and 2003. It was home to the largest local chapter of ATTAC-Belgium, counting up to 500 members, and hosted the biggest local Social Forum in the country. The two powerful national trade unions became more involved in the alter-globalization movement in Liège than anywhere else, sometimes even taking positions against their national

offices. Active in ATTAC-Liège since 1999, these unions participated in the mobilizations around the European economic and
financial ministers' summit in Liège in September 2001 and then
in the Coordination d'Autres Mondes (Other Worlds Coalition),
the local Social Forum.

'Barricade'[7] has been active as an 'alternative and autonomous
social and cultural centre' since 1996 in a working-class neighbourhood in the centre of Liège. It first aims to be a 'convivial
space', where people are invited to come along, to read or to have
a discussion over one of the many special beers available at the
bar. The accent is on 'quality human relations'. Renovated by the
activists, the centre's two houses host a multitude of cultural and
social activities organized by committees which emerged from the
initial project: an alternative bookstore; a convivial bar; a feminist reading group; a 'cyber-centre' that promotes open software
and offers introductory computer courses to unemployed workers;
a theatre company; a choir; and a Collective Purchasing Group.
The multi-faceted project aims, on the one hand, to bring together
different cultural and social milieux on the basis of convivial
relations and, on the other, to transcribe political demands and
a questioning of neoliberal policies into everyday life activities.
In this way, around twenty people meet each Monday to address
agricultural and food problems through a 'Collective Purchasing
Group', ordering their food directly from engaged local producers. The project aims to demonstrate the possibility of 'alternatives to the supermarket and to a productivist agricultural policy'.

Constructing a space to favour the (re-)creation of social ties,
developing other forms of relationships and lived experiences,
constitutes the heart of every project promoted by Barricade. The
public which frequents the centre shares 'the desire to learn and
discover, the refusal of mindless evenings in front of the television, and the inclination to leave the cocoon and open one's
spirit'.[8] Instead of the passive leisure of the consumer society,
'Barricaders' are invited to take an active role and become actors
again; debating, singing in the choir, developing free software,
or becoming a 'consum-actor' with the Collective Purchasing
Group. In each activity, there is the same will to assert one's own
subjectivity and to resist consumer society. In opposition to
supermarkets that engender cold and anonymous relationships,
the Collective Purchasing Group insists on meeting the producers

and maintaining contact with them. Similarly, the welcome afforded to artists passing through Barricade and the opportunity to 'spend a convivial moment' with them are what counts. This conviviality of relations is not simply a fortunate by-product of the centre's activities, it is the very reason for the projects in the first place.

Because their activism is centred on experience and relationships, the participation of each person in concrete organizing and in the evaluations, debates, and decisions of the group is essential. This way of organizing requires a lot of energy and constant learning. In the Collective Purchasing Group, a task rotation was established, allowing members of the group to become familiar with the different aspects of the project and forcing them to acquire the necessary skills. As M. Louviaux (2003) shows, these principles of self-organization are tempered by a certain tolerance, permitting a flexibility around the involvement of each person. Taking into account individual specificities, engagement is connected in certain respects to new forms of more fluid and individualized involvement. The objective of these 'approaches to self-organization' in Barricade's activities is to limit the distinction between a few *entrepreneurs of mobilization* and ordinary activists; or, in their own words, 'between the initiators, *those who carry* the project, and *those who are carried*': 'The goal is to avoid falling back into an instrumental relationship between client and provider of goods and services.' However, in practice, avoiding the emergence of these two categories is a permanent challenge.

Engagement and autonomy

Barricade's general philosophy results from disenchantment with attempts to engage in 'the politician's politics': 'At the beginning of the 1990s, I was involved in this project of a united left. Since then I have been vaccinated against electoral alternatives.' Barricaders want to 'question traditional practices' and engage 'in a reflection on oneself'. Activists' habits have been transformed by these new forms of engagement and new organizing methods. While, for many experienced activists, common appeals, platforms and charters symbolize the quest for convergence and alternatives, at Barricade there is distrust of 'traditional platformist activists': 'When you make a platform of demands, which other civil society organization and social movements try to put in place, it is no longer "other worlds are possible", but "one other world is possible": "Moreover, as Demand 6.4 on page 14 states, we have decided that . . . ." To me, you are already somewhat dead when you have frozen all of your demands like that.' The Barricaders continue to 'seek the road' and try to build it by experimenting with concrete practices. 'Reflection on what is lived' thus prevails over technical debates about macro-economics. Learning by trial and error is a central aspect of the different projects, which are constructed 'by feeling around'. In addition, they highly value any opportunities for learning through the exchange of experience with invited artists, activists from other cooperative anarchist communities, or visitors to Barricade.

Autonomous from political parties, Barricade also maintains a certain distance from national coalitions, and notably from the Belgian Social Forum. There is strong distrust of 'what comes from above', and particularly from Brussels: 'We don't much like the national which says to the local, "You should do this! You should do that!" without any real tie to local community life.' However, global issues are not absent from Barricade's projects. The social centre was the key actor in the local Social Forum between 2001 and 2005. Barricade is also very concerned with raising public awareness about alter-globalization issues. But macro-economic and technical questions are introduced from the starting point of everyday problems: from the lives of ordinary people to WTO negotiations; and from the daily meal to food and agricultural policies. To inform people about the 'dangers of the General Agreement on Trade in Services', a 'theatrical performance' by Barricade and the Liège alter-globalization coordination staged the privatization of a pedestrian bridge in Liège in order to demonstrate in a playful manner the issues at stake in these international negotiations. Through a series of small theatrical actions, it was able to challenge passers-by about the importance of defending public services and the dangers of privatization. The message was conveyed not by deploying a long series of figures, but through irony and ridicule. Using the same tone, Barricade organized a series of actions at the Christmas market to challenge the political unanimity around a tax decrease. Barricade activists demanded instead that the finance minister 'take back his fiscal Christmas gifts'. On both occasions, it was a matter of 'linking creativity, the message to be transmitted, a festive aspect and a media event' (a Barricade organizer). Other actions, which testify to the cultural centre's embeddedness in the neighbourhood, don't go beyond a local target, such as the struggle to save a community garden, or the fight against the construction of an addition to the courthouse.

As a cultural centre, Barricade embodies an expressive and subjective movement not so much because it hosts plenty of cultural activities, but because it embraces a political culture and a specific philosophy which place resistance and alternatives at the centre of its local and daily activities, from consumption to leisure. By doing this, it puts the construction of an autonomous space to foster personal experience and convivial relations at the heart of its projects. However, this approach also has its limits. As numerous civil society actors have experienced, the desire to be open to the poorer classes is not so easily achieved. Situated in a poor neighbourhood in the centre of town, Barricade essentially attracts those possessing high cultural and educational capital, especially among its entrepreneurs of mobilization. Moreover, the evolution of Barricade, and particularly the institutionalization of certain of its activities, has increasingly oriented the organization towards a service-centred self-help model (Kriesi, 1996): a social circle with activities mostly organized by seven paid staff who have been hired since 2003. This evolution has sometimes distanced it from the more explicit and reflexive opposition to neoliberal globalization, with activities centring on the construction and maintenance of sociability, as well as the social re-integration of unemployed people, for which it has received subsidies from the regional government and the European Union.

Alter-activist youth[9]

Categories of alter-globalization youth

Young people are widely perceived as little concerned by politics and exhibit a general loss of confidence in democratic institutions (Galland & Roudet, 2005). However, analyses that equate a lack of formal democratic participation with apathy overlook alternative forms of political engagement (Hurrelmann & Albert, 2002; Gauthier, 2003; Youniss et al., 2002). Rather than exhibiting a disinterest in politics, some young people are developing alternative ways of getting involved, less institutionalized, and distanced from traditional political actors. Many young alter-globalization activists are extremely critical of formal political and civil society organizations, including political parties, unions and large NGOs, which they often view as hierarchical, bureaucratic and distant from any grassroots base.

It would be a mistake, however, to consider young activists as necessarily innovative. Old and new practices co-exist within alter-globalization movements, just as many younger activists participate in traditional leftist organizations. The great strike at the National Autonomous University of Mexico in 1999 was, for example, dominated from the start by innovative practices, before other, more traditional ones, progressively gained ascendancy. A student who was active at the time explained in this way: 'During an assembly, after many members had already left the group, certain people spoke, discussing the "necessity of a second purge of the group"' (interview, 2002). Without going as far, a group of young activists regularly tried to infiltrate different Parisian networks, using techniques which might bring back old memories: 'They drag out the general assemblies on trivial points and ideological speeches and then, when everyone has left, they call for a vote on key issues' (a young Vamos activist).

Hence, it is important not to overlook the diversity of youth activism. Youth differ according to their mode of involvement, relation to political institutions, vision for society, social origin and educational level (Muxel, 2001: 46). Moreover, some are more open to global networking while others emphasize a radical anti-capitalist critique and local self-management. In each country where we have conducted research, we have, however, identified five categories of young alter-globalization activists, which are neither rigid nor exhaustive.

Young revolutionaries From Chavez' party in Venezuela to the British Socialist Workers' Party, traditional parties of the extreme left still have significant influence with many young people due to their radical goals, simplified visions of the world, and, for the most traditional ones, strategies of infiltration. Younger revolutionary actors are committed to state-oriented strategies of change, anti-capitalism and more traditional forms of member-ship, recruitment and belonging.

NGOs and institutional youth actors Many young activists within the alter-globalization movement belong to, volunteer with or work for leftist political parties, unions, NGOs and other formal associations, either directly or as part of their youth sections, as is common in Latin America. Some behave similarly to their older counterparts, while others bring a 'fresh approach' that enables productive collaborations between their dynamism and the experience of older activists.

Poor and minority youth Paradoxically, this group, including young immigrants and people of colour who suffer most from neoliberal policies (Blossfeld et al., 2005), is often less visible in the alter-globalization movement. This issue has long dominated debates in the USA (Martinez, 2000; Starr, 2004; Juris, 2008a), although youth of colour have been more involved in recent mobilizations, such as the protest against the Free Trade Area of the Americas (FTAA) in Miami and the first US Social Forum in Atlanta (Juris, 2008b). Anti war marches have also provided an opportunity to demonstrate for poor and minority youths in European countries, but, with the exception of in the UK, this has not led to their further involvement. Even during the 2003 ESF, which was held in the Parisian suburbs, young people from the second or third generation of migrants remained widely excluded from the event, which was dominated by intellectual middle-class activists. Similarly, few young slum dwellers took part in the WSFs in Porto Alegre, Mumbai and Nairobi, the latter being particularly problematic as organizers closed their fences to people unable to pay the admission fees.

Libertarian youth Groups of libertarian youth are organized around small, anti-capitalist collectives and include squatters, anti-militarists, alternative media practitioners, and others who stress local struggles and collective self-management. These autonomous activists reject all forms of hierarchy, stressing independence from parties, unions, NGOs and representative institutions. They are extremely critical of what they perceive as more institutional alter-globalization events, including world and regional Social Forums. As a counterweight to the official Social Forums, autonomous youths have organized their own 'libertarian' spaces and forums in Porto Alegre (2003), Paris

(2003), London (2004), Caracas (2006) and Malmö (2008). At the tactical level, libertarian activists tend to engage in militant direct action, including black bloc tactics targeting corporate targets and the police (Dupuis-Déri, 2005).

Young alter-activists Critical of institutional sectors and the Marxist left, alter-activists stress horizontal coordination, direct democracy and contingent, flexible forms of commitment. However, whereas libertarians emphasize the local and are wary of forging wider alliances, alter-activists are committed to an ethic of openness, local–global networking, and organizing across diversity and difference. They participate in larger global justice events, including regional and world Social Forums, but they do so by keeping 'one foot in, and one foot out', maintaining a critical attitude toward internal hierarchies and non-democratic practices. Moreover, as we shall see, alter-activist culture is characterized by creative forms of action and an emphasis on process and experimentation.

Although they are more prevalent in Europe and North America, this type of critical-minded alter-activist – mostly coming from the middle classes, and often students – seems particularly globalized. We were able to encounter them in every city in which we carried out our research: from London to Managua, and from Mumbai to Mexico. In most of the cities of the global south, they were chiefly to be found among students and more 'westernized' sectors of the population. Living in different countries, these middle-class youth are, however, connected to the same rebel world: they inform and are informed by Indymedia, which is now active in more than forty countries; they take part in discussion networks; they are strongly influenced by Zapatista philosophy; they mobilize against summits of global institutions; and they meet each other in international camps. The remaining part of this section will focus on this category. Its practices are, however, not exclusive and are partly shared by activists from all the other types.

'One foot in, one foot out'

Coming, as many of them do, from the student milieu, young alter-activists are deeply marked by the alter-globalization

movement and its international gatherings. This has not prevented them from remaining critical of the ways these events are
organized: 'We, young people, came to this forum to give it a
different thrust and turn it more towards action. Because the
forums usually stop at discussion, at the theoretical creation of
another world, but don't do a lot in practice' (activist youth
from GAS9, Mexico). Many alter-activist youth demand greater
transparency of organization, more room for participation, and,
above all, they wish 'to mix spaces of discussion and activities'
(report back from WSF 2004 by a Vamos activist). They criticize
'NGO and activist professionals [for] traveling from one corner
of the world to the other to chase their forums' and for 'distancing themselves from what is happening locally' (young Belgian
activist). The difference in forms of political engagement often
establishes a reciprocal distrust between youth and alter-globalization organizations. This has become, on the one hand, an
excuse for certain leaders of ATTAC-France to keep their distance from younger activists between 2000 and 2006, and, on
the other, the basis of a sometimes exaggerated suspicion of all
forms of institutionalization. However, the 2005 World Social
Forum showed that certain initiatives taken by activist youth
were able to have a real influence on the evolution of 'adult'[10]
organizations (see pp. 195–6).[11]

Unlike more traditional actors, alter-activists stress grassroots
participation and personal interaction in the context of daily
social life. Movement gatherings, neighbourhood relations and
protest camps thus become spaces to *experience and experiment*
with alternative ways of life. A document issued by the Parisian
alter-activist network 'Vamos' explains: 'We do not separate our
practices and aims. We choose a horizontal, anti-sexist, self- and
eco-managed way of operating' (see p. 38). This clearly differenti-
ates alter-activists from NGOs and other global justice activists
who are criticized for 'not being aware of the idea of process,
which means there is no difference between means and ends. Our
manner of working has to reflect the values we are defending as
part of our resistance' (interview, Liège). Their emerging living
utopias combine elements of certain traditional ideologies, such
as the emphasis on internal democracy and autonomy that has
been a core feature of the anarchist tradition (Dupuis-Déri, 2005;
Graeber, 2002), deep influence from recent movements like

Zapatism and feminism, and a commitment to openness and collaboration.

Creative direct action

Alter-globalization activist youth display little enthusiasm for taking part in long negotiations of draft statements or platforms. Workshops in alter-activist spaces are often about 'talking through experiences of struggle' (Spanish activist, WSF 2002): 'In Seattle, we succeeded in taking care of this and that; on the other hand, we had these problems that we were able to resolve in Quebec by using this tactic . . .' Action, moreover, constitutes the heart of their political engagement. They often elect to escape a day of workshop at the World Social Forum to participate in the occupation of a building or the destruction of a GMO[12] field. *Active non-violence* is a difficult form of action but it is adopted by a growing number of youth, self-proclaimed 'disobedients'. Without recourse to violence, these protesters try, for example, to enter restricted zones during international summits or block routes leading in. The struggle against consumer society and its omnipresent advertising is also increasingly important in their networks. 'Ad-buster' campaigns are carried out in the subways of numerous cities around the world in order to 'free public spaces from the chains of consumer society'.

Democratic and egalitarian structures (Polletta, 2002) and a network-based organization (Castells, 1996–8; Juris, 2008a) both strongly favour tactical innovations, collective creativity and the ability to adapt to fast-changing environments among social movements. The tactics employed by young alter-globalization activists produce theatrical images for mass-mediated consumption. Beyond their utilitarian purpose – shutting down major summits – mass actions are complex cultural performances, which allow participants to communicate symbolic messages to an audience. During the 2007 protest against the G-8 summit in north-east Germany, the International Clowns Company was an important and hilarious actor that helped to decrease the tensions with the police. In this sense, alter-activism is not only festive; it also reflects the emphasis on creativity, diversity, innovation and symbolic protest among young activists.

Be the media

A creative and particularly effective use of new communication technologies is another feature of youth alter-activism. They are employed to express one's creativity and subjectivity or to organize actions, share information and coordinate activities. Internet sites and chat rooms have become an important means of debating, spreading information, exchanging experiences and preparing international actions, camps and meetings.[13] Each international forum and mobilization has its alternative media centre. The people involved often gather for several days before such events to share practices in an 'Alternative Media Forum'. Pirate radio,[14] campus newspapers, mailing lists and Twitter are all employed. Video-cameras are also put to use by activists during various actions: in order to construct their own experience (McDonald, 2006) as well as to defend themselves against repression, the presence of a camera having a calming effect on the police. There have been actions by cyber-activist hackers (Picot & Willert, 2002; Aguiton & Cardon, 2007), and electronic civil disobedience which has been used against websites of transnational corporations, international institutions and the Republican Party. Other aspects of the reappropriation of and free access to knowledge, information and communication include free software and operating systems.

While mass media 'manipulate subjectivities', once 'reappropriated' by users media can transform into a privileged space for the expression of subjectivities, creation and exchange. 'Don't hate the media, be the media' was adopted as the slogan of the main alternative information network, Indymedia. Established during the anti-WTO protests in Seattle with the aim of 'allowing everyone to participate and be active in the media' (according to one of its founders, WSF 2002), the network enjoyed a rapid success and, within a few years, local collectives were active in more than forty countries, allowing alter-globalization activists to create and circulate alternative news and information. During mass actions and gatherings, hundreds of activists take to the streets to record video footage, snap photos and conduct interviews.

Network-based organizational forms

Whether in a project, an ephemeral network or a more structured organization, youth are generally involved through affinity groups: college friends, activists from the same local chapter, people encountered on the bus before a protest, a group of more timid or more action-oriented activists, etc. This fluidity and the lack of requirement for long-term commitment correspond to the culture of contemporary society (Bauman, 2000; Sennett, 2006) but also meet the contingencies of young, student life. Job opportunities, the burden of university studies, friendships or the unforeseen blossoming of a love affair can make activist involvement a shifting variable. Not without its merits, this individuation of political engagement has its drawbacks, particularly in the area of continuity, transmission of past experiences, or the inscription of movements within the social and political landscape.

Alter-activists are generally wary of traditional forms of social organization and protective of their autonomy. Eschewing large organizations, they tend to work in overlapping, restricted groups organized around specific projects and connected to each other through informal networks and personal affinities. Alter-activists have developed decentralized, network-based organizational forms, including highly flexible, diffuse and often ephemeral formations, which bring together many alter-activist youth in a broad network of disparate local committees instead of a single, unitary movement organization. Examples include the Direct Action Network (DAN) in the United States, Reclaim the Streets, the Movement for Global Resistance (MRG) in Catalonia, Vamos in Paris and GAS9 in Mexico City.

Alter-activist networks challenge representative logics. Rather than identifying with a specific organization, for example, activists are committed to the wider movement and its guiding values. Participation is thus individualized, but still concerned with collective goals and collaborative practice. In this sense, alter-activist networks provide open spaces for communication and coordination around concrete projects, favouring open participation over rigid membership. Finally, alter-activist networks have no formal hierarchies, elected positions or paid staff, and decisions are taken by consensus. For example, as we have seen, the organization of alternative camps, including the 'Intergalactic Village' during the G-8 summit in 2003, the Mexican youth camps in Cancún or the camps during the 2007 G-8 in North Germany, is open and participatory. The organizational structure of Vamos involved up to 200 activists during preparatory meetings of the anti-G8 camp. Although these are not always the most time-effective ways of operating, alter-activist networks value horizontal structure and democratic process as political ends. This leads to an egalitarian, dynamic and flexible form of activism and non-representative logic (McDonald, 2006). At the same time, horizontal networks have limitations. For example, they can be highly unstable, given the lack of formal structure and clear chains of responsibility. Despite their efforts to create a horizontal and participatory space, the initiators of the alternative and self-organized village during the G-8 summit in Evian were disappointed: 'In the end, many things fell to us.' The most important aspects of organizing the space fell to a handful of activists; participants became involved only to a limited extent, and then generally only in the more pleasant aspects.

Unlike more formal organizations, networks are not born and do not die, but mutate according to circumstances and campaigns. Frequently re-baptized, they grow, shrink and transform according to the major project driving them – generally the organization of an alter-globalization event. This flexible dynamic generates a large turnover of membership in networks. In the network of Parisian alter-activist youth, only two of those who were active in 2001, when the name of the network first appeared, were still involved in Vamos at the end of 2004. The name had changed several times, but the network had persevered: meeting methodology, conceptualization of actions and general philosophy remained very similar. In addition, several references were made to past actions, particularly the 2003 camp at the G-8 at Evian (France) and the autonomous space at the Paris ESF later the same year. The website had also remained identical, constituting a virtual anchor for the continuity of a network with a very high turnover. But this logic of project-based political engagement and individuation does not encourage long-term organizing. Between actions, everyone returns to their jobs, until the group dies away or re-emerges, more beautiful than ever, for a new mobilization sparked by a few people. Other enthusiastic initiatives rapidly fall away. This was the case, for example, with the 'Intergalactika' network which was enthusiastically launched during the 2002 World Social Forum with the aim of maintaining communications and strong relations among alter-activists' networks. However, when everyone returned home, no one really worked on the project, which, in the end, was never established – until, a year later, a similar initiative was again launched, with no more success. Nevertheless, concern about sustainability of groups and coordination beyond projects weighs heavily on some young movement entrepreneurs (McCarthy & Zald, 1977). At Porto Alegre, a young Brazilian responsible for the 2002 camp lamented that the 'exchanges are amazing and the camp is very well run, but we have a hard time doing something more permanent than camps'. Less pessimistic, a young Parisian noted: 'The movement may disappear without much outcome, but those young people who took part in it have learned many things and will get mobilized much faster for the next movement.'

Vamos and GAS9

Decentralized networks involve new forms of political commitment and participation. For one, alter-activists tend to prefer more temporary, ad -hoc coalitions. At the same time, many alter-activist networks that began as temporary coordinating vehicles to bring people to alter-globalization demonstrations continued to operate over time. For example, MRG was created to mobilize Catalan activists for the protests against the World Bank and the IMF summit in Prague in September 2000. After nearly three years of organizing actions, gatherings and workshops, the network finally 'self-dissolved' in January 2003, 'to abandon the dull politics of Porto Alegre, the false representations and the petty struggles for power'.[15]

Paris-based Vamos started by organizing buses to take students to the anti-G8 protests in Genoa, 2001. Back in Paris, they constructed stands and gave talks on campuses about the neoliberal agenda of multilateral summits. In 2002, Vamos led numerous symbolic direct actions on issues such as migration, the war in Iraq, transnational corporations and neoliberal reforms. From there it expanded in a new direction with the yearly organization of a week of talks and exchanges, about alter-globalization issues, on Paris campuses. Vamos also brought two buses of French activists to the June 2002 Seville counter-summit. A year later, during the G-8 summit at Evian, France (near Geneva), the alternative camp organized by Vamos and a similar network from Lyon hosted more than 4,000 European activists. Allied to the jobless, migrants and precarious workers' activist networks, Vamos later helped put together a self-organized space on the margins of the ESF in Paris. These two events constituted *spaces of experience* in which alter-activist youth discussed, prepared actions and experimented with concrete alternatives in the areas of collective management of speaking, cleaning and gender equality. In contrast to the rooms and auditoriums of the 'official' ESF, Vamos' space was also a place to live, meet and party, which offered free lodgings and allowed space for music bands to perform. In the course of pulling together these events, Vamos activists organized themselves into a very functional network based on targeted actions, division of tasks, working groups and individualized participation. Vamos activists claim a certain influence from the Zapatistas and international alter-activist trends, combining an advertised distance from traditional social organizations with collaborations with numerous civil society actors.

In Mexico City, the GAS9 network was also founded around a global mobilization, namely against the 2003 WTO summit in Cancún. With a core of a dozen students from the National Autonomous University of Mexico, the GAS9 network hoped to make the Cancún mobilizations a 'springboard to awaken youth and social movements to the problems of globalization'.[16] Working in a city in which debates on neoliberalism had been limited to a few intellectuals and NGOs, they carried out an important work of conscientization and promoted a broad convergence. Some 'Youth assemblies towards Cancún' involved more than 200 young people from diverse backgrounds – students, libertarians, militant communists, NGO workers and educators. Dozens of people spoke at these gatherings to share their ideas, present their plans of action, organize the trip or convey information. GAS9 carried out diverse actions at Cancún, notably managing to block access to the WTO convention centre for two hours. Returning to Mexico City, the group changed its name several times, but remained active despite a heavy turnover of participants. The network took part in several local initiatives and in the heavily repressed march against the summit of the Inter-American Development Bank in Guadalajara in March 2004, where some of its members were arrested. GAS9 has since gradually re-oriented around three main activities: an alternative media centre; support for the Zapatista movement (through spreading information, organizing cultural events and the participation of many young activists in gatherings and events called by Subcomandante Marcos); and, finally, in support of these other two areas of activity, a group of drummers active in protests and alter-globalization events modelled after Seattle's 'Infernal Noise Company', which they saw at the protest marches in Cancún. For example, these drummers led their parade through the streets of San Cristóbal in an attempt to inform the population about the importance of the Zapatistas' 'Other Campaign'.

Protest camps as spaces of experience

The 2002 No Border camp near Strasbourg especially focused on self-organization and set the standards for many of its followers. Youth camps at the WSF have also become points of reference, gathering some 2,300 activists in 2002, 15,000 in 2003 and 30,000 in 2005. In June 2003, the 'Intergalactic Village' during the mobilization against the G-8 summit in Evian involved over 4,000 activists and had a deep impact on young French alter-globalization activists. In Mexico, in 2005 alone, national and international autonomous youth camps were organized in Oaxaca, along the US–Mexico border and near Mexico City. In 2007, during the protest week against the G-8 summit in Heiligendamm in north-east Germany, the three main camps hosted over 10,000 activists. They were conceived as bases for direct action against the restricted area around the G-8 summit as well as places to sleep, eat, meet other activists, debate and discuss. In the evening and part of the night, the camps were lit up by hundreds of discussions and songs around small fires, screenings of alternative movies and techno parties. The days were dedicated to protest marches, the planning of direct actions to block the roads to Heiligendamm, or organizing meetings or workshops where activists shared experience. Drawing on the experience of previous alter-activist protest camps, which have taken place in many countries, as well as the long tradition of self-organization by German activists, the autonomous organization of the various *barrios* (neighbourhoods) and of the camps as a whole was both participative and efficient, being at the same time experimental and functional in most aspects of camp life – from biological vegan foods, camp security, workshops and cleaning to training for blockade actions. Since 2007, 'Climate Camps' have become widespread. Loose networks of young activists, including a wide proportion of teenagers, even set up a climate camp in the heart of the City of London during the 2009 G-20 meeting. Although it was removed by the police during its first night, it is recalled as a convivial space of exchange and a strong experience for a new generation of activism.

Alter-activists conceive these camps not only as a base to prepare and lead actions or to host workshops on alter-globalization issues, but as spaces of experience, laboratories where alter-activists can experiment with new ideas, practices and forms of social action: 'One of our objectives is to implement a complete vision of the world(s) we're fighting for in the here and now, and right down to the smallest details of daily life.'[17] Camps are opportunities for experimenting with different forms of participation and social interaction. In this sense, youth camps are organized along direct democratic lines: there are no formal leaders, decisions are made collectively, and all residents are encouraged to take part in the construction, organization, and daily administration of the camps. For example, the 2002 No Border camp in Strasbourg (see Juris, 2008a) and the 2003 Intergalactic Village near Evian employed a decision-making structure based on a network of self-organized neighbourhoods or *barrios*. Each 'neighbourhood' would manage its affairs through a local assembly, while decisions affecting the entire camp, including those related to infrastructure, security, media or collective actions, would be taken through larger spokes-council assemblies, or *inter-barriales*, involving delegates from each *barrio*. At the Intergalactic Village, as in many other camps, a notice-board called for participation in numerous tasks: cleaning, cooking, organizing discussions, etc.

While celebration and the pleasure of living an alternative experience are at the heart of these activist spaces, the will to encourage more participative forms of organization demands considerable investment. Strolling around the 2005 WSF youth camp in the evening, journalists and participants would doubt-lessly retain party images and sounds of samba. However, just a few steps away, and while the majority of activists were unwind-ing on downtown terraces, youth from the alter-activist space 'Intergalactic caracol' met well into the night to organize the fol-lowing day together. Several internet meetings before their arrival in Porto Alegre enabled a group of around ten activists from Europe and the Americas to establish certain parameters. However, in order to allow everyone to participate, decisions had to be made on-site: each person spoke and each idea was dis-cussed until 2 or 3 a.m.

Beyond opposing neoliberalism, these camps provide spaces for socializing, sharing ideas and experiences, celebrating, mixing private and public, making friends and struggling for a better world. Alter-activist camps provide a time out of time, a com-munal space where hierarchical relations are suspended. Indeed, such spaces of experience are particularly productive moments for experimenting with alternative ways of life, new social identi-ties and novel forms of interaction. At the same time, despite their utopian thrust, alter-activist camps also present complex, often intractable, challenges, including the rise of informal hierarchies, the necessity to delegate despite the emphasis on participation, differing levels of involvement of residents, and the emergence of political divisions. Moreover, these camps are ephemeral: once they end, groups tend to dissolve and networks unravel. Nevertheless, such camps represent important moments in which individual lived experience intersects with collective history. Thus, to take part in an alternative camp reinforces political involvement and commitment to the alter-globalization movement in the long term. However ephemeral, such an intense experience of political activism during one's youth can transform social identity and political beliefs in fundamental ways (McAdam, 1989).

A youth culture activism?

Both in daily practices and during large gatherings, alter-activist youth culture creates new forms of political engagement centred

on concrete projects, affinity groups and networked organization, but also a cult of experience lived in the moment. Outside
grand ideologies, activist youth create decentralized and non-
hierarchical networks in which groups from different areas of the
world share similar practices and ideas about political engagement. Although they engage in public mobilizations, they renounce
neither their deep disenchantment with the structures, institutions and traditional actors of political and social life (Forbrig,
2005) nor their own individuation. The innovative practices of
alter-activists provide a potential basis for a new culture of political participation. However, these forms of political engagement
are not without their limits. Most of the time, they have scarcely
any impact on public debate. With the exception of black bloc
sporadic actions, they have remained largely invisible to the
media and public opinion, which are more attuned to media
campaigns managed by NGO communication experts.

Youth, and particularly middle-class students, attraction to
alter-activism partly depends on life-cycle and generation effects.[18]
Youth are more deeply influenced by the characteristics and
values associated with the information society (Castells, 1996–8)
in which they grew up. The values of autonomy, self-realization
and creativity defended by young alter-activists conform closely
with contemporary shifts in capitalism (Sennett, 2006). Indeed,
several surveys show that, in comparison with the overall population, young people value more flexible and autonomous forms of
commitment and are faster in adopting new information technologies (Hurrelmann & Albert, 2002; Galland & Roudet,
2005). Today's youth are also part of the post-Berlin Wall generation, characterized by a deep disappointment with traditional
politics and activism.

Life-cycle effects reinforce this trend. Alter-activist values,
practices and experiences are particularly compatible with a specific period of life which has been called 'emerging adulthood'
(Arnett, 2004). Indeed, youth sociology has often associated this
period of life with many of the characteristics that are visible in
alter-activist culture, such as the thirst for lived experience and
experimentation (Weber, 1963 [1919]: 96). Moreover, youth-
specific patterns of social interaction – which are more flexible
and informal than among working adults with families – have a
significant impact on their mode of political participation (Muxel,

2001). Their often insecure jobs (Blossfeld et al., 2005) and lower level of professional and familial responsibilities allow more free time and make them more likely to engage in horizontal networking. In addition, young people tend to adopt more radical positions, and are less involved with more institutionalized social and political actors. Finally, as with young alter-activists today, cultural and festive aspects of protest and the insistence on democracy and participation were critical elements of various student movements in the 1960s. For example, the Mexican student movement in 1968 (Alvarez Garín, 1998) placed a major emphasis on democratic, participatory organization while calling for democratization of the state. Many young Germans engaged in counter-cultural projects while Italian anti-military camps were similar in many ways to alter-activists' camps today. Moreover, apropos of the festive aspects of contemporary alter-activist protests, Daniel Cohn-Bendit, leader of the French students in 1968, once remarked: 'It's simple. You order the police to evacuate and you reopen the Sorbonne. I find three or four orchestras and the party begins. People will dance, drink and be happy' (Gomez, 1998: 32).

From the Zapatistas to alter-activists

When two Barricade activists took stock of the differences between current movements and the labour movement at the end of the 1950s, it was a series of quotations from Marcos which came to mind: 'The road is made by moving forward. No path is mapped out'; 'Questions must be asked while walking, as and when we advance in our projects.' Similarly, when twenty Latin American, North American and European alter-activist youth organized an autonomous space at the 2005 WSF youth camp, they called it the 'intergalactic *caracol*' in reference to the Intergalactic Gathering which took place in Chiapas in 1996 and to the Zapatistas' 'Good Government Councils', called *caracoles*. From all over the world, they rallied around the Zapatista inspiration: 'the common ground we found among everyone was a reference to the Zapatistas, who embody a will to autonomy and other forms of struggle' (contribution to the inauguration of the *caracol*). From the French Intergalactics to the Italian Ya Basta, different youth movements have similarly named themselves after the rebels of Chiapas.

How to explain this fascination with the indigenous, rural community movement that is Zapatism on the part of urban, alter-activist youth with a hyper-individualized lifestyle? Beyond their differences, the alternative social centres, alter-activist youth and indigenous Zapatistas share a similar, experience-based concept of social change and political engagement, which forms the way of subjectivity of the alter-globalization movement. The interest the Zapatistas, the social centres and the alter-activist youth have in each other and their gatherings is not accidental. In his poetic style, Subcomandante Marcos seems to have succeeded better than most in describing the logic of the spaces of experience established by these activists: active participation by all, conviviality of social relations, learning by trial and error through experimentation, construction of autonomous spaces, an anti-power logic and the valorization of diversity within the movement.

Having delved into the logic of experience drawn from three actors who act according to different modalities of the way of subjectivity, we will turn, in the next chapter, to an examination of these actors' concepts of social change, the social conflicts they wage, and the inherent limits of this trend of the alter-globalization movement.

4

Expressive Movements and Anti-Power

A concept of social change

As Tito, the teenager from the suburbs of Mexico City, broke into his third song during the 'Meeting of the Zapatistas comandants with youth and civil society' at around 3.20 a.m., a Trotskyist, a long-time supporter of the Zapatista cause, moved closer to me and began to fidget: 'This is all very well, but what use is it? What points can be drawn from these successive speeches and songs? What text will come out of this meeting?'

From the point of view of institutional politics, social actors following the path of subjectivity appear quite limited in outcome. The multiple Zapatista mobilizations for constitutional reform clearly failed at the politico-legal level. From the same perspective, what is the political impact of 'tagging' advertising in New York subways? It would be considered useless – or even counter-productive, in that it impairs the functioning of a public service. Theories of 'contentious politics'[1] would see nothing in these actors but a movement too weak to carry its demands successfully to the political sphere. At worst, they would see symptoms of declining participation in the mechanisms of political life or attitudes leading to a 'dissipation of social movements' (Phelps-Brown, 1990). At best, they would regard the characteristics of these movements as indicative of an early phase of the *cycle* or *development* of social movements, in which innovations multiply, creating 'relatively open spaces for new collective experiments' (Tilly, 2003: 105).

The dynamism of the actors examined in the last two chapters, however, suggests not so much decline or the deficiencies of an immature movement, as the emergence of a new political culture and other forms of participation. These subjective and expressive movements seek to 'increase capacity for action and free choice. [They] want to change life a lot more than transform society' (Touraine, 2000 [1997]: 96). Within relationships and in the midst of everyday life, alter-activist youth, Zapatistas, social centres and some *piqueteros* movements create new spaces allowing each person to play an active role in the course of their lives, whether in consumption or in active citizenship. While only a limited number of actors are involved, these spaces of experience respond to a qualitative logic of social change rather than political outcome and regulation measures. Against the hold of the dominant ideology and markets, these actors seek to produce their own forms of cultural life, to self-transform, and to assert themselves through their creativity, without manipulation by or subordination to the market hegemony and its cultural industries. Activists thus devote a substantial amount of their energy to building the movement itself; to experimenting with concrete, local alternatives, and developing a lifestyle which strives to be different from that imposed by capitalism. The figure of an expressive and subjective movement does not imply a lack of economic and social demands, but tends to articulate construction of the self, cultural issues and social justice around a concept of change perceived as a process which begins with society and individual behaviour more than with the decisions of policy makers and institutions.

Instead of an abrupt and radical break in the course of history (the traditional idea of revolution), these activists consider social transformation to be an ongoing collective process. The 'other world [which] is possible' will not arrive tomorrow, after 'The Revolution', but begins here and now, in the interstitial spaces of our societies, (re-)appropriated by actors and transformed into alternative and autonomous spaces of experience. It is no longer by influencing institutional politics, nor by seizing political power, but by putting the movement's values and alternatives into practice, reaffirming local forms of sociability, constructing autonomous spaces and defending them against the influence of the state and the market (Held & McGrew, 2007: 199–201) that individuals will be able to take charge, act, and thereby realize themselves as subjects.

As we have seen in the previous chapters, the consistency between practice and defended values is at the centre of the experimentation processes and is the starting point of any social change. Activists of the way of subjectivity believe that the movement must be organized to reflect its alternative values: horizontality, participation of the greatest number possible, limited delegation, rotation of tasks, respect for diversity, etc. Rather than messianic visions or a pre-established project, these activists focus on everyday practices: 'We are feeling our way, seeking out concrete and emancipatory paths toward the transformation of social relations.'[2] There are neither over-arching models, nor 'prefab' social projects, nor pre-established plans. Alternatives decline in the plural: 'We don't have a model to propose but many alternatives. For me, it's not "another world is possible". Happily not! It's other worlds' (Barricade activist). What they want to build is 'a world in which many worlds fit' (Le Bot & Marcos, 1997). Thus neither the Zapatistas nor the participatory budget of Porto Alegre present *models* to be followed as such, but represent sources of inspiration which must be adapted to local realities and the specificities of actors: 'It is not a transportable, pre-built model but a source of inspiration to rethink our democratic practices' (activist from a London social centre, 2003; see also Khasnabish, 2008).

A distinct approach of the structure of movements flows from this concept of social change. Convivial relationship, active participation of each member and horizontality is in many cases only possible in the context of a relatively restricted group.[3] Rather than enlarging its various groups and committees, Barricade seeks to 'swarm': 'After twenty, it is better to create a second group, because once this limit is passed, different problems arise and it becomes difficult to maintain the same relations among members.' Activists of Barricade clarify that 'We don't seek to build a big organization but many, many small organizations, each maintaining its specificities.' Activists of the subjectivity path do not want their organization to grow until it reaches global proportions. They believe a global change will arise from the multiplication of diverse, autonomous spaces of experience. The idea here is the 'swarm': other, similar but autonomous, networks being created in other neighbourhoods and cities.

Thus, when someone becomes interested in Barricade's Collective Purchasing Group, activists respond, 'rather than join us, better go and see what is happening in your neighbourhood. If there is no collective purchasing group in your neighbourhood, build it.' This discourse echoes Marcos' words: 'The best way to support the Zapatista struggle is to lead your struggle where you are.' The young Zapatista sympathizers gathered in Cancún (2003) approved of this message: 'The most important thing I've learnt from Marcos is that you have to live Zapatismo and resist wherever you are.'

Disenchantment with previous forms of social transformation led activists to develop a strong distrust of all forms of power. They believe that 'neoliberalism must be criticized, but it is also necessary to contest the idea of power which is a legacy of former leftist social movements. . . . The politics we want is no longer about delegation to political parties' (Italian activist, 2004 WSF). Rather than to take power or develop countervailing power, they wish to create spaces of experience 'free of power relations through the dissolution of power-over' (Holloway, 2002: 37),[4] outside the domination of market ideology and communalism and without ties to 'power-domination'. In order to distinguish these practices from those aiming at countervailing power (the 'counter-power' of Montesquieu), we will use the term 'anti-power' in this context.[5]

The indigenous Zapatistas, Barricade activists, alter-activist youth and *piqueteros* emphasize resistance to social control. Autonomy is central to the spaces of experience which resolutely position themselves outside the political and the institutional – not only to evade power relations but also because these actors believe that capacity for change does not stem from political and institutional power. They thus call for change 'from the bottom', based on everyday practices and the participation of everyone: 'It isn't Lula who is going to make things happen, but actions from below' (Mexican activist youth). World transformations 'could not come from above but must already be built from below' (interview with a *piquetero*), in their lives and neighbourhoods rather than through the study of international economic measures. Change is not limited to the local, but it resolutely unfolds 'bottom-up': starting with practical solutions and without the certainty of knowing the direction of history. Building different social relations, convivial and non-competitive, assumes a great importance, as well as transforming one's own personality: 'We can't change the world if we don't start with ourselves, helping our neighbours, seeing how things are going in our neighbourhood . . .' (a young Mexican activist, 2003).

In this conceptualization, the near and the local become essential; the world is transformed by a multitude of alternatives based on experience, participation, everyday life, local movements and self-transformation. Change is thus conceived as both very short- and very long-term. On one hand, it occurs in limited spaces where the implementation of practical alternatives brings very concrete, rapid changes to a limited number of participants. But, at the same time, these spaces are part of a larger movement which struggles against the current system and transforms values through a decades-long labour of sedimentation. Previous distinctions between reform, revolution and anarchism thus lose their relevance.

While not always explicit, the legacy of some anarchist thought is very much present (Dupuis-Déri, 2005) – particularly in its self-organizational aspects. Likewise, the emphasis on consistency between practice and defended values was central to the philosophy of several prominent activist figures of the twentieth century, such as Gandhi, Martin Luther King and Nelson Mandela, as well as feminist movements since the 1960s (see Nava, 1992; Lamoureux, 2004; Rowbotham & Linkogle, 2006). While they are never referenced, this trend also continues some aspects of the movements in Eastern Europe in the 1970s, particularly the idea of 'anti-politics': 'Through self-organization, it was possible to create autonomous spaces in society. . . . The aim was not to *replace* power with another kind, but rather under this power – or beside it – to create a structure representing other laws and in which the voice of the ruling power is heard only as an insignificant echo' (Kaldor, 2003: 55–6; Havel, 1985; Konrad, 1984 [1982]). Actors of the way of subjectivity revive and adapt such practices and carry forward their discussions in a process by which this political culture continues to invent itself through reflection, concrete experience and exchange. However, in many cases, the memory of past protest movements has barely been transmitted, leaving alter-activist youth with the impression that they have invented wholesale a form of political engagement and a political culture, several of whose core elements were already present in previous resistance movements.

A social and subjective engagement

While personal and community realization are central, inequalities remain no less crucial for a majority of the world's people. Alter-globalization activists combine the subjective dimension with social and economic demands. New feminist networks, deeply involved in the alter-globalization movement, are particularly clear on this point. World March of Women (WMW)[6] activists claim to 'unite struggles against three oppressive systems: patriarchy, capitalism and racism' (D. Mate, coordinator of the World March of Women, WSF 2002).[7] With figures and experience to back them up, these feminists denounce both distributive injustices, of which women are the main victims (the WMW considers that '70% of the world's poor are women', WSF 2002), and problems stemming from the lack of recognition of women as subjects (violence against women, discrimination, patriarchy, etc.), the links between these two levels being generally established. However, they do not identify as victims: 'Obviously neoliberal globalization has exacerbated the effects of patriarchy, but we must be careful to avoid always victimizing women. In reality, the women's movement is currently the largest social movement in the world. Everywhere, women are struggling and organizing themselves' ('Women and globalization', position paper of ATTAC-Paris, 2001).

This fight for equality and recognition doesn't end with utopic visions of another world to come, but is waged within alter-globalization groups themselves – both to ensure that 'the gender dimension is better taken into account' (Italian activist, WSF 2002) and to counter discrimination and sexist practices within the movement. At the same time, these alter-globalization feminist activists refuse to confine themselves to this activist dimension of their life: 'We give life, we work, love, create, struggle, and have fun' (extract from the 'Women's Global Charter for Humanity'). Far from limiting their demands to women's rights, the 2001 International Meeting stressed that 'it is impossible to achieve different conditions for women without changing the world'. The WMW has since been extensively involved in the alter-globalization movement and endeavours to 'offer a global project of a fair and equal society for everyone, men and women'.[8] Adopted in more than 100 countries around the world in 2004, their main reference text is indeed called the 'Women's Global Charter *for Humanity*'.

Numerous organizations close to this way of subjectivity combine social and economic struggle with the promotion of subjective transformation. Jobless workers' movements in Europe and Argentina, minorities in the United States, indigenous people in Latin America all aim to go beyond stigmatization and blame. They provide their activists a space both to rebuild their self-esteem and to become again actors in their life and their society. In this way, the 'No Vox' movements' networks strive to move beyond blame and assert the dignity of the unemployed, against the 'stigmatizing idea that the unemployed can't find work because they aren't looking for it' (Flores, 2002: 41). Unlike theoretical knowledge, access to experience is not tied to the possession of certain resources, notably cultural capital and higher education. People who are excluded or marginalized often have little expertise and few theoretical arguments but strong experience. It is on this base that they build innovative movements within the way of subjectivity.

Illusions of anti-power and diversions of spaces of experience

In addition to the diversions related to the overemphasizing of subjectivity and experience, some limits to the way of subjectivity should also be underlined when it comes to its concept of social change. While often effective, 'spaces of experience' are also fraught with illusions such as the existence of groups freed of power relations and the utopia of a space outside society and politics. Moreover, the spread from social change in a limited group to larger scale transformation remains a blind-spot.

The illusion of the end of power

Activists of the way of subjectivity have developed a concept of change which refuses 'the language and logic of power and does not accept the concept of realism on which political power relies' (Holloway, 2003). While an impressive creativity and a renewal of social thought result, the utopic nature of this idea of a space without power-domination must be interrogated. The idea of a space purified of all power relations, 'without leaders and fundamentally horizontal' (Antentas et al., 2003: 31), a space freed of structure, power and exclusion is clearly utopian (Pleyers, 2004, Polletta, 2005; Teivainen, 2008). As in all social spaces, structures and power are very much present in alter-globalization networks and spaces, although in less formal ways than in more hierarchical organizations. M. Crozier and E. Friedberg (1980: 254) concluded their studies on organization with an analysis of self-organization, pointing out that

> Power is impossible to eradicate, and relations of power are essential components of cooperation and human relations in general. As long as self-management's partisans refuse to admit this, any action they undertake will run the risk of producing an effect opposite to what they wish to achieve. Power can be regulated and moralized only by flushing it out into the open, in order to prevent the consolidation of positions of strength and the crystallization of dependency relationships around these positions.

Romanticization of horizontal networks and autonomous spaces should be avoided. Lack of formal hierarchy should not be confused with a total absence of hierarchy. In the absence of explicit rules about decision-making and formalized power, prominent people may acquire considerable influence. Within alter-globalization gatherings, the influence of each participant varies according to their vocal leadership, social capital and ability to participate in previous meetings (which can prove crucial to grasping certain issues). Additionally, activists are confronted with very immediate problems related to the highly variable level of involvement of participants or the many challenges posed by cultural and political diversity.

The place of the adversary

In this way of subjectivity, the pole of opposition (Touraine, 1978) is the least well established. Not that the adversary is totally absent, but the relation to it is either too strong or too weak. Activists waver between an overly diffuse image of the adversary and a radical, definitive rejection, which prevents a social conflict from being established. In the former case, the adversary becomes omnipresent, infiltrating the very personality of activists: 'the enemy is not only external, it is also our own ways of thinking' (a *piquetero*). It hence becomes a matter of 'changing oneself'. In the latter case, the adversary becomes an enemy with whom all dialogue is rejected. Activists evoke a disconnected adversary, who rapidly becomes full of phantasms: a cohort of powerful actors who deliberately organize the domination of subjectivities and human beings, embodied in several big transnational companies or in international institutions – the WTO, World Bank, IMF – or countries – United States – which impose neoliberal policies, war and the capitalist system. Opposition is such that these enemies are kept at a distance and dialogue refused. Unlike NGOs, activists of the way of subjectivity refuse, for example, to participate in international summits whose legitimacy they contest. This is the meaning of the destruction of symbols of capitalism by black bloc groups and of some speeches during the Zapatista 'Other Campaign': 'We want a world where there is a place for everyone, even for the rich. In our world, they will have a place: prison' (Subcomandante Marcos, *La Jornada*, 2 February 2006).

The way of subjectivity oscillates between these two extreme poles of opposition, each of which effectively makes conflict disappear. In both cases, the relationship with the adversary is not deemed important. The pole of opposition is weakened to the point of removing the movement from '*contentious politics*' (McAdam, Tarrow & Tilly, 2001), towards a self-centred expressive movement:[9] 'It is in transforming ourselves, in changing our relationships and our concrete spaces for living that we will change the world' (an Argentinian activist).

Illusions of a space outside society and the political

The question of how to move from change at the individual or local level to global transformations generally remains a blind-spot for these movements and theorists of anti-power. Moreover, when transformation of the actors themselves and the improvement in their conditions of everyday life become the alpha and omega of the movement, global issues can be forgotten in self-focused activism. Withdrawal into identity alone or into internal movement issues can reduce the movement's functions to one of self-help (Kriesi, 1996). As we have seen, actors can also withdraw into a hedonistic experience of activism. Desire for social ties can sometimes translate into an attraction to community relations, even in an urban setting.

While expressive movements can contribute to profound social change, they can also lead actors towards a withdrawal from society: adopting Hirschman's 'exit option' (1970) and retreating to the margins of society rather than challenging the way in which it is organized from the inside. But does withdrawal from society suffice to achieve the change the activists desire? In some situations, it can, on the contrary, help to reproduce the system. If the actors of this path withdraw from conflictive engagement in the arena of institutional politics, retreating from political debate and turning their backs on state institutions and power, don't they effectively abandon the field to their adversaries? Indeed, M. Hardt and A. Negri (2000: 265) warn: 'Battles against the Empire might [not] be won through subtraction or defection. This desertion does not have a place; it is the evacuation of the places of power.' The logic of subtraction from political and economic power seems far less sound to the extent that the transition from these limited spaces to the global level remains extremely vague. To what extent can small collective purchasing groups really offer a global alternative to large-scale distribution? Can the experiments with horizontal organization and alternative social relations in the ephemeral camps or in the interstitial spaces of society have a deep impact on future society? Will the multiplication of local spaces of experience spread to lead to larger-scale transformation? How to move from the alternative organization of a few indigenous communities to global change? The limits of changing the world 'from below' and 'without taking power' have become more striking in Mexico, one of the countries where this alternative trend has been the most innovative. Numerous rural communities have set up autonomous municipalities, often with very innovative practices. Some have been working for decades, notably in the state of Oaxaca. The Zapatista movement and, on the opposite side, the intransigence of the government on agrarian issues and towards social movements have encouraged a multiplication of such spaces in the first decade of the twenty-first century. As innovative as they were, these autonomous spaces and communities have impeded neither the repressive and conservative evolution of Mexican politics nor rising inequalities and the strong decline of most Mexican living standards.

Moreover, as J. Scott (1998) showed, national political authorities are generally very wary of the development of autonomous spaces. The economic logic of global markets as well as the political logic of governments generally seek to intervene in these spaces, whether to monopolize resources or to impose the rule of law. Since the state's means of repression are measured on an entirely different scale from the defensive capacity of autonomous communities, a certain tolerance on the part of state authorities normally proves indispensable to their survival. Defending and sustaining autonomous spaces consequently requires that action be taken outside these spaces, within the very political arenas from which they claim to have escaped and in which purely local dynamics are inadequate.

Facing the political

Mistrust of, distance from and ambiguity towards the state

Mistrust is especially strong regarding state institutions, which embody top-down logic. It generates an overall rejection of political actors and state institutions. In Mexico, the campaign around the Zapatista Sixth Declaration retained a strong dimension of political rejection. Subcomandante Marcos reserved particularly strong language for all political actors and parties during the electoral campaign, including the centre-left candidate who eventually lost the election by a tiny margin and in a context of strong suspicion of fraud. Likewise, 'Que se vayan todos!' ('Throw them all out!'), the battle cry of the Argentinian revolt in December 2001, led numerous groups of *piqueteros* to advocate abstaining from voting in elections, believing that 'they [the politicians] are all the same. . . . Nothing can be expected from them' (a woman from the Unemployed Workers Movement (MTD) 'Teresa Rodriguez', interview 2003); 'None of the parties represent workers. Political parties have no role to play in social change! . . . It is clear to us that politics will not bring solutions' (activist from MTD 'Quilmes', suburb of Buenos Aires, 2003). Similarly at Barricade, people claim to have been 'vaccinated against party politics'. This disenchantment is widely shared among young alter-activists: 'I no longer believe in democracy as it exists. What I am looking for is a different way of reaching consensus, with more participation by the people' (Mexican activist); 'I don't have hope in traditional politics any more. I have no hope that institutions, the government or political parties will change anything' (young Spanish alter-activist).

Indeed, several actors that adopted this way of subjectivity have developed a one-dimensional vision of the state and its institutions, believing that the latter's main objective is to weaken and *tame* (Kaldor, 2003) social movements. The total rejection of political actors can, however, bring about a depoliticization of activists locked into local and cultural issues. But this firm rejection of the political and of institutions at the level of discourse often becomes much more ambiguous in practice (Svampa & Pereyra, 2003). Despite their proclaimed intention to maintain autonomy and the strong rejection of the state in their discourses, many spaces in fact survive on state support. This contradiction was particularly marked in the Argentinian movements which emerged after the 2001 financial and social crisis. The discrediting of institutions and political actors and the desire for autonomy were central elements in the discourse of the autonomist *piqueteros* from 2001 to the beginning of 2003. However, the majority were holding weekly demonstrations to get broader access to state subsidies as unemployment benefits or support for public canteens. Similarly, after only a few months of autonomous operation, many worker-occupied and worker–run factories in Argentina called for 'nationalization under worker control'.[10] While, in Liège, the alternative and autonomous nature of Barricade did not prevent the board from accepting, after prolonged debate, public subsidies, which saw it move from zero to seven employees in 2003. As for the Zapatista experience, it illustrates both the possibility and the limits of local autonomy without institutional support. The movement has set up an innovative political and social organization, building new institutions 'from below' and more adapted to the local realities and demands (see chapter 9). However, it has not been able to set up a sustainable alternative economy and to improve material living standards significantly.

Participation rather than representative politics

Disenchanted with current forms of representative democracy, activists of the way of subjectivity create new practices of participation. By establishing practices and empowering participants, their spaces of experience allow ordinary people to become actors in their life more and to contribute to social change in very concrete ways, starting with their everyday lives.

The desire to 'change the world without taking power' focuses on society rather than the higher realms of politics: 'What we are seeking is for the people to make the changes more than the politicians' (Mexican activist). The whole point for these activists of the way of subjectivity is precisely to move away from a politics of representation to one of direct participation: 'To those who accuse them of being "anti-political", the activists respond with a concept of politics as an activity based on 'strong' forms of participation of all citizens rather than as delegation to a few professionals' (Della Porta, 2005: 201; cf. McDonald, 2006).

Unlike unions and actors of the way of reason, the perspective of these activists focuses on social spaces rather than state, institutions and the political. From this perspective, Subcomandante Marcos described himself as a 'social rebel' rather than a 'revolutionary':

> a revolutionary basically plans to change things from above, not below; the opposite of a social rebel. . . . The revolutionary tends to convert back into a politician, but the social rebel never stops being a social rebel. When Marcos or the Zapatista movement are converted into a revolutionary project, that is, into something resembling a political actor in the political class, Zapatismo will have failed as an alternative project. (Marcos, interview in Michel and Escárazaga, 2001: 145)

The turn towards the social and society *from below* is the core meaning of the 'Other Campaign', launched by the Zapatistas in the summer of 2005. One year before presidential and legislative elections, with all of Mexico – particularly the press, television and intellectuals – completely absorbed by the electoral duelling, the Zapatistas attempted to turn attention towards society, towards the multiple local actors who provide the country with its energy and dynamism.

The rejection of debate with traditional political actors can thus be interpreted as a sign of wanting to pursue another path of social change. However, in believing that 'the government is not an interlocutor to address if you want to see things done differently in Europe' (protester during European summit, at Brussels, 2001), in avoiding difficult but important debates and in focusing on the logic of anti-power, have these actors chosen an effective way to bring about the changes they desire? To what extent can they bypass political intermediaries and arrive at social transformation that is concrete, less transitory and of a certain scale? Moreover, the issues raised by the forms of political participation in the spaces of experience are not easily incorporated by political and social actors, including part of the alter-globalization movement. The lack of representation, rejection of delegation and reluctance to build more structured organizations make it difficult to communicate demands to policy makers.

Conclusion

Rather than a struggle against globalization, this way of subjectivity is first and foremost a call for the freedom to choose one's existence, at the individual and collective levels, against the logics of power, production and mass consumption. The core of this activism which valorizes experience is located in the creation of spaces in which each individual and each collectivity can construct themselves as subjects, as actors in their everyday lives as well as in their society. Indeed, it is not experience in and for itself which lies at the heart of this way of subjectivity but experience linked to the will to become an actor.

While movements of industrial society believed that change would come from the fields of political power or production, the actors of the way of subjectivity look towards the private sphere, everyday activities and the local – areas largely ignored by their predecessors. By transforming their leisure activities, consumption or modes of transportation, everyone can become more of an actor in their own lives and an agent of change in the world. Their movements are rooted in experience, subjectivity and creativity rather than abstract figures and expertise. The struggle against the globalizing and homogenizing system is carried forward by the assertion of particular subjectivities which defend the existence of 'a world in which there is a place for all worlds' (Le Bot & Marcos, 1997) against market domination and communalism. Zapatistas, *piqueteros*, activists of social and cultural centres and alter-activist youth thus share the centrality of lived experience, a concept of social change based on subjective and cultural transformation, the valorization of diversity and the implementation of concrete alternatives and social relations.

Innovative as it is, this path also has its limits and diversions, stemming from the concentration of actors at the single pole of the movement identity. The defence of communities against market logic can give way to a withdrawal into localism, communalism and closed identities. The assertion of subjectivity through experience can drift into the diversions of hedonism, disconnected from its initial orientation towards social change. Individuation of involvement and commitment can undermine the continuity and unity of the movement, dissipating in sporadic activism. The way of subjectivity contributes to the renewal of politics but its expressions can be diverted into an *anti-political movement*, replacing an ambiguous relationship to politics with an opposition to all types of political actors. The concept of social change adopted by these activists is also fraught with illusions such as the existence of groups freed of power relations or the utopia of a space outside society and politics, while the distance between change in a limited group to larger-scale transformation remains a blind-spot. Finally, in most cases, the adversary of the movement either remains extremely vague or is considered to be an enemy with whom all dialogue must be refused. Each of these issues highlights the importance of linking such spaces of experience to a dimension better able to influence a broader political community.

Part 3

The Way of Reason

Clinging to matters of the heart or good intentions would
mean handing over the best weapons to partisans of the
current system: 'heartfelt, for sure; but so little mind...'
(Passet, 2001)

5

Expertise for Another World

Resisting through reason

The media often dwell on the festive and demonstrative aspects of alter-globalization mobilizations. But the success of issues deemed 'tedious' or 'forbidding' by activists themselves is also very impressive. Apart from occasional demonstrations in the streets, most alter-globalization activists spend most of their activist time in auditoriums, conferences, lectures and numerous meetings. Thousands 'slog' (term used by an activist from Liège) through arduous lectures on international finance and gather in halls to listen to the explanations of a couple of experts. By calling themselves *citizens*[1] rather than *activists*, they express their disenchantment with previous forms of activism and their interest in reformulating ways of political engagement on the basis of an active concept of citizenship. To oppose neoliberalism, become actors in globalization, and participate in decisions which affect their lives, they have chosen the *way of reason*, founded on technical and abstract knowledge, expertise and popular education.[2]

A brief analysis of a text which is clearly inscribed within this way of reason allows a preliminary illustration of its main constitutive features. The article 'A humanitarian tax for Asia' by J. Nikonoff, then president of ATTAC-France, was published in the French daily *Libération* on 4 January 2005, just a few days after the tsunami which left more than 250,000 dead in South-East Asia.

Reason instead of emotion Rather than allowing ourselves to be overwhelmed by emotion in response to human suffering and to the terrible images broadcast from Asia, actors of the way of reason seek to 'rationalize' and 'think', because if 'something is not right, [. . . it is that] this immeasurable catastrophe is not thought'. The cold rationality of numbers and policy questions replaces the warmth of human relations and emotions. The tsunami is explained by – and reduced to – a series of objective factors: the 'major size of the earthquake', 'its suddenness', the 'biblical symbolism of the flood'. Reason, not emotional reaction, should guide citizens: 'Let's not forget that, each day, according to the Food and Agricultural Organization, hunger and malnutrition claim the lives of 25,000, chiefly children. . . . One could not sustain, each day, an emotional shock of the same intensity in response to diffuse dramas, atomized throughout the world, resulting from a slow agony, difficult to translate into a "scoop" of media images.' The status of precise data, calculated by experts from international bodies or from the alter-globalization networks, proves to be particularly important in these discourses, especially as a means of arousing the indignation of citizen activists.

The possibility to act rather than inevitability of fate While the tsunami is 'presented as an inevitability of fate, justifying all the present, past and future impotence of national and international public officials', the president of ATTAC-France links the extent of the damages to the economic situation. The assertion of the possibility of acting, which is at the heart of the alter-globalization movement, is exemplified here by a proposal for a series of short-, medium- and long-term actions, from the boycott of a Dutch bank (see below) to global taxes which 'will require years' to implement. Similarly, in response to the 'diffuse catastrophe' of world hunger, concrete actions are possible and require comparatively limited means, relative to sums invested elsewhere by governments, the cost of the Iraq war being the example most frequently cited. For the tsunami as for world hunger, alter-globalization activists assert that solutions do exist. To achieve them, 'it is political will that counts'. While 'it is necessary to give' to help regions devastated by the tsunami, the donation, inscribed within an emotional register, is entirely insufficient. 'Nice feelings' must thus 'give way to real measures capable of responding to real problems'. J. Nikonoff consequently proposes 'mobilizing' around a series of economic objectives in the medium and long term. An exceptional tax levy – '0.05 % of global stock market capitalization' – to aid the tsunami victims is in this way considered a first step towards world taxation.

Deconstructing myths and axioms of the market Alter-globalization intellectuals never seem to miss an opportunity to contradict a neoliberal axiom – in this case, the optimal allocation of resources by free markets: 'If this were true, we would have seen the immediate and spontaneous flood of capital towards Asia, a kind of financial tsunami to help the region recover.' The delegitimization of the market continues as the lack of compassion and humanity in market rationality – in which human beings appear to constitute one factor among others in the tourist economy – is accentuated:

> Throughout the drama, business continues. No morals, no reserve, no decency; it's business as usual. Sure, the Tsunami killed tens of thousands of people and devastated the entire country, but the Indonesian and Indian stock exchanges beat records, borne along by an economic climate deemed favourable. According to Eddie Wong, chief analyst for Asia at the ABN Amro Bank: 'Damage sustained by the better hotels does not appear serious, and there have also been economic gainers, such as cement producers.' One could also add coffin-makers!

For sure, the economist at ABN Amro does reduce reality to economic data. But doesn't the president of ATTAC share the same will to 'rationalize' the situation, to bypass emotions and privilege the economic perspective?

A similar statement arises from an analysis of the arguments developed by the activists of the way of reason against the war in Iraq, which focused on abstract analysis and on the economical dimensions. They emphasize the collusion between the Bush adminstration and the financial interests of the military-industrial complex, oil companies and private armies and companies related to provisioning the US army or 'reconstructing Iraq'. From the same perspective, they assert that the solution to terrorism lies in the economic plane: 'cruise missiles and stealth bombers are powerless in the face of the turmoil of societies dislocated by inequalities, poverty, pandemics, and – frequent corollary – 'worked on' by fundamentalists' (ATTAC, 2004b: 8). Hence, the Jakarta Peace Consensus which arose from the main international gathering against the war that brought 200 delegates[3] from five continents in May 2003, stressed 'the important links between globalization and militarism . . . We see the invasion of Iraq as part of the on-going economic war against peoples of the South. Under the rules of the IMF/World Bank and WTO, our world is becoming increasingly unjust and unequal.'

Spaces of expertise

Legitimacy of expertise

Unlike experience, which refers to 'mental states appearing to involve an immediate relationship between the mind and the fact and whose contents are intrinsically subjective and qualitative',[4] the way of reason passes through objective, quantifiable and technical content, which must be acquired through training. The latter then represents a substantial part of activist efforts: 'In order to act, we must first become familiar with the mechanisms we claim to fight, and this demands a minimum of *work*' (ATTAC, 2002: 110). The abstraction and the universal nature of the measures advocated also encourage the privileging of a global outlook, which is indeed very much present in the discourse and the alternatives proposed by the actors of this way of reason: 'To bring about citizen-based economic regulation, it is necessary to work at the global level, to set up global economic regulations' (Dierckxsens, 2001: 138).

Expertise is at the core of this alter-globalization trend. It is on expertise that the legitimacy of actors of this way of reason reposes, and through which their will to act and to participate in public decisions passes. 'Expertise' here designates *technical knowledge of a precise subject or area*, such as the GATS, third world debt, education or the Tobin-Spahn tax. This term will not be used to imply the elitist character of a knowledge mastered by only a handful of experts, but to indicate knowledge of an abstract, theoretical and generally universal character. Activists use the term to mean 'a subject on which a technical knowledge has been acquired', a 'field of competence':

> This refers to [topics] which do not concern our main field of expertise, such as access to land, which is Via Campesina's domain. (Activist from the third world debt cancellation campaign)
> A journalist asked me what I thought of trade union positions on Arcelor. I replied, 'But on those questions, the unions have the *expertise*, not me!' (Activist from Liège)

Alter-globalization has chiefly mobilized economic expertise; although the entire field of knowledge – from environmental science and communications to biology – has been harnessed, particularly on such questions as Genetically Modified Organisms. There has also been a substantial investment in the field of law, which activists consider 'not as a defensive barrier for given situations, but as a factor of change within an historical process' (F. Houtart, interview, 2003; see also Habermas, 1997). In Mexico and Central America, a number of human rights NGOs have thus expanded beyond their original specialization in political rights to encompass 'Economic, Social and Cultural Rights' and joined alter-globalization national networks on this basis.[5] The Committee for the Abolition of Third World Debt (CATWD, 2004), for its part, perseveres in advancing the demands of the movement by requiring the implementation of existing international law and agreements.

Actors of the way of reason have constructed their credibility and acquired recognition among the activists' networks, in public opinion and with political actors and international institutions, on the basis of the quality of their expertise: 'Whether or not you agree, when you have a document written by the Transnational Institute, you know it is serious' (a European expert, interview, 2002). Therefore, 'from our flyer to our book to our petition, the requirement for rigour must be permanent' (ATTAC, 2002: 110). Within the civil society organizations close to this way of reason, those who take on the role of spokes-people for the movement base their legitimacy on their expertise:[6] 'Many people said that Benjamin was starting to take up too much space. But he's the one with the expertise. . . . I don't mind that someone who works hard is put in front' (activist in Liège Social Forum).

Alter-globalization activists of the way of reason challenge the monopoly of expertise by international institutions in global governance, especially in the area of political economy. Alter-globalization activists mean to counter IMF or European Commission experts with their own experts, 'who are at least as good as the [European] Commission's' (B. Cassen during a talk in Paris, 2002). While they rely on experts themselves, they consider the influence of experts in global governance to be disproportionate, and highlight the lack of respect for the limits proper to practices of expertise. They also denounce the fact that many opinions are issued without the possibility of validation, without proper consideration for the rules of scientific validity. The trappings of scientific discourse are assumed in order to gain authority in debates which have more to do with ideology than with science (Sapir, 2002).

Faced with their counterparts in international institutions or transnational companies, alter-globalization experts claim popular support as an additional source of legitimacy: 'Isn't their legitimacy expressed by the response of crowds, who regularly demonstrate in support of their initiatives?' (R. Passet, *Grain de Sable* (ATTAC online newsletter) 415, 8 April 2003). This popular support is also demonstrated in petitions: with 24 million signatures collected between 1998 and 2000 in 166 countries, the petition for the cancellation of third world debt gathered the greatest number of signatures in history.

Spaces of expertise

The production of specific expertise in each issue area is the core objective of alter-globalization *spaces of expertise*: *groups of activist–experts, who specialize in relatively precise subjects and enjoy a certain authority on that question within the movement.* Some groups are devoted to economic measures or to following international negotiations. Others focus on education, law, culture, the position of women or migrants. There are different degrees of such expertise: some groups enjoy international recognition while others bring together local activists slightly better informed than others on a particular question.

The concrete forms assumed by these spaces of expertise vary. Some are integrated into a larger organization, like ATTAC's 'Women and globalization' committee. Others constitute an organization in their own right, such as Focus on the Global South or the CATWD. The latter formed in 1990 around Eric Toussaint, an activist–expert who gradually gained access to the financial resources necessary to assemble a team around him. Five paid staff analyse developments on the issue and help to spread awareness of the third world debt problem around the world. Based in Belgium, the committee developed an international network throughout Europe, Africa and Latin America, whose activists have become experts in their own right. E. Toussaint, who, thanks to the CATWD, has become an alter-globalization globetrotter, was also one of the founders of ATTAC-International and then the World Social Forum. Under his influence and that of the Jubilee South campaign, the issue of the third world debt has continuously gained importance within the international networks and especially the World Social Forums.

ATTAC (Association for the Taxation of Financial Transactions for the Aid of Citizens) was initiated in 1998 by a group of French intellectual-activists who essentially wanted to develop a space of expertise which could construct an alternative discourse to the 'one way thinking' (i.e. neoliberal ideology) they denounced, particularly in the monthly *Le Monde Diplomatique*. They were surprised by the popular success of the organization and by the creation of local committees; its first president, B. Cassen, even acknowledging that 'when ATTAC was created, there was no thought of local committees'.[7] More than a space of expertise, ATTAC rapidly came to embody a *model of convergence* capable of bringing together very broad opposition to neoliberal globalization in a relatively generalist organization. After three years, it counted 27,000 members in France and local committees in about forty countries. The organization dominated the alter-globalization landscape in France until 2003, when it entered a gradual decline.[8] Strong internal conflicts marked the following years and eventually led to the election of a new leaders' team (see chapter 7) in December 2006. ATTAC could never regain its initial dynamic, however.

The Mexican Action Network against Free Trade (ReMALC[9]) is another example of a space of expertise. Created in 1991 to oppose the free trade negotiations then taking place between Mexico, the United States and Canada, it later broadened its field of action to challenge the neoliberal model of development in operation in Mexico, proposing, for example, an alternative economic programme in 1995. ReMALC then specialized in opposing trade negotiations at the international level – especially the Free Trade Area of the Americas (FTAA), but also free trade agreements between Mexico and the European Union, and the WTO. Its activities have developed around three central goals. The first objective is to 'critically analyse economic and trade policies', to propose alternatives and to 'raise awareness of Mexicans about these issues' (interview with a ReMALC spokesperson, 2003). In this capacity, it is largely dominated by an affinity group of intellectuals and experts, though other groups are not without representation. Secondly, before its failure at the 2003 mobilization against the WTO summit in Cancún, ReMALC acted as a *convergence space* for the Mexican alter-globalization movement and contributed to spreading information on the issue to numerous organizations. In this way, it linked around 100 organizations, including unions, intellectual groups, NGOs, ecology networks, and peasant and citizen groups. In practice, delegates of half a dozen organizations take responsibility for the network and thirty others occasionally take part in meetings deemed important; the rest are involved only formally. Finally, one of ReMALC's main functions is its *participation in international alter-globalization networks*. Closely networked with similar actors in Canada and the United States (Arroyo et al., 2002; Massicotte, 2004), ReMALC helped found the Hemispheric Social Alliance against the FTAA and, as a delegate of this Alliance, used to be the only Mexican organization in the International Council of the WSF.

However, most spaces of expertise transcend the limits of organizations and constitute disparate networks, such as the orientation and steering committees of the campaign against International Financial Institutions or the 'Decent Work' campaign. One of the functions of large organizations and forums is precisely to encourage meetings and collaborations among experts specialized in the same fields. For example, fifteen intellectuals close to ATTAC met to debate the question of development (ATTAC, 2004a). The 'specialized' seminars and workshops during the Social Forums are privileged venues permitting such spaces of expertise to emerge or to be reinforced.

Beyond workshops geared to a general public, the most important exchanges take place through more informal conversations among members of these spaces, who learn to know and appreciate each other. Positions drafted collaboratively and emails sent analysing recent developments in issues of concern to the network then become the privileged means of continuing these exchanges. The European network against transnational corporate lobbies offers an interesting example. A number of organizations such as Friends of the Earth and the Corporate Europe Observatory had worked on this issue for years. Several of their experts collaborated to organize workshops on the topic at the European Social Forums. At the 2004 ESF in London, the workshop was followed by a 'campaign assembly' whose objective was to organize 'actions against the influence of transnational corporations on the European agenda'. Groups from Scandanavia, Italy and Catalonia then converged with this network, which originally comprised a few British and Dutch experts. After discussing the issues, they assembled the various activities proposed by each group into a joint calendar – which eventually sparked a collaborative dynamic.

Specialization, coordination and competition in civil society networks

An activist or a single organization can't develop an accurate analysis of the full range of questions tackled by alter-globalization. Specialization is consequently an essential element of movement efficiency (Wahl, 1997). This is particularly the case for experts, but is also true of grassroots activists, who must choose among hundreds of workshops and talks during each Social Forum: 'During this forum, I will attend the workshops on water, privatizations and the WTO' (a green activist on her arrival in London for the 2004 ESF).

Once their expertise is recognized within the movement, these spaces of expertise see their analyses taken up by a broad network of actors and playing a decisive role in the positions and actions of other organizations. In this way, ATTAC's local groups participated in various protests – related to food security, illegal migrants or GMOs – without developing their own expertise in each area, but relying on specialization: 'For housing, we go to DAL [Droit au Logement (Housing Rights)]; for GMOs, to the website of the [Peasant] Confederacy' (Parisian activist).

Although indispensable to the development of expertise, specialization of knowledge occurs at the price of fragmentation. The challenge is thus managing to combine specialization and coordination. In discourses, the urgent need for cooperation is highly emphasized. In practice, however, spaces of expertise compete over subject areas without always being able to converge or merge (Keck & Sikkink, 1998; Dumoulin, 2003). The creation of new groups of experts, along with new organizations, progressive expansion of the field of competence claimed by a group of researcher-activists, divergent positions or personal interests of leaders can all help to generate overlap or even encroachment into spaces of expertise. In this way the explosive arrival of ATTAC on the scene challenged the Parisian expert NGO Observatoire de la Mondialisation in its areas of expertise and eventually led to its dissolution. In most cases, relations between groups of experts working on the same issue are characterized by a mixture of partnership and competition. This is the case, for example, between the international networks of CATWD and Jubilee South. Both specialized in the third world debt issue and with a largely common approach, the two spaces of expertise nevertheless maintain some distance in order to justify their respective existence. Although Jubilee South is far bigger, the CATWD insisted on developing its own international network in Africa. This 'competition' does not prevent them from occasionally collaborating, however; for example, they co-organize a part of their workshops at each World Social Forum.

Functions of spaces of expertise

The essential role that spaces of expertise play in the way of reason can be resolved into six principal functions. The first consists of *analysing policies and current debates in a precise area*. Spaces of expertise follow the most recent developments in their subject-area and 'monitor' international institutions (an anti-WTO network expert, 2002). In some cases, this leads to their also having a *function of 'alert' and orientation of public debate*: 'if debate does not occur spontaneously on these issues, it is up to ATTAC activists to provoke it' (B. Cassen, 19 January 2002). Informed about recent progress in political negotiations, spaces of expertise are best placed to judge the most opportune timing for bigger mobilizations in civil society networks: 'the Collective for the defence of illegal migrants has expertise in this area, so when it says that we really need to protest, we follow. And it is its discourse which counts on this issue' (Liège activist). Spaces of expertise also bring to light negotiations which are taking place and expose information which often remains confidential. The 'Dracula strategy' – 'drag the WTO negotiation into the light of day and it will wither and die' (Observatoire de la mondialisation, 1998; see also George, 2004: 197) – has proven particularly effective during negotiations of the Multilateral Agreement on Investment. By mediatizing these hidden processes, spaces of expertise reinforce democracy and participate in an alert system equipped with 'antennas highly sensitive to society's problems', which is the core mission of civil society (Habermas, 1989) and counter-power actors (Rosanvallon, 2006).

Their next function is to *construct 'rational' theoretical alternatives* and show the relevance and *feasability* of these alternatives, in order to prove that it is possible to act, and that rational and coherent measures can be taken. This labour of expertise allows, at least in theory, the definition of relatively precise and measurable objectives, in contrast to the often simple utopian ideas promoted by some alter-globalization actors, particularly those of the way of subjectivity: 'more time must be spent making measurable and operational proposals than throwing out slogans' (a leader of ATTAC-France, WSF 2004).

Alter-globalization experts must also *arouse indignation*; for example, by using data to illustrate world suffering. Activists of the way of reason get mobilized by learning that a child dies every 15 seconds due to lack of access to drinking water (Petrella,[10] 2001). Spaces of expertise also play an important role in the area of *popular education*. Alter-globalization experts hold numerous lectures and training sessions in order to share their knowledge with the greatest number of people. The Transnational Institute, ATTAC and Friends of the Earth developed their action in this perspective. Social Forums also assume this function; they resemble vast campuses in which each room is taken over by a studious public, 'eager to know and to understand' (ATTAC, 2000a: 14). While alter-globalization expertise often seems to address policy makers, one of its major purposes is to teach and convince the movement's own activists, which is important for two main reasons. Active citizenship – which is at the heart of the alter-globalization movement's way of reason – requires a certain knowledge, whether on technical issues about political economy and finance or on how to manage a city. In addition, the strong individuation (Ion, 1997; McDonald, 2006) of political involvement within the alter-globalization movement redoubles the importance of convincing each activist, through well-founded argument, of the relevance and feasibility of the advocated position.

Finally, alter-globalization experts are often chosen to *confront opposing experts* and to *convince policy makers* on the basis of a 'rational analysis of the situation'. As the president of ATTAC-Liège (interview, 2003) explained, 'The second main role of the organization [the first being 'education and self-education'] is to put pressure on the policy world. So we define ourselves a little like a counter-lobby. Given that there is such proximity between the policy makers and the financial or industrial lobby, particularly at the European level, we need to take up the role of counter-lobby.'

Convincing policy makers is in fact one of the primary tasks for activists of the way of reason. With the proliferation of international bodies and negotiations, new spaces have opened for (counter-)lobbying activities, in which international NGOs and other alter-globalization actors have invested, though to a much lesser extent than transnational corporations. This can go as far as editing texts in collaboration with governments of the global south or the participation of alter-globalization experts in delegations from such countries as India or Malaysia to the WTO ministerial at Cancún. But also, at the local level, activists 'send [their] analyses to those politicians who want it; analyses which are generally extremely reliable, credible and convincing' (ATTAC activist). This work is all the more important because, as even the French Senate acknowledges, 'France is experiencing a lack of independent counter-expertise in areas as crucial as taxation policy, macro-economic analysis, social policy, and education.'[11]

Alter-globalization 'counter-lobbying' is not, however, without its contradictions: it opposes the growing impact of lobbying by transnational companies and economic interests,[12] while attempting to develop its own lobbying capacity. It is nevertheless to be distinguished from other lobbying efforts – notably those carried out by corporations and NGOs – by the mass mobilizations which support it. The latter reinforce the positions put forward by experts, whose task it is to transform the claims and aspirations expressed by protesters into concrete technical proposals. The alter-globalization marches around international summits clearly share classical advocacy objectives: to influence political decision-makers. R. Passet even writes about 'lobbying by the people, carried out in the streets' (*Grain de Sable* 415, 8 April 2003). Alter-globalization activists' efforts to exert political pressure rely on a rather traditional repertoire (Tilly, 1986, 2004) which includes demonstrations, petitions, and more direct challenges to elected representatives: 'We write letters to representatives or, when we meet them, we question them directly' (ATTAC activist). But activists also draw on more recent innovations such as symbolic actions directed at the media.

Information and popular education

In the information society, 'the critical resources are individual and collective capacity to learning and training' (Willke, 1998: 29). The primary purpose of many organizations is thus to endow their members with the tools necessary to understand the world in ways which escape the hold of the dominant neoliberal ideology and to provide them with the means to debate political trends, especially in the areas of economics and finance. Learning – which is based on experience in the *way of subjectivity* – is in this context essentially a matter of the diffusion of expert knowledge through lectures and popular works. As the packed rooms of the Social Forums and the ATTAC universities indicate, activists of this way of reason possess a great thirst to learn and understand. A local ATTAC chapter is, above all, 'a group of people in a process of learning'; to be a member of the network against the debt means to 'inform oneself on the issue of debt, reading documents . . .' (interview with a French activist).

The counter-power of the way of reason draws its strength from the support of public opinion resulting from media exposure of decisions, negotiations and facts considered unacceptable. As U. Beck (2005: 442) outlines, power 'is founded on the way in which facts are systematically passed over in silence and denied by leaders – of states as well as big groups'. In a second phase, alter-globalization activists then establish their counter-expertise, broadcast through the newsletters of each organization.

Participation cannot be disassociated from information, which constitutes an essential precondition. These alter-globalization activists consequently consider information and reliable media as key elements of democracy. The creation of media empires in the hands of a few wealthy financiers and industrialists with links to economic and political power (Klinenberg, 2007) greatly concerns alter-globalization activists. Silvio Berlusconi, Rupert Murdoch and Fox News figure among the activists' main targets. The acquisition of *Le Figaro* by a rich French arms manufacturer reopened the debate in France in 2004. Media bias in the coverage of the early stages of the Iraq war was also roundly denounced. Alter-globalization activists considered 'disinformation strategies'[13] the root of American public support for the war on Iraq: 'They are ill-informed. They believe that Israel is occupied by the Palestinians, know nothing of the bombing of Sudan or the sanctions on Iraq' (S. George, during a conference, 2002).

Through popular education, alter-globalization organizations seek to encourage 'a shift in mindset', 'a necessary detoxification after two decades of neoliberal brainwashing' (ATTAC, 2000a: 14). Through alternative media, lectures and various gatherings, popular education attempts to reinforce the autonomy of citizens and their capacity to analyse and counter 'the hegemony of neoliberal thought [which] is exercised through the media' (French activist). The spread of alternative information and analyses is thus a crucial task of alter-globalization networks. It takes place through diverse channels: alternative newspapers and magazines,[14] reading and reflection groups, colloquiums, books, films, online magazines, information bulletins,[15] etc. The internet constitutes an extraordinary tool on which activists rely. The *Grain de Sable* (Grain of Sand), ATTAC's online, twice-weekly magazine used to reach over 50,000 activists in France and was published in several countries and six languages.[16] Many politically engaged retired people have taken up computing in order to 'be able to follow the movement'. Various more entertaining activities are organized in an attempt to disseminate the issues to a broader public. For activists of ATTAC, the alter-globalization festive parade in Liège, an activist, festive procession through the city's streets, is not seen as a space to express one's subjectivity but as an opportunity to 'approach people on the sidewalks. It is a time of information for all citizens' (General Assembly of ATTAC-Liège, 2003).

The ambivalence of expertise

Expertise and participation

While experience cannot be delegated, the construction of solid, scientific arguments which embody expertise requires a certain specialization and hence a delegation.[17] Therein resides a major difference between the two paths of alter-globalization. No activist can be an expert in the entire range of issues tackled by the alter-globalization movement. Activists are consequently obliged to base their judgement on the expertise of others. Expertise thus implies a certain number of 'black boxes': 'we are prepared to trust specialists on a range of matters and to regard as true all kinds of statements which we cannot submit to critical analysis because we lack the time and the necessary cognitive skills' (Boudon, 1989 [1986]: 116; 1998). Here a fundamental tension surfaces between two core elements of the way of reason: the *active participation of citizens in decision-making* and a *necessary delegation to experts*. Alter-globalization activists have rebelled against the 'domination by international experts' as anti-democratic, and denounced the delegation of choice in the areas of political economy and trade to experts working for international institutions – but, at the same time, they are forced to rely on experts themselves.[18]

For alter-globalization activists, to become familiarized with alternative expertise is a way to become an actor in the global age. While the discourse is often heavily economic, the objective is clearly political: 'to reappropriate together the future of the world' (ATTAC founding platform subtitle); 'to ensure that citizens recover an influence over decisions which affect their lives' (Parisian activist). Expertise is then considered to be an *instrument* on which a reinforced and more active citizenship and a more democratic governance can rely. The words of a Dutch expert from the Corporate Europe Observatory are particularly explicit in this respect:

> Our idea of democracy is very important. Citizen participation is a basic idea of democracy. Of course we can try to do it by trying to be an expert and trying to do this type of work, and of course we also do it. But I think that it is very important to bring this debate into the public at large. And that's why we write articles in the newspapers, and so on. And we try to expand the debate so that people understand that there is a problem here, that the political power of transnational corporations is a problem. Because if we leave it only to the experts, we might be capable of success, but it would not be based on broad support. I think that in a democracy . . . first off, it is very important to have these types of discussions, these types of debates, and it is a bit the objective of the Social Forums on the whole: political debates . . . Our goal is to oppose the power of multinationals. Why? Because we want a better functioning democratic system, particularly one with more participation. (interview, ESF, 2004)

The alter-globalization movement aims to make 'the economic and financial mechanisms that are presented to us as domains reserved for "experts"' (ATTAC, 2002: 31) accessible to citizens. This was a major significance of the events of Seattle: the WTO is not only a matter of experts. Thousands of 'ordinary citizens' seized hold of the debate and made their voices heard, challenging the influence of experts in their elaboration. Alter-globalization thus decisively positions itself as an *anti-technocratic movement*, agitating in favour of an expansion of democracy though greater citizen participation. It is the 'first global social movement against public technocracies which are denounced as complicit with business' (E. Cohen,[19] 2001: 95).

The objective is not to transform each member of ATTAC into a Tobin-Spahn tax expert, versed in the technical detail which would allow its implementation. Rather, popular education aims chiefly to provide each citizen with the elements necessary to grasp what is at stake in policy measures and political negotiations in order to be able to position themselves in the debate. The activist seeks to 'equip herself with the expertise necessary to evaluate the meaning and significance of a measure' (Cassen in ATTAC, 2000a: 15). Activists of this way thus endeavour to constitute themselves as personal subjects, capable of forming opinions with a full knowledge of the facts and deciding when to mobilize: 'People no longer allow themselves to be carried along by slogans. . . . They want to understand for themselves, to be able to reflect themselves' (a Parisian union official, very active in alter-globalization networks, 2001). The importance of individuation[20] and the autonomy of activists increases the significance of education. The objective of alter-globalization popular education is consequently 'not primarily about transmitting knowledge to people who don't have it, nor about dispensing formulas or tools to people who will absorb them like blotting paper. It is about allowing each person to act by herself, to recover the quality of *free subject* (as opposed to object or "the public"), and to act with others, in solidarity. It is to promote the emancipation of people' (D. Minot, ATTAC Summer University, 2004).

Alter-globalization activists are not the first to have recourse to expertise. Since the 1980s, environmental NGOs have relied heavily on scientific analysis in their awareness-raising and advocacy campaigns. However, what is unique about alter-globalization is the alliance of expertise and active participation by a great number of citizens. While the vast majority of members of NGOs like Greenpeace limit their participation to an annual donation, delegating action, the construction of expertise and lobbying to a few professional activists, the alter-globalization movement encourages the active participation of all its members in the debates. Through broad distribution of knowledge and expertise, the distance between experts and 'ordinary citizens' is limited. Once involved in the movement, some activists rapidly become experts on some issues, to the point of gaining recognition in the field. Identifying himself in 1999 as 'an ordinary citizen interested in these issues', two years later Arnaud Zacharie had become one of the foremost alter-globalization experts in Belgium.

Diversions of expertise

While they can be complementary, the logic of expertise and the logic of participation can also enter into tension and opposition. Participation by the greatest number and the elaborating process of a careful expertise are not always in happy harmony: 'Ultrademocratization sometimes leads to things . . . The scientific committee of ATTAC [Wallonia-Brussels] drafted a document and circulated it to everyone and to ATTAC-Liège, everyone made a critique. And the committee and its experts who worked weeks on the document had to deal with critiques from *the man on the street*' (Liège activist, 2003). On the contrary, when the logic of expertise begins to prevail over that of participation, the mechanism at the heart of the way of reason inverts and the movement comes to reinforce technocracy rather than fight it. It reproduces within itself a pattern of domination by a few experts which it denounces in international institutions: the grassroots activists' will to become actors is thwarted by the experts, who consign them to a passive role and come increasingly to limit their political involvement, to the detriment of democratic practices. The paradoxical result is to suffocate the subject that alter-globalization has brought into being.

The *diversion of expertise* thus consists of overextending a logic which is essential to the functioning of the movement (expertise) to the point of dissociating it entirely from the perspective of the initial purpose of the movement (to increase citizens' participation): 'Rather than being at the service of the actors, rational knowledge becomes the heart and engine of their political engagement' (Wieviorka, 2003: 47). Intellectual elites then occupy the centre of the movement, and are more and more separated from grassroots activists, particularly through a process of institutionalization of the movement's organizations and the installation of intellectuals as spokes-people for alter-globalization. As we will see in the following chapter, this technocratic diversion contributes to the development of a cosmopolitan activist elite, in close contact with political and international governance actors but distant from its base, at times even adopting an elitist vanguard's logic.

Alter-globalization is thus transformed into an intellectual pressure group, focusing more on counter-expertise than popular education, and on experts more than citizens. This diversion of expertise also tends to promote an institutionalization of the movement and to dissolve its conflictual nature: close relations between alter-globalization experts and their adversaries encourage integration into the institutional sphere and the institutionalization of some civil society actors as part of a 'taming process' (Kaldor, 2003).

'The danger of being overwhelmed by NGOs'

The diversion of expertise offers an insight into certain attitudes which might otherwise appear paradoxical, such as a suspicion of NGOs on the part of activists who are themselves the heads of NGOs or similar organizations. Many grassroots networks insist on the 'huge difference between NGOs and grassroots struggles' (an activist of the 'No Vox' network, 2003). Such criticisms are more surprising when they are taken up by the leaders of several small but committed organizations, who fear 'that the movement could be overwhelmed by NGOs that may share similar preoccupations but are not directly linked to social struggles'. Surprisingly, these words, spoken at the 2003 WSF, are those of François Houtart, a long-time activist and leader of the 'Tricontinental Centre', an activist research centre organized around a well-known expert, possessing an extremely tiny social base, and relying on donations and grants from the Belgian state to fund its activities. It clearly resembles the impugned NGOs in many aspects. Yet the opinions of F. Houtart are echoed not only by numerous activists but also by heads of major NGOs. Questioned on this issue in 2002, S. De Clerck, director of Oxfam-solidarity Belgium, developed arguments in the same direction. Similar statements were made in Mexico, where NGOs had more influence on the alter-globalization movement than 'mass organizations'. A leader of SERAPAZ, a peace and human rights NGO which leads a civil society network against neoliberal policies, explained the 'necessity of rethinking the concept of civil society starting from social movements. . . . The social movement demands its sovereignty, its capacity to take the initiative in the face of political parties and NGOs. We at SERAPAZ are very attentive to this phenomenon.' (interview in Mexico City, 2003).

These warnings by NGO leaders about the dangers of NGOs assuming a disproportionate influence over the alter-globalization movement do not refer to NGOs as concrete actors nor to the form and structure of NGOs, which they have adopted in their own organizations. F. Houtart, S. De Clerck and the leader of SERAPAZ are in fact addressing the *diversion of expertise* evident in some NGOs which display certain symptoms – most palpably, technocracy; hyper-mobile leaders disconnected from social bases; and institutionalization. While their mode of organizing, resources and efficiency make some global civil society organizations generally better placed to respond to needs linked to a degree of institutionalization of the movement organizations, numerous alter-globalization activists decry their lack of commitment to social conflicts, considered to reflect an *apolitical* stance adopted by NGOs and humanitarian networks (Kaldor, 2003). The institutionalization of movement organizations, the privileged place assumed by experts, and lack of grassroots membership together encourage a retreat from the anti-establishment pole of the movement and from grassroots social struggles.

Conclusion

The way of reason of the alter-globalization movement relies on expertise to encourage the emergence of an active citizenship in the global age and the formation of social actors who are both autonomous and engaged in public debate. Expertise and democratization can mutually reinforce each other: experts share their knowledge with citizen-activists and benefit in return from the legitimacy of a social base and the influence of numbers as well as expertise. However, the logic of participation and that of expertise can also enter into tension and subject actors of this way of reason to different and even conflicting imperatives. Expertise by itself can lead to the privileging of efficiency over participation. Experts can quickly become disconnected from local activists and even coopted by political parties or international institutions with whom they share this valorization of expertise. An inverted figure of the movement then reinforces technocracy – the power of experts over society – rather than combating it. In the reality of organizations and events of the way of reason, these two aspects often play out side by side: tendencies which lead to the diversions of expertise, and others which constantly reinforce the moorings of 'active citizen', participation and empowerment of the greatest number. The relationship between 'citizens', grassroots activists of the movement, and their leaders, whether experts or intellectuals, thus proves to be of central importance. This will be the focus of the following chapter.

6

Citizens, Experts
and Intellectuals

Introduction

The defining feature of the way of reason of alter-globalization is the partnership of committed experts and citizens in projects aimed at encouraging a more active citizenship, requiring a certain knowledge, especially in the area of political economy. As an expert from a network against the WTO explained in an interview in 2001,

> there was something new in the fight against the MAI, and then in the mobilization in Seattle: experts, researchers, intellectuals found themselves with trade unionists and activist groups, radical networks. It is the first time. In fact, we see researchers becoming activists, and ATTAC is to some extent the proof of this; but also activists who become researchers, and this has a huge impact on mobilization.

Indeed, ATTAC strongly embodies this tendency of the alter-globalization movement, particularly in France, where it had its beginnings. Providing an overview of the purposes of ATTAC, its president and founder claimed 'to have leapt over the symbolic barriers between the "ivory tower" and the "ground" by systematically mixing scholars, researchers, trade unionists engaged in struggles, activists from various backgrounds and ordinary citizens' (ATTAC, 2000a: 15). The experts and intellectuals who founded alter-globalization organizations and events were surprised and overwhelmed by the 'citizen dynamics'. This was particularly the case with the hundreds of local committees of ATTAC whose emergence had not been foreseen by the intellectuals who founded the organization. In the same way, the World Social Forums, conceived and organized by and for progressive scholars, were flooded by thousands of activists coming from very diverse struggles.

A citizen movement

Citizens in the way of reason

The way of reason is not limited to intellectuals and experts. It is also shared by thousands of 'ordinary citizens' who attach a strong importance to learning in their activism. They believe that more active citizenship and the advent of a fairer world require a knowledge of some technical, abstract issues – particularly in the area of economics – which would allow them to grasp the issues, sustain debate and throw the Washington Consensus into question.

Diverse activities correspond to different levels of expertise which activists may have attained; while discussions with national political authorities are reserved for a few experts, giving a lecture on a specific theme to a local ATTAC group is within reach of many others. Hundreds specialize in a specific issue area, gradually becoming 'experts' in their own right – the objective then being to share their knowledge with other activists. The goal is for each activist to have sufficient knowledge on alter-globalization issues for them to be able to talk in their own circles, 'to debate with their neighbour or in their workplace' (activist from ATTAC-France).

In contrast to the way of subjectivity, to practise the way of reason and acquire knowledge on often highly technical issues requires certain resources, particularly in cultural capital. Statistical research has demonstrated that, in western societies, the majority of people who are politically engaged come precisely from the middle class with higher cultural capital (Bekkers, 2001).

Organizations involved in the way of reason are no exception to this rule. In many countries, and particularly in France, ATTAC thus has the reputation of being an 'organization of intellectuals'. This is in fact confirmed by various studies.[1] In 2002, 71 per cent of ATTAC-France members had a graduate degree (Cours-Salies, 2002). Teachers represented almost a quarter of its activists (23 per cent). Indeed, one of the organization's leaders estimated that 'at ATTAC, the average activist is a high school economics teacher'. Conversely, only 3 per cent of its members were from the working class, and ATTAC members who didn't have a university degree were quite rare (Cours-Salie, 2002).

Despite declared intent and the presence of five organizations representing the most insecure sectors of society (illegal migrants, unemployed workers and people living in bad housing) among the founders of the organization, ATTAC has never really managed to integrate working-class milieux. Certain limits to alter-globalization's 'popular' education are apparent: 'There is, in my opinion, a problem due to the way our texts are drafted. No matter how hard we try, at times, to vulgarise, it's a big challenge given the subjects we tackle, they are quite complicated issues as well . . .' (an activist from ATTAC, 2004). The gulf between those who frequent working-class milieux and activists of the intellectual middle class (Bourdieu, 1984 [1979]) leads to numerous misunderstandings. A dynamic group of women activists from ATTAC-Liège regularly went to outdoor markets in the region in order to raise awareness about alter-globalization issues outside the usual circles. At the opening of 'La Batte', the big Sunday market in Liège, they unfurled a banner reading 'No to the dictatorship of the market!' Surprised by their relative lack of success, they were finally accosted by passers-by who thought that they wanted to close La Batte market.

Citizenship at the heart of alter-globalization identity

The term 'citizen' is now omnipresent in documents and interviews with actors of the way of reason, particularly among those whose first political involvement was alter-globalization. Many alter-globalization organizations use the term in the name of their group – such as ATTAC or the French Citizen Coordination for the Control of the WTO. The reinstatement of citizenship is at the core of the identity of and alternatives proposed by these actors of the way of reason: 'Today, it is *"Citizens of the world, unite!"'* (activist from ATTAC-Liège).

Excepting labour unions and peasant organizations, individuals in the alter-globalization movement do not mobilize on the basis of a worker identity. Citizenship thus offers a new point of reference.[2] Sufficiently abstract and vague to unite beyond the internal diversity of activists of the way of reason, the figure of the citizen proves at once more universal and more individualized than the categories offered by movements of industrial society.

Like 'activist' in the way of subjectivity, the choice of the term 'citizen' rather than 'militant' by numerous actors of the way of reason aims at creating a distinction from traditional forms of political participation deemed corporatist, partisan or ideological. Many alter-globalization activists maintain that, unlike *'militants* [who] mobilize chiefly to defend their personal interests or their jobs', *citizens* 'are not corrupted by the system and apparatus' of traditional movements. To a young leader of ATTAC-Liège, 'being a citizen implies that you have the interests of a citizen and you must defend them'. In interviews and activist speeches, the reference to citizenship is almost systematically linked to the emergence of new forms of political engagement and a questioning of 'traditional' forms of activism often associated with the predominance of large trade unions, the centrality of labour relations tied to companies, the nation-state as the context for struggle and negotiation, and privileged relations with leftist political parties (Wieviorka, 2005).

The reference to citizenship also throws into question the image of the career activist and her dependence on an organization. The 'citizen' is placed in the public sphere with minimal mediation; organizations are essentially considered to be instruments, places to seek information and resources necessary for citizenship. The term 'ordinary citizen' expresses this independence and distance from any organization whatsoever. It is often used during introductory go-rounds at the beginning of meetings and in some interviews: 'I was obviously there as an *ordinary citizen*, so I didn't represent any movement organization. So I am one of those people who maybe would never have been active and

would never have been politicized if ATTAC hadn't existed'
(ATTAC activist).

In the interviews, *citizen* was also used frequently in contrast
with *politician*. Thus, those who are involved in the new organizations consider themselves to be 'citizens who are completely fed
up with [traditional] politics. They are arriving without ideological bias' (interview, 2004). The ambiguity of relations with political parties can be traced to this will of alter-globalization activists
to combine involvement in the public sphere with a certain rejection of traditional politics. The concept of citizen embodies this
double-intent. While distinct from an engagement in a political
party, the reinstatement of citizenship was, in the first place, a
response to political apathy. For alter-globalization activists, the
'big problem is that the man in the street is no longer interested
in what will change his life. But for us the democratic debate is
fundamental' (GA of ATTAC-Liège, 4 June 2003). In activist
discourses, the idea of citizen reflects, 'people who have nothing
in particular [but who,] after having abandoned the public sphere
to the sole care of career activists and politicians, suddenly wake
up to the catastrophes that are happening to them' (an organizer
with the CATWD); 'It is a citizen movement which becomes
conscious of the problems and says, "Things must change and
we, citizens, we have something to say about it"' (an ATTAC
activist, 2000).

As evoked in activist texts and discourse, the notion of 'citizen'
does not refer to membership in a particular political community
nor to the national context traditionally associated with the notion
of citizenship. Frequently urban, individualized and produced by
a rather intellectual middle class, most activists often have little
attachment to cultural or national identities. The challenge facing
alter-globalization activists is how to advance citizenship at the
same level of global integration as that of economic actors, while
no international institution is presently capable of promoting and
providing a framework for citizenship at this level. The situation
appears somewhat different in a region like Catalonia or in Latin
American countries, where the national context has a much
greater influence on movements. Starting a week of primary
school in the Zapatista communities or a general assembly at the
anti-neoliberal organization 'El Barzón' in Monterrey is unthink-
able without the Mexican national anthem. The reinforcement of

active citizenship was seen as a fundamental element of national transition to democracy by Mexican activists.

Citizens of the way of reason distinguish themselves from *activists* of the way of subjectivity in that they assign a central place to *institutions* (see chapters 7 and 9). However, rather than the idea of a social contract between citizen and state which gives rise to rights and duties, alter-globalization activists hold a view of citizenship in which each person can take a more active part in democratic life. Thus, citizenship primarily plays out on the register of active participation and conflict with the state (Giddens, 2000; Habermas, 1989; Rosanvallon, 2006). We move from the perspective of the citizen subject of a state to a view of the state as an instrument of citizenship. The call to a new citizenship came to crystallize a re-enchantment of the political and of political engagement which takes place through a greater individuation.

Committed intellectuals

Intellectuals as entrepreneurs of the alter-globalization movement

Intellectuals and experts hold a privileged place within the way of reason of the alter-globalization movement. Their role was crucial in the initial stages of the movement, during which their work helped to arouse the indignation of citizens over the consequences of Washington Consensus policies. Building and internationalizing the new movement relied largely on the prestige and fame of committed intellectuals, on their legitimacy as experts in their fields and on their international affinity networks. Since its foundation in 1994, the International Forum on Globalization has played a leading role in South Asia and North America. It defines itself as an alliance of 'leading activists, economists, scholars, and researchers providing analysis and critiques on the cultural, social, political, and environmental impacts of economic globalization' (www.ifg.org/about.htm, accessed 1 June 2010). Among its distinguished members figure Maud Barlow from the Council of Canadians, Vandana Shiva from the Indian Research Foundation for Science, Technology and Ecology, Walden Bello from the Bangkok-based Focus on the Global South,

Lori Wallach (USA) from Global Trade Watch and Martin Khor (USA) from the Third World Network. In France, the popularity of alter-globalization owes a lot to intellectuals such as Susan George and Bernard Cassen.

Hundreds of intellectuals built the movement around the world, sharing the conviction to represent 'true public opinion and to be the best interpreters of general causes' (Charle, 2001). They are thus dominant in a large number of alter-globalization organizations of the way of reason. ATTAC, the Committee for the Abolition of the Third World Debt, Global Trade Watch, the Mexican Action Network against Free Trade, the Continental Alliance against the Americas Free Trade Area and Focus on the Global South were all founded by intellectuals and scholar activists. This was also the case for some major alter-globalization events, including the World Social Forum and several national forums. In Austria and Russia, the national Social Forums started in a university research centre which remained their dominant actor for years.

Intellectuals have been defined as 'a special category of people who defended political positions based on arguments of social authority, i.e. their competence as thinkers, historians, scientists, professors, writers, or artists' (Charle, 2001: 7628). Through their work, they acquired certain values (reference to truth, universalist values, criteria of validity), methods of thought, tools and the discipline (Weber, 1963 [1919]: 111; also Maclean, Montefiore & Winch, 1990; Cardon & Granjon, 2003) to form wise judgements. The numerous, cultivated alter-globalization public, moreover, created an interesting 'market' able to provide these intellectuals with recognition and a certain legitimacy, as well as to guide some intellectual projects (Boudon, 2004).[3] Since knowledge is highly valued by the way of reason, it is hardly surprising to discover a large number of intellectuals among alter-globalization actors.

It was after they had gained recognition for the quality of their analyses in relatively precise fields (within the logic of expertise) that figures such as B. Cassen (geopolitics; American culture), E. Toussaint (specialist in the issue of third world debt) and L. Wallach (legal expert and economist) became involved as intellectuals and organizers of the movement. This did not lead them to abandon the production and dissemination of expert knowledge. During the two days we spent following Eric Toussaint at the 2004 World Social Forum, he moved back and forth between the role of expert, presenting specific aspects of the third world debt issue, and that of entrepreneur of alter-globalization mobilization, in his capacity either as head of the international CATWD network during internal meetings, or as an active member of the International Council of the WSF.

Two generations of activists

Many alter-globalization experts and intellectuals are long-time activists, having accompanied protest movements for decades. Several made the transition from anti-colonial third world solidarity to alter-globalization, while retaining a Marxist bent or their roots in dependence theories. They generally read the alter-globalization movement in the line of their previous struggles. Some, such as the Argentinian James Petras (2000: 57), even consider it to be a 'movement which has taken up and developed Marxism in new circumstances, adapting it to new class actors and using it in new types of struggle'.

However, a new generation of experts and intellectuals also emerged with alter-globalization. Often in their thirties, they challenge civil society cleavages forged in past struggles. More pragmatic and less ideological, this new generation relies on constantly tracking developments in global economics and trade negotiations. At times disputes erupt between the two generations, some of the oldest fearing a 'drift towards social democracy' by their younger fellows, who, for their part, do their best to differentiate themselves from a Marxism they deem 'outmoded': 'I personally did everything in my power to absolutely avoid all the old Marxists in this journal issue' (interviews with two activists from the same small alter-globalization research centre). Nevertheless, new and old experts generally collaborate; the youngest can thus benefit from the networks established by their elders, while the latter support the revival inspired by the new generation, although without always really grasping it: 'I really don't know how to describe what is new in ATTAC, but Arnaud [Zacharie] can tell you. He won't say it like that, but everything he will tell you is new' (interview, 2000).

The trajectories of Bernard Cassen, Lori Wallach and Arnaud Zacharie well illustrate different types of alter-globalization intellectuals and experts. Born in 1937, *Bernard Cassen* obtained a Masters degree (*aggrégation*) in English at the Ecole Normale Supérieure in Paris. Teaching at the Sorbonne, he participated in the founding of the University of Paris-VIII in 1968, where he taught until 2000. He began a parallel career in journalism, which brought him to the monthly *Le Monde Diplomatique* from 1973 and saw him become one of its directors in 1996. Meanwhile, he played a role in the Mitterrand administration between 1981 and 1985 as the director of the inter-ministerial mission of scientific and technical information. Close to the former French minister J. P. Chevènement, Cassen is a republican intellectual with sovereigntist leanings. He follows a more political line than most alter-globalization activists and always expressed his keen support for Latin American progressive regimes. He played a defining role in the creation of ATTAC in 1998. His commitment to popular education was apparent from the beginning of the 1970s and led him to give this orientation to ATTAC: 'We don't want to see people parading in the streets without really knowing why.' The statutes of ATTAC-France and its highly centralized and hierarchical structure also bear his mark. Acting president between 1998 and 2002, he later placed J. Nikonoff at the head of ATTAC, maintaining a very strong influence in the organization himself as honorary president and with the mandate for international relations. Notably, he was deeply involved in the campaign against the Treaty establishing a Constitution for Europe in 2005. Cassen was also among the founders of the World Social Forum (Cassen, 2003) and exercised a major influence over its development, as well as within the International Council, until the end of 2006. ATTAC's internal elections fraud in June 2006 led to a strong victory by the opposing team in a new election held in December 2006. There were unquestionably hard blows for Cassen. Far from resigning himself, he and J. Nikonoff founded the opposition 'Avenir d'ATTAC' ('Future of ATTAC') which continues to develop his line of thought, challenging the newly elected leadership.

Lori Wallach was born in 1964. A Harvard-trained lawyer, expert in international law and economics, she has devoted her skills to fighting against the liberalization of international trade and for fairer trade which respects the environment, labour and agriculture. She was first involved in Ralph Nader's Public Citizens, then, in 1995, became head of Global Trade Watch, an alter-globalization think tank. In 1997 and 1998, she contributed to blocking a 'fast track' procedure which would have permitted the US president to have international trade agreements adopted more rapidly and practically without debate by Congress. Involved in different international networks of alter-globalization experts, including the International Forum on Globalization, she contributed to the derailing of the Multilateral Agreement on Investment in 1998 and of the Free Trade Area of the Americas project. In 1999, her organization also played an important role around the 'Millennium Round' of WTO negotiations in Seattle. Lori Wallach, moreover, specializes in analysing and following negotiations of sector privatization and deregulation within the WTO, an organization that she believes is currently close to a 'terminal crisis'. Wallach has played an important role in fostering the growing debate about globalization and trade liberalization. Her writings on the ravages of globalization and on the WTO have become reference points. Her work has had significant national and international echoes. Recognized for the quality of her expertise and the relevance of her analyses, Lori Wallach has often appeared in the media and has testified before more than twenty US congressional committees as well as in the European Union Parliament and several foreign Parliaments. She rejects the global standardization implied by current international norms and proposes, instead, that the people should participate in the elaboration of international trade rules and overall decision-making. In this way, she strives to rehabilitate the full exercise of democracy, in order to achieve social justice and democratically accountable governance.

Born in 1973, *Arnaud Zacharie* began his political involvement at the age of twenty-five. He joined ATTAC-France online, before holding a meeting at his home with a dozen activists who later participated in founding the local chapter of ATTAC in Liège, Belgium, in 1999. He embodied the revival of political engagement in Liège: based on expertise, and outside political parties and old quarrels among activists. Very active with ATTAC-Liège, he was 'discovered' and then quickly hired by Eric Toussaint, president of CATWD, where he began publishing.

This fruitful collaboration did not impede Arnaud Zacharie from maintaining his autonomy from Eric Toussaint, keeping his distance from the latter's loose Trotskyist affiliation and adopting more pragmatic, 'less radical and revolutionary' positions. In 2001, he became the spokes-person for ATTAC-Wallonia-Brussels for three years and then left the position to 'avoid having a few individuals permanently installed at the controls of the alter-globalization movement' (interview, 2004). A renowned expert and good speaker, he is as comfortable explaining the problems of neoliberal policies and the WTO to a high school audience as to experts in ministers' offices. Participating in various international gatherings, including the World Social Forums, he has remained sceptical of the 'centralism of ATTAC France' and feels closer to the Scandinavian and German representatives of the organization. Holding a BA in communication studies and two Masters degrees in international relations, and a daily reader of the *Financial Times*, Arnaud Zacharie is a dedicated worker and author of eight volumes between 2001 and 2006. At twenty-nine, he was offered the post of head of the research department at the 'National Centre of Development Cooperation', a coalition of around 100 Belgian NGOs. Six years later, he became director of the whole organization.

Predominance of intellectuals within the International Council

Many academics and committed intellectuals have become major 'entrepreneurs' (McCarthy & Zald, 1977) of alter-globalization mobilization. They played a determining role in the emergence, development and internationalization of the movement. Since then, they have held a good number of key positions in the movement organizations and networks. Among the most active members of the WSF's International Council between 2002 and 2005 were many scholars and 'committed scholar–activists networks'.[4] These include: E. Taddei, then director of a broad Latin American network of social scientists, who participates in the name of the Americas' Continental Social Alliance; A. Buzgarin from the University of Moscow, the founder of Alternative Russia; F. Houtart from the World Forum for Alternatives and Professor

Emeritus at the Catholic University of Louvain (Belgium); S. Amin, director of the Third World Forum, president of the World Forum for Alternatives and former Professor of economics at the University of Paris; L. Gabriel, Professor at the Ludwig-Boltzmann Institute for Contemporary Research on Latin America; W. Bello, director of Focus on the Global South and Professor at the University of the Philippines; B. Cassen of ATTAC, Professor at the University of Paris VIII; and the scholar–activist Network Institute for Global Democratization. Several other member organizations are think tanks, small activist research centres, or NGOs which are composed mainly of engaged intellectuals, such as several 'centres of alternative information'. Almost all of these 'organizations of intellectuals' enjoy a very limited – often non-existent – social base in their countries.

The function of the International Council is, however, unconnected to any specialization of a *space of expertise*. Its role is to 'ensure the openness and diversity of the World Social Forum' (B. Cassen, meeting in Paris, 2004). How then to explain such a predominance of intellectuals in the organizing bodies of the international movement? The high value conferred on knowledge and intellectuals, which characterizes the way of reason, and the central role played by intellectuals in the formation of the alter-globalization movement are evidently factors. However, the strong presence of intellectuals at the international level is reinforced by two heavily correlated factors. First, the capacity of experts and intellectuals for abstraction and their facility with universal categories gives them a greater ability to think on a global scale. Some of them even believe that 'experts are the only ones able to think and manage conceptual tools at the global level'.[5] Possessing a special interest in global issues, intellectuals become more involved in international alter-globalization networks, convergences and events. Moreover, working for NGOs or the academy, intellectuals possess the necessary time and resources, both social capital and financial, to attend international forums and preparatory meetings, which leaders of grass-roots movements generally lack.

Second, as C. Tilly (2004: 153) pointed out, social movements rely on 'mobilization professionals' far more at the global than the local level. Indeed, the internationalization of the alter-globalization movement relied largely on the prestige and fame these intellectuals had gained, on their legitimacy as experts in their fields, and on their international affinity networks. In the mid-1990s, years before the larger alter-globalization gatherings were organized, scholar–activists and engaged intellectuals began creating their own international networks (e.g. the International Forum on Globalization, the World Forum for Alternatives, etc.). These networks and the resulting affinity groups were later to take a leading role in the foundation of alter-globalization networks, forums and events. With these decision–making groups generally expanding on the basis of contacts established by the founders and other influential members, intellectual activists have maintained a leading role in groups like the International Council of the WSF. As C. Tilly (2004: 152) pointed out: 'Expansion of social movements along existing interpersonal networks excludes those who don't belong.' The movement's global orientation and internationalization and the position of intellectuals as elite international activists hence reinforce each other. The weight and influence of experts and intellectuals within the movement strengthen its tendency to be globally oriented. In turn, the movement relies heavily on these intellectuals as international elite activists.

Theories of another world and practices of expertise

Intellectual leaders and democratic deficiencies

In contrast to the way of subjectivity, the logic of expertise and the – more political – logic of older leaders of movement organizations have little concern for consistency between practice and values of the movement. Problems relating to internal democracy and strong leadership have arisen in movement organizations founded by scholar–activists in every country in which this field research was conducted, at both national and international levels. Many activists interviewed cited the rather authoritarian personality of a leader, or political cultures and national traditions tending towards the 'iron law of verticalism and caudillism' in Mexico Zermeño, 1996, or Jacobinism in the French style: 'I don't know whether it is due to the political imaginary of the French, very centralized. ATTAC has a way of presenting itself as though it is the avant-garde of the movement' (activist from Liège).

Many collaborators, employees of alter-globalization think tanks and committed intellectuals decry the 'strict control [their leader] imposes on every document and initiative that comes out of the organization' (a young employee of a Belgian activist research centre). These terms recall the portrait of Cassen published in the daily *Libération* on 21 January 2002: then acting president of ATTAC, he 'drafts all the texts, as a "matter of credibility and rigour". Overwhelmed by the demands, crushed by the workload, he strives to get a grip on his *vampirish culture of control*, relaxing his pedagogical and vertical concept of power. He *resigns* himself to launching a democratization project internally that the organization defends externally.'

Explanations in terms of personality or national culture prove inadequate in light of the number and similarity of the cases encountered. The frequency of these observations indicates a structural problem, inherent to this way of reason: its *ambivalence towards experts*. The latter have an essential role and privileged place in the way of reason. At the same time, alter-globalization also aims to encourage the participation of the greatest number and opposes 'domination by experts'.

Recognized experts in their fields, committed intellectuals who become leaders of an organization often have a tendency to behave like strong leaders internally, closely watching the work of their collaborators and having difficulty accepting criticisms of their organization or even of the entire alter-globalization movement. Cocooned by the legitimacy of expertise and their knowledge, the majority of alter-globalization experts and intellectuals show scant concern for the internal democracy of their organizations. Some young activists openly described their supervisor as a 'real internal dictator'.[6] Many small alter-globalization think tanks and NGOs are built by and around a committed intellectual who presides as lifelong president. Even larger organizations headed by intellectuals do not always manage to address adequately the question of internal democracy. In 2006, the leadership team of ATTAC was even convicted of fraud in the organization's internal elections (Passet, 2006).

Certainly, several committed intellectuals and leaders are deeply preoccupied by the movement's internal democracy and openness (e.g. Albert, 2004). However, most consider internal democracy to be a secondary problem which the importance of current struggles and campaigns prevent from being properly addressed. The urgency of the situation is often evoked to justify the lack of democracy, openness and representativeness. When asked about the democratic weaknesses of the WSF International Council, Cassen defended himself in this way: 'The International Council was conceived in a hurry. It is useless to seek criteria and principles that guided its construction. There were no criteria behind the choice of its participants.'[7] While the criteria of democracy may not be relevant in spaces of expertise, the same cannot be said of spaces dedicated to organizing a movement fighting to reinforce democracy in society.

Active citizens and passive activists

Strongly rejected by activists from the way of subjectivity, the distinction between 'grassroots activists' and intellectual leaders is clearly assumed by many engaged intellectuals: 'The alter-globalization movement is like a human body. Committed researchers are the head of the movement and the masses that mobilize for events like Seattle are its legs.'[8] Indeed, many committed intellectuals assume they are more competent than grassroots activists to assess global challenges and develop alternative expertise, proposals and clear programmes for the international movement.

This perspective often limits the role of local activists, making them local informants and recipients of the wisdom and political culture produced by intellectuals who comprise the movement elite (see p. 148). Their chief role becomes one of demonstrating popular support for the leaders of the movement in order to assure them greater political impact.

This top-down approach of the organizational process and the dominant position of cosmopolitan intellectuals have created a contradiction between the message promoted by the alter-globalization movement and actual practice: while encouraged to become 'active citizens', activists are often kept in a passive position, as consumers of events and ideas conceived by a few leaders. The elaboration of the movement's discourse is thus reserved for experts. An activist very involved in the secretariat of ATTAC-

Liège learned this the bitter way. She spent several months editing an introductory text for the organization only to see her work greeted by harsh criticism from several leaders and recognized experts. *Why?* Unwittingly, she had trespassed on an area of competence of ATTAC-Liège's experts – writing documents. Surprised and disappointed, she ceased playing an active role in an organization she had served zealously for four years.

This distance between citizens and intellectual leaders is reinforced by the rapid professionalization of brilliant new experts[9] and by the multiplication of international meetings which cultivate the formation of an international alter-globalization elite. As happens in other sectors of global civil society (Chandhoke, 2002: 48), once immersed in this 'international alter-globalization', most leaders gradually draw away from their social base and become unaccountable to their membership. However, a leadership assumed by a small affinity group of committed intellectuals over alter-globalization events and networks is in fact often contested on this basis. As we will see in chapter 8, grassroots activists seldom limit themselves to this passive stance – they set up diversion strategies or simply don't show up.

When the Mexican Network against Free Trade (ReMALC) imposed itself as the coordinator of the 'People's Forum' that was expected to unite all the protest events against the WTO summit in Cancún, 2003, other participant organizations and activists were reduced to a passive audience during the preparation meetings while ReMALC experts took all the leading roles. Many voices soon denounced 'these NGOs and intellectuals who want to talk in the name of the movements but have no social base' (a Mexican farmers' union activist, 2003). However, when the time came to start the counter-forum in Cancún, no one showed up, leaving the ReMALC leaders alone in their forum, which was soon cancelled.

This 'People's Forum' offered a striking illustration of the gap that separated intellectual leaders from the Mexican civil society that they claimed to represent. Collaboration between citizens and experts/intellectuals thus remains a constant challenge for the alter-globalization activists of the way of reason. This is especially the case for ATTAC-France and the World Social Forums, both having been conceived as spaces of expertise by their founders.

ATTAC-France, an organization conceived as a space of expertise

As we mentioned, ATTAC was founded as a space of expertise by a group of French intellectuals who didn't foresee the creation of local committees and of an active citizens' participation within their organization. Nevertheless, ATTAC rapidly came to embody a *model of convergence* capable of bringing together a wide range of activists and 'ordinary citizens'. The logic of expertise, however, remained dominant until the end of 2006, leading to structural deficiencies in the organization at the level of internal democracy. It was notably illustrated by the internal election process.

In 2002, B. Cassen managed to impose his choice of candidate, J. Nikonoff, as his successor at the head of the organization. He retained the international relations mandate for himself, in the process purging a few dynamic activists whose loose Trotskyist affiliations displeased him. Despite strong opposition and with little charismatic appeal, Nikonoff held the presidency until the end of his mandate in 2006. Tensions within the organization were such that ATTAC-France was then polarized between partisans and adversaries of the Cassen–Nikonoff duo. These two proclaimed victory in the internal elections held in June 2006. But suspicions of fraud were quickly confirmed by three independent expert reports (Passet, 2006). New elections were called for December 2006 and the former leadership obtained only four of the twenty-four seats in the administrative committee of ATTAC-France.

While it disappointed thousands of activists and surprised journalists, because ATTAC defined itself as a civil society organization which fights for a 'reinforcement of democracy', this electoral fraud was inscribed within an extension of the logic which had dominated ATTAC-France since its inception and which is encountered in many organizations of the way of reason: the resurgence of an avant-garde attitude by leading intellectuals. ATTAC-France was shaped by a top-down and authoritative approach to organizing a movement, in which intellectual leaders indicate the way forward without much consideration of internal democracy or local chapters. The distance between 'intellectual' leaders of the organization and 'grassroots activists' is taken for granted among the members of the executive team, as the following extract from an interview in 2001 with an ATTAC-France administrator, chosen by Bernard Cassen, indicates:

> There is obviously a difference between grassroots activists, who join ATTAC to get a political culture, and the members of the scientific council who are academics and directors of newspapers and magazines. There is obviously a gap. But I think there is a mutual enrichment. People in the executive committee and in the scientific council work to produce research documents and information. The local sections are useful because they are on the ground and can inform us about what they observe in their region. They see things at this level, in their region, in their town.

Grassroots activists are thus essentially reduced to playing a relay role: a matter of 'informing' the head of the organization. In return, they receive knowledge and a political culture which they are supposed to spread. This organizational logic is, to say the least, astonishing in an organization which purports to promote a new culture of involvement and 'active citizenship'. According to this leader of ATTAC, the principal task of not only the scientific council, but also the executive committee and the headquarters team, is to 'produce research and information documents'. However, while the former is indeed a space of expertise, the role of the other two bodies is coordination and leadership of the organization, requiring functions and attributes different from those of a space of expertise.

In some respects, ATTAC-France operated like an NGO in which a dozen salaried professionals based in Paris had to '*manage 27,000 members*', to quote one of the employees of the headquarters in a 2002 interview. In addition, like all of the founding texts of the organization, the platform was the work of a journalist from *Le Monde Diplomatique* – in this case, Serge Halimi – rather than a product of an activist assembly. Similarly, on 17 January 2002, ATTAC-France's 25,000 activists discovered that their organization had a new platform, on which they had not been consulted, for either content or relevance. The text had been written by a few intellectuals in consultation with the organization's ruling president. No prior internal consultation was held to elaborate or approve it.

The Jacobin and very centralized logic of organization emanating from the top of the organization is very far from the 'network, without hierarchical structures nor geographic centre' cited in the international platform of ATTAC.[10] Members register at the national level before joining local chapters, leaving 75 per cent of their membership fees at the national level in the process. Representation of local chapters at the national level, unforeseen at the beginning of the organization, wasn't recognized until 2001. Even then, the assembly of local chapters was restricted to offering 'advisory opinions', the president of the time having explicitly refused to grant them decision-making power at the national level. The lack of democracy and the dominant position of ATTAC in the alter-globalization field in France focused much criticism on the organization – on the part of some experts and intellectuals disturbed by ATTAC's 'competitiveness', and those closer to the pole of subjectivity: 'It's strange to be forever talking about participative democracy and not start by applying it to ourselves.'

While this structure led to democratic deficiencies, its centralization and the domination of a few leaders also lent ATTAC-France a solidity and strong visibility which made the organization central to French alter-globalization between 1999 and 2002. Moreover, grassroots activists acknowledge the efficiency of the national bodies and the primacy of the logic of spaces of expertise. Numerous actions organized by national leaders additionally proved very successful with the membership – whether fund-raisers, actions or meetings. In January 2002, ATTAC filled the famous Parisian concert hall 'Le Zénith' with more than 7,000 supporters. Leaders took this as a sign of their legitimacy, and felt themselves to be 'strongly supported by the base' (interview, 2002).

For sure, the Paris headquarters enjoyed significant power. However, 'even with Cassen, at ATTAC, it has never been the president who makes the organization' (interview with a dissident employee from central headquarters, 2003). From its inception, ATTAC brought together the energies of very diverse networks and activists around its federating platform, combining the efforts of committed experts, civil society activists and 'ordinary citizens'. Alongside the dynamic set up by the organization's leaders, and despite a strong concentration of resources at the national level, local chapters have established a different dynamic, that of a 'citizen movement'. Possessing much autonomy (but scant resources), most of the local chapters managed to bring together long-time activists, citizens disappointed by previous political involvements, and others with no prior engagement. Many popular education activities and diverse mobilizations have been organized. Spaces of expertise also emerge at this level, such as the 'Women and Globalization' group which came out of a local chapter of ATTAC in Paris. Since its beginning in 1998, the organization has thus been fraught with a tension between a logic privileging the efficiency of a limited number of experts and another, which accords greater importance to internal democracy and local committees. The 2006 elected leadership attempted to reorganize ATTAC on the basis of the latter. They started new campaigns and supported several collective initiatives, notably concerning sustainable development and climate change. With the global financial crisis, its talks, lectures and 'popular education' activities have enjoyed real successes in many towns and on campuses. ATTAC-France has, however, not regained the dynamism, prestige and place it previously held in the alter-globalization movements in France and internationally. The organization's reputation had suffered lasting damage, the impact of which has been even more dramatic as the initial success of ATTAC largely relied on the image of a 'citizens'' organization that promoted a renewal of activism beyond classical divisions and the quarrels of the political left (see pp. 191–3).

Internal democracy and passive participation at the World Social Forum

Prominent committed intellectuals were also behind the World Social Forum, which was initially conceived as a conference for experts and intellectuals. The first WSF, in January 2001, was supposed to bring together a few hundred people in a university in Porto Alegre. Instead of the 2,000 expected one month prior to the event, 15,000 people attended. Event organizers were completely overwhelmed by the crowds and the enthusiasm of participating activists. However, certain aspects of this now annual gathering remain deeply embedded in the logic of expertise rather than that of participation and internal democracy. Prominent intellectuals were chosen to speak at the main panels while 'normal participants' were relegated to the role of passive audience. The International Council held its sessions behind closed doors, with security guards. The clearest illustration of the distinction assumed between elite and grassroots participants was to be found in the VIP lounges provided in 2001 and 2002. This hierarchy was particularly visible at the third World Social Forum. Gathering 100,000 people in Porto Alegre, it represented a major organizational challenge. Rather than regarding WSF participants as the dynamic force of the movement, however, the organizing team perceived them as a problem, wondering how they would be able to 'manage the crowd', to quote a member of the WSF Brazilian organizing committee at an International Council meeting before the forum. Their solution was to hold more events for a mass, passive audience. Up to 11,000 people attended the speeches of cosmopolitan intellectuals like Arundhati Roy and Noam Chomsky, while over 100 workshops were cancelled to allow over 60,000 people to listen to Lula, the newly elected Brazilian president.

Participants in the WSF deplored how this dynamic fostered the 'emergence of big spokespeople who are taking too important a position in the movement. Some of them gave up to five talks in three days' (a Belgian activist, 2003). Others even warned: 'we must be very careful not to allow the development of a class of "intelligent and well-educated" international NGOs and large organizations with lots of resources within the WSF, while the real actors, the "mass movements", become increasingly marginalized and removed from the process' (Korean activist, Cancún, 2003).

The vanguard tendency of some leaders and the sense that they constitute an elite distinct from the mass movement have been expressed most clearly in the elaboration of some manifestos and programmatic documents written by small groups of leading intellectuals deliberately avoiding any participatory process with the forums' grassroots activists. In 2005, nineteen prestigious intellectuals, including some Nobel Prize winners, wrote and signed 'The Manifesto of Porto Alegre'. They presented it to the press in a five-star hotel. The 170,000 WSF participants were given no opportunity to discuss and amend the text, framed as a major document of the forum. A year later, the Bamako Appeal was drafted by intellectuals of the same network, provoking a new salvo of criticisms (Sen & Kumar, 2007). As happens in other international movements, such a separation from the mass movement can quickly lead to the empowerment of cosmopolitan leaders who 'represent themselves as speaking for "the people" without developing a base of any depth or the means for ordinary people to speak through them' (Tilly, 2004: 152).

WSF bodies, and particularly the International Council (IC), are subject neither to representativeness nor to democracy, and their way of functioning has more in common with that of the decried WTO than with the principles of participatory democracy of alter-globalization ideals. Since 2003, criticisms of this governing body 'which concentrates lots of power but is accountable to no one' (delegate of the Italian trade union COBAS, WSF, 2004) have constantly grown. To most activists, the organization of the forum appears 'so opaque that it was nearly impossible to figure out how decisions were made or to find ways to question those decisions' (Klein, 2002b: 204). Even the international peasants' organization Via Campesina, which figures among the WSF-IC's influential founding members, questions its legitimacy (Nicholson in Antentas et al., 2003: 136). Mandated to ensure the openness and diversity of the forum, the WSF-IC is not in any way an open, free and democratic space. Held in closed sessions, its meetings bring together about 150 heads of 'international networks'. The selection process of its members is not governed by any precise criteria, which leads to over-representation of certain sectors, notably intellectuals. It is necessary to possess not only considerable economic capital to attend their meetings around the world, but also – and most importantly – social capital to join, and even more to take a truly active part. Appointed rather than elected, with no clear mandate, members are not accountable to any social base.[11] While complete internal democracy may be illusory, these deficiencies are particularly problematic because the renewal and reinforcement of democracy constitutes a cornerstone of alter-globalization alternatives and utopias (Mestrum, 2004). The WSF has thus been exhorted to become 'an active process through which we can experiment, learn and see what democracy organized by the people looks like' (activist from Korean People's Action against WTO, WSF, 2004). Growing criticisms were expressed both by 'citizens' of the way of reason and activists of the way of subjectivity. Chapter 8 will show that, combined with a cross-fertilization process that led WSF leaders to become more sensitive to internal democracy and grassroots active participation, these criticisms fostered a considerable change in the WSF dynamic, which became more open, horizontal and participatory in its 2004 and 2005 gatherings (see pp. 194–8).

Conclusion

While the alter-globalization movement contests dominant and elite-driven globalization, it is itself partly ruled by elite activists who share a top-down approach to social change and organization. Encouraged to become 'active citizens', activists are often kept in a passive posture as consumers of events and ideas conceived by a few leaders. This throws into question the credibility of a movement which is represented by many activists and scholars as 'globalization from below' (Bandy & Smith, 2005; Brecher, Costello & Smith, 2002).

Nevertheless, even the organizations and events conceived by and for intellectuals have never been limited to this top-down logic. Each one has been overwhelmed by the enthusiasm and energy of grassroots activists. In the WSF, ATTAC-France and countless other alter-globalization organizations, the 'citizen' (rather than 'expert') trend has succeeded in gaining the upper hand and greatly transforming these events and organizations. As we will see in chapter 8, the fight against domination by experts and 'residual forms of avant-gardism' (Glasius & Timms, 2006: 235) plays out within the alter-globalization movement. The numerous criticisms were partially integrated by organizers after the 2003 WSF. They have since tried to privilege small workshops which represent spaces for active participation and exchange of experience between activists from around the world. Thus, as we will see in chapter 8, for the 2005 Forum only a handful of events were organized by the International Council; the rest were delegated to participating organizations and took place in less enormous tents.

The question of the place of intellectuals within a democratic system and projects of social change has been around as long as democracy itself. The Greek philosophers and playwrights dedicated philosophical discussions and theatre plays to the relation between elites and democracy early on (Zumbrunnen, 2004; Wallach, 2001). Thinkers of the Enlightenment for their part put their hope in despots capable of leading their subjects towards Progress. Over the past two centuries, many political or revolutionary movements have put their faith in the intellectual avant-garde, from the British Fabians to Leninists. More recently, the power of 'experts' was tackled by Habermas in 1968 and became a focus of criticism in the following decades, notably by the anti-nuclear movement (Touraine et al., 1980). Experts have, however, seen their social role reinforced with the rise of the risk society (Beck, 1992 [1986]) and the growing role of international institutions. Similarly, in the alter-globalization movement which aimed to oppose this technocracy, experts, 'research activists' and intellectuals have occupied many key positions in its organizations.

In *The Mandarins*, Simone de Beauvoir used to ask whether it was really the business of intellectuals to run social movements to reform the world just 'because they know how to hold a pen and are good at playing with ideas'. Are alter-globalization intellectuals in a better position than others to make good decisions about movement strategy or how to achieve the desired other world? The skills necessary to organize a movement do not coincide with those which allow one to become an expert on a particular issue. While effectiveness and scientific criteria preside in the logic of expertise, more participation and democracy are called for to build the movement's organizations and events. When the logic of expertise takes precedence over all others, the movement is inverted and becomes technocratic.

7

Reason, Democracy and Counter-Power

A movement against neoliberal ideology

Having studied the logic of expertise and the relations between intellectual leaders and grassroots activists within the way of reason, the third chapter of this part will turn to an analysis of the concepts of social change and social conflict underlying this trend of the alter-globalization movement.

The indignation of activists of the way of reason is aroused not by experience but by figures representing world suffering, marshalled by alter-globalization experts to counter the image of successful neoliberal globalization: 'Two billion people live on less than two dollars a day; one billion on less than one dollar' (ATTAC expert); 'In a three-year period, Washington Consensus policies have caused more deaths than World War II did in six years!' (A. Boron,[1] talk at Guadalajara, 2002). But the heart of alter-globalization is found in the evolution of the discursive regime from poverty and suffering to inequality, allowing a transition to the logic of social conflict and an assertion of the possibility of acting. Alter-globalization experts aim to demonstrate that neoliberal policies have led to a growth of inequality over the past decades: 'Increased average wealth has been accompanied by an exacerbation of the gap between the two extremes. The ratio of the incomes of the richest 20 per cent of the world's population to the poorest 20 per cent went from 30 in 1960 to

78 in 2000' (Passet, 2003: 37). Hence, the global situation appears to be even more appalling in that 'there has never been so much wealth produced as today, and there have never been so many poor' (English activist, ESF 2004). This assertion leads to the naming of clear adversaries – transnational corporations and financial, trade and economic institutions (WTO, IMF, World Bank and World Economic Forums) – out of which they have constructed simplified and homogenizing images. In the minds of activists, these institutions have come to embody both neoliberal ideology and the technocratic aspect of the new global governance.

Alter-globalization activists within the way of reason oscillate between two logics in the relationship with their adversaries. The first is *dichotomous* – clearly denouncing an adversary, often on the basis of a simplified representation of reality. This is particularly present among an older generation of activists who reproduce old schematics, often close to Marxism. Other activists, particularly those whose political engagement is with alter-globalization, believe that the domination and oppression exercised by ruling actors stem less from their will than a *systemic logic* and the constraints of an interdependence in which every actor is embedded and by which freedom is limited: 'Bill Gates certainly does not want children in Africa to die of hunger on his account, nor does he want the system to be the way it is. . . . It's clear that Bill Gates can't do much at this level. He only follows the system' (Zacharie, 2003). R. Petrella (1996: 20–1) also maintains that business people are neither prepared for, nor interested in governing the world. In this perspective, the threat to democracy does not arise from a will to control, but from transnational companies' will to sell (cf. Barber, 1996). Activists thus repeatedly evoke images of a system that is now out of control, comparing it with 'a train moving increasingly fast, but heading towards a cliff', 'markets which are on auto-pilot, in which everything accelerates without anyone asking where it is going'.

Rather than opposing the 'masters of the status quo' or dominant social actors, alter-globalization activists of the way of reason actually oppose the elites who direct change. The crucial issue is the management of the transition to a more globalized society. The way of reason thus embodies an *historical movement* (Touraine, 2001 [1999]) which challenges the hegemony of neoliberal ideology in the name of an objective and rational analysis of the situation and of the results of neoliberal policies. Alter-globalization activists struggle against the 'neoliberal ideology' and the Washington Consensus more than against the – in any case, ill-identified – 'neoliberals'. They believe that the battle against neoliberalism plays out primarily in the realm of ideas; ideological change being considered the basis of sustainable social transformation: 'From the point of view of development, it is not so much money which counts, as ideas. The World Bank has gained an intellectual hegemony. They have *gained the 'obvious'* since everyone rallies to what they say' (G. Massiah, talk, 2001).

At the heart of the way of reason of the alter-globalization movement is this challenge to the hegemony – in the Gramscian sense – of neoliberal ideology, which has imposed its approach to the transition to a more globalized society as 'natural' and 'without alternative' and so it is thus barely debated: 'The parliamentary debate is stifled and liberalization established as a dogma' (ATTAC-France's 2002 *Manifesto*).

French sociologist of science R. Boudon (1989 [1986]: ch 9) maintains that the 'truth' of economic theories has more to do with their capacity to forge a provisional consensus than with their always highly debatable scientific validity. In this context, the deconstruction of 'neoliberal rationality' becomes essential in challenging this hegemonic thought.[2] Not only alter-globalization activists but even some of their opponents have considered since the late 1990s that this might be the weak point of neoliberalism. A few days before the WTO congress in Seattle, the US Trade Representative, C. Barshefsky, asserted that 'the lack of support from public opinion is the chief threat to the system of multilateral trade' (*Le Monde*, 23 November 1999).

Alter-globalization activists attempt to re-insert democratic debate about topics – from economics to new technologies (GMOs, intellectual property rights, trade, etc.) – which were presented as the domain of experts and limited to the single question of maximizing efficiency. From the main texts expressing the critiques, demands and proposals of the alter-globalization activists of the way of reason written between 1989 (for the precursors) and 2005, as well as 400 lectures and numerous interviews, it emerges that, after the injustice of neoliberal policies is denounced, the major criticisms formulated rest on two central values that alter-globalization activists share with their adversaries: *rationality* and *democracy*. For instance, alter-globalization activists attempt to demonstrate the irrationality of neoliberal policies and denounce the lack of democracy in the institutions they oppose.

Rationality at stake

Alter-globalization activists and neoliberals each attempt to present their model of development as the more rational. The neoliberal ideology is based on the postulate of the superior rationality of markets over public authorities, while alter-globalization activists attempt to demonstrate the irrationality of organizing globalization on the basis of domination by markets and finance. They do so by pointing out the disfunctionality and aberrations of contemporary capitalism, as well as the 'rationality and coherence of globalization with a human face' (title of *Grain de Sable* 415, 8 April 2003). They proclaim themselves better defenders of economic rationality than the neoliberals, whom they accuse of 'privileging the interests of the few and rich' (Petrella, talk, 2002). The delegitimization of the neoliberal economic model and a call for another economics (Laville, 2007) represent major thrusts of the alter-globalization struggle. Alter-globalization thus aims to expose the problems and contradictions of the hegemonic neoliberal discourse. As R. Boudon explains (1989 [1986]: 86 and 92), 'there has only to be an open attack on the fashionable idea for its authority to be undermined . . . As Kuhn rightly argues, paradigms tend to be overthrown when a surfeit of problems has built up: it is then that doubt begins to appear, and one begins to question what before was undisputed.'

Critique of value-oriented rationality: means became ends

Alter-globalization activists attribute increasing inequalities to the fact that the Washington Consensus has made economic and financial growth the central criterion for evaluating economic performance. Autonomized and dissociated from the political and the social, the economic system becomes its own end, operating outside any control. In light of the main objectives they attribute to the economy, alter-globalization activists believe that it is irrational to evaluate the economy solely on the basis of its own instrumental rationality. Alter-globalization economists see the economy as an 'instrument' to reduce poverty and satisfy human need: 'Humanity is thus the final end and there is no other measure of economic progress than the degree to which this end is achieved' (ATTAC, 2000a: 21). This central idea is expressed in the slogan 'People, not profits'. Alter-globalization activists reproach economists and experts from international financial institutions for forgetting that, 'behind the macroeconomic indicators, there are dramatic human realities' (an activist from Friends of the Earth, WSF, 2002): 'Economists are very far off in their calculations when they do not take into account that their adjustment variables are human beings!' (A. Zacharie, WSF, 2003).

From the same perspective, since its very beginnings, alter-globalization activists have challenged the GDP as an indicator of wealth and the well-being of the population. This position was echoed by the Commission on the Measurement of Economic Performance and Social Progress (Stiglitz, Sen & Fitoussi, 2009). Its report states that 'It has long been clear that GDP is an inadequate metric to gauge well-being over time particularly in its economic, environmental, and social dimensions, some aspects of which are often referred to as sustainability' (p. 8); 'We often draw inferences about what are good policies by looking at what policies have promoted economic growth; but if our metrics of performance are flawed, so too may be the inferences that we draw' (p. 7).

Alter-globalization experts endeavour to show that, contrary to neoliberal postulates, growth does not necessarily lead to the satisfaction of the needs of the greatest number. An increasing number of activists and experts promote an economic 'de-growth' (Latouche, 2002), particularly to protect the environment. The idea of 'alter-growth' (or 'a-growth') is also gradually gaining voice: 'the real problem today is no longer producing more, it's a problem of distribution'.[3] It is a question of evaluating the economy according to the well-being of the greatest number rather than according to economic growth. The latter is neither good nor bad;

everything depends on the way in which goods are produced and then divided, and on access to a certain number of 'common goods and services' such as drinking water, education and health care.

Critique of instrumental rationality: the test of facts

Since a central element of scientific rationality consists of testing theories in the light of facts, alter-globalization activists demand an evaluation of neoliberal policies applied by international financial institutions (particularly the IMF and the World Bank) according to the objectives and criteria of success established by these same institutions: namely, poverty reduction, macro-economic and financial stability, and economic growth.

Poverty reduction figures among the essential elements of the World Bank's mandate, notably through its 'Poverty Reduction Strategy'.[4] Promoters of the free flows of capital have framed their approach as a means to decrease poverty, claiming that freedom of capital movement means more resources at the disposal of developing countries (IMF, 2007; Animat, 2002). However, data on poverty from international institutions and prominent scholars (UNDP, 2006: 263; Wade, 2007) dampen enthusiasm for the Washington Consensus policies, showing that, outside China, poverty has increased in the world, despite economic growth in the 1990s (Held & Kaya, 2008).

Macro-economic and financial stability is the core objective of the IMF. Here, too, alter-globalization activists draw up a damning account of the policies which have been pursued. The succession of financial crises throughout the 1990s contradicted the claim that free movement of capital necessarily brings greater financial and macro-economic stability. The founders of ATTAC link the organization's birth to a 'diagnosis: the confirmation, in the Asian financial crisis, of the malignance of markets and of their hegemonic role in neoliberal globalization' (Cassen in ATTAC, 2000a: 12). According to S. George (talk in Mexico, 2003), 'we can't find a single case where structural adjustment plans [imposed by the IMF and World Bank] have succeeded'. Financial scandals such as the Enron affair in 2001, and the Madoff and the Goldman Sachs scandals in the aftermath of the global crisis, as well as the subprime mortgage crisis starting in 2007, have since reinforced these ideas. To alter-globalization activists, 'the market is no longer regulating, it amplifies instabilities' (ATTAC, 2001a: 39). The scale of the global crisis in 2008 and 2009 appears to prove them right. The crash in Argentina in 2001–2 is considered as another irrefutable proof of the failure of neoliberal policies. In the 1990s, the country was regularly designated as 'IMF's darling' (*American Prospect*, 28 February 2002) for its careful implementation of the IMF recommendations to open, liberalize and privatize. It eventually led it to an unprecedented economic crisis. The UNDP calculated that the average annual income per resident dropped from US\$ 8,950 in 1997 to US\$ 3,194 in March 2002,[5] plunging half of the Argentinian population below the poverty line in 2003.

While they do not consider *economic growth* to be an objective in itself, alter-globalization experts try to show the limitations of neoliberal policies even on this level. After the North American Free Trade Agreement (NAFTA), A. Charlton and J. Stiglitz, former vice-president of the World Bank, argued (Stiglitz & Charlton 2006: 22) that, 'if there were ever an historic opportunity to demonstrate the value of free trade, it was Mexico'. They show that the test clearly failed. A quarter-century after the Mexican turn towards neoliberal policies in 1982, and fifteen years after the entry into force of NAFTA, the average growth of GDP per person there has not exceeded 0.4 per cent per year from 1982 to 2002,[6] while the inequality of the distribution of wealth has significantly increased. Certainly, NAFTA facilitated recovery from the monetary crisis of 1994 and 1995, but real wages in Mexico have fallen, the net balance of jobs is negative, inequality and poverty have grown (Zermeño, 2005), and NAFTA made Mexico one of the countries most vulnerable to international crises, as the 2009 7.1 per cent fall in its GDP demonstrates. On the other side of the border, E. Duflo, from the MIT, states that, while NAFTA contributed to accelerated growth in Canada, the numbers of jobs for workers decreased more rapidly in the liberalized sectors. She argues that 'it is senseless to contrast long term benefits to short term costs if those who pay the costs are not compensated'.[7]

Activists also consider certain of the axioms on which neoliberal experts rely to be false or obsolete: 'One of the most dangerous confusions is the mixing of elements essential to economic common sense with irrational content coming from hypothetical postulates' (A. Ferrer, *Grano de Arena*[8] 101, 15 August 2001). Among the chief of the axioms at issue are Ricardo's theory of comparative advantage, Say's assumption of natural resources as free goods, and the idea that more appears better (Ricardo and Pareto). Alter-globalization activists argue, for example, that nature, whose reproduction is currently threatened, can no longer be conceived of as 'a free good' (that is, available in unlimited quantities and at no cost) and removed from the realm of economic calculation, as it has been since J. B. Say.[9]

Moreover, alter-globalization activists consider the neoliberal free market model to be based on 'a narrow, strict approach of rationality identified with individual rationality' (Bourdieu, 1998: 108). The model of market-oriented behaviour of individuals seeking to maximize personal interest is considered by these activists to be incapable of integrating long-term thinking, taking the common good into account or sufficiently integrating economic, social and ecological limits. For this reason, alter-globalization activists propose restoring power to social, political and institutional actors who can counter-balance the irrationalities of self-regulated markets and thus reinforce economic rationality.

From the irrationality of neoliberalism to the possibility of acting

The irrationality of neoliberal policies, the influence of non-proven axioms and the failure to test facts have led alter-globalization activists to denounce Washington Consensus precepts as failing to comply with scientific criteria: 'The economic reasoning is in reality ideological and political and not scientific' (F. Müller, German alter-globalization expert, WSF, 2001). Alter-globalization activists oppose 'the myth of the dominant economy, which lives on fictions' (R. Passet, talk in Paris, 2002), and 'the interpretation of reality from the starting point of presuppositions which are not empirically verifiable' (A. Ferrer, *Grano de Arena* 101, 15 August 2001). From neo-Keynesian economists to the most leftist activists,[10] all alter-globalization trends focus on 'the madness of markets'. In 1998, Susan Strange entitled her book *Mad Money*, while for J. Stiglitz (2002) capitalism has 'lost its head'. From there, it is a short step to comparing neoliberalism to religion:

> Neoliberalism has its 10 commandments proclaimed by the G7, its prophets (Hayek and Friedman) and its spiritual guides (Reagan and Thatcher). (R. Passet, ATTAC Summer University, 2002)
>
> To be understood, the neoliberal discourse must be analysed as a religious discourse: it is dogmatic and simplistic; it has its holy trinity of economic growth, free trade and globalization; it has its Vatican of the IMF, the World Bank and the WTO, which, like the Vatican, believe themselves to be infallible and, for our salvation, impose their solutions on us. The outcome is obvious: paradise is so far away that we will never be able to do the reckoning. (M. Neef, Chilean economist, *Grano de Arena* 175, 20 January 2002)

By putting neoliberalism to the test of its outcome on its own criteria, alter-globalization activists attack the core legitimacy of the neoliberal ideology, which rests on the assertion of the scientific nature of the policies advocated and on the promise of results. Critical economists have made clear that neither scientific criteria, nor economic efficiency on its own, can justify the support which the precepts of the Washington Consensus enjoy. Since the mid-1990s, the Nobel Prize winner P. Krugman (1996) has also been questioning the 'obsession with competition' which he attributes to goals that are external to economic debate, such as forcing through unpopular measures (see also Randeria, 2007). The implementation of neoliberal policies is thus a matter of political choice and not the outcome of a clear economic rationality.

The emphasis alter-globalization activists place on the relatively limited amounts needed to implement alternative policies further underlines the political nature of current economic choices and affirms the possibility of acting against injustice.

> Calculations by Harvard's Linda Bilmes and Nobel-prize-winning economist Joseph Stiglitz remain most prominent. They determined that, once you factor in things like medical costs for injured troops, higher oil prices and replenishing the military, the war [in Iraq] will cost America upwards of $2 trillion. That doesn't include any of the costs incurred by Iraq, or America's coalition

partners ... Consider that, according to sources like Columbia's Jeffrey Sachs, the Worldwatch Institute, and the United Nations, with that same money the world could: eliminate extreme poverty around the world (cost $135 billion in the first year, rising to $195 billion by 2015); achieve universal literacy (cost $5 billion a year); immunize every child in the world against deadly diseases (cost $1.3 billion a year); ensure developing countries have enough money to fight the AIDS epidemic (cost $15 billion per year. ... [All that] for a cost of $156.3 billion this year alone – less than a tenth of the total Iraq war budget.[11]

Relying on expertise and analyses based on economic rationality, alter-globalization activists thus move the debate from the field of economic expertise towards that of social and political debates. They reaffirm the possibility of acting to influence the direction of globalization and economic mechanisms formerly thought to be controlled by the invisible hand of the market.

Democracy at stake

Critiques of neoliberalism in the name of democracy

The lack of transparency of trade negotiation processes as well as the lack of accountability and democracy in global institutions that promote neoliberal policies constituted the second volley of critiques levelled against neoliberalism. Just as with economic rationality, alter-globalization activists and neoliberals confront each other over a value that both claim to defend: democracy. The neoliberal ideology links the advance of democracy to that of the market economy, presenting the combination as an optimal, even natural, system (cf. Laïdi, 1994: 61), asserting that 'capitalism is the transcription into the economic order of a principle which, in the political order, is called democracy' (Baechler, 1995: 102). They argue that the intensification of global economic exchange engenders democratization globally, as illustrated by the advent of democratic regimes after the fall of communism in Eastern Europe (Huntington, 1991).

Alter-globalization activists reject this coupling of market and democracy, pointing out, for example, the lack of respect for human rights in countries with capitalist economies such as the

Gulf states (Davis, 2007) and China (Kin Chi, 2005). Having drawn lessons from the Soviet terror, alter-globalization activists are committed to strong democracy as a central value of the alternatives proposed by their movement; they seek to foster a more transparent and democratic system of global governance (Patomäki & Teivainen, 2005). They denounce the lack of public debate on economic decisions considered to be fundamental: 'It's a parody of democracy: parliamentarians speak for days about the opening of the hunting season and dispatch in two minutes, without debate, the proposals on GATT'[12] (I. Ramonet, ATTAC at Le Zénith, 19 January 2002). Similarly, J. Bové rebelled against the fact that 'there wasn't even a parliamentary debate before GMO crops were authorised in the fields' (WSF 2006, Bamako).

The hegemony of neoliberal ideology made its positions appear natural and without alternative. Alter-globalization activists' task was consequently to 'put this globalization back into debate'. However, the secrecy maintained around international economic and trade negotiations prevented debates from happening. The lack of information about the Central American Free Trade Agreement (CAFTA) in 2003 was questioned in this regard: 'We are three months away from signing a Free Trade Agreement with the United States and, in this country, no one knows the content of the treaty. . . . And moreover, the Guatemalan government is claiming that the policy of the Costa Rican government is holding up negotiations!' (interview with a scholar–activist, San José, July 2003). A few days earlier, on 15 July 2003, the national Nicaraguan daily *La Nación* summarized the findings of a survey as: '52% of Nicaraguans accept the treaty without knowing the content'.

The adoption of supra-national agreements inspired by the Washington Consensus, the neoliberal ideology of *laissez-faire*, and the delegation of decision-making power to independent administrative bodies have, in the name of free trade, considerably limited government capacity to act (Grinspun & Kreklewich, 1994). The analysis of I. Bizberg (2003) and the case studies presented by L. Carlsen, T. Wise and H. Salazar (2003) emphasize the restrictions that NAFTA-imposed rules placed on Mexican authorities' capacity for action. S. Randeria (2007) highlights similar constraints placed on the Indian state by the WTO. Her study of NGO campaigns shows that the limited capacity of national governments to act is a result not only of the terms of treaties but, foremost, of a lack of political will on the part of state actors to make use of the recourses still open to them.

As an anti-technocratic movement, alter-globalization activists believe the dominant influence of non-elected experts in international decisions to be particularly undemocratic (Teivainen, 2002). The influence these experts enjoy results from two parallel developments. First, the technicality and increasing complexity of the issues that international economic bodies deal with require specialization. Second, experts were supposed to act in a longer-term perspective than political actors,[13] as economic Nobel Prize winners F. Kydland and E. Prescott (1977) and R. Barro (1986) had demonstrated. By the end of the 1980s, a strong consensus thus emerged on the independence of central banks in Europe: 'it seemed necessary to shelter their management from the vicissitudes of political life' (Quaden, 1990: 183): the impact of election periods, budgetary excesses and corruption, and of placing the technical management of the economy in a longer-term perspective.

Taken together, these two elements encouraged a blanket 'blind trust': elected officials handed over a multitude of negotiations and decisions to expert independent administrative bodies. Social and political actors then have little influence over their own representatives, a state of affairs which appalls alter-globalization activists: 'Citizens have come to understand that very often decisions are taken at the supranational level over which politicians have no control; for example, by European commissioners, who don't have any real democratic legitimacy' (activist of the Corporate Europe Observatory, 2006).

The neoliberal globalization and development model is based on a combination of the market economy, representative democracy and expert input deriving from a 'technical and apolitical' concept of modernization. In contrast, alter-globalization activists of the way of reason want to foster citizens' input on decisions which are now delegated to a few experts. They have developed a model based on stronger regulation of the international markets under the monitoring of citizens and civil society organizations such as Global Trade Watch or ATTAC. The lack of public consultation on cultivation of GM crops and the ratification of free trade agreements are often raised in this context. It is a matter of 're-conquer[ing] the spaces lost by democracy to the financial sector' (ATTAC platform). The alter-globalization activists thus give more political than economic significance to the technical measures they promote.

In addition, the discrepancy between mechanisms of the welfare state and democratic participation, organized at the national level (Held, 1995; Held et al., 1999), and the fact that increasing numbers of major decisions are taken at the international level, threaten to empty democracy of all its content (Altvater, 1997). Activists of the way of reason thus consider the building of a global democracy and some global institutions to regulate economic globalization as an urgent challenge.

Stance towards international institutions

As the major bodies managing the transition to a more global society, some international institutions occupy the place held by the state in previous generations of historical movements (Tarrow, 1999; Tilly, 2004; Touraine et al., 1980). The debate around global governance and the reform of international institutions hence constitutes a privileged battlefield.

Alter-globalization activists of the way of reason adopt different positions relative to three sets of international institutions. They do not recognize the legitimacy of the World Economic Forum and the G-8, which they see as expressing the 'will of the richest to govern the world'. Therefore, the World Social Forum has consistently refused to dialogue with its counterpart in Davos. At the same time, alter-globalization activists support processes aimed at creating or reinforcing institutions of international governance. They support the creation of international bodies able to impose social and environmental standards, to strengthen international law and to empower ratified international treaties, such as the Human Rights Declaration or International Labour Organization conventions. They demand the reinforcement of the ILO and the UN,[14] especially in relation to economic bodies, and support new regional institutions like the 'Bank of the South' in Latin America. The position towards the European Union is distinct. While they are pro-European,[15] alter-globalization activists nevertheless oppose the dominant direction of the European

Commission, which they consider to be neoliberal. They deplore, for example, the fact that the European treaties focus on free markets and are weak on social protection. This was the reason that alter-globalization activists marched against the European summits between 1997 and 2004 and why a majority of alter-globalization activist organizations opposed the Treaty proposing a European Constitution and the Lisbon Treaty.

The World Bank, IMF and WTO summits gave alter-globalization activists opportunities to stage a confrontation between the two concepts of globalization and development. Because they possess mechanisms to sanction violations of their norms, these three institutions dominate global governance. The strongest criticisms of the three institutions relate to the technocratic, opaque and anti-democratic way these bodies function: voting is rare, there is an imbalance of power between countries, and delegates have 'no accountability to their populations' (see Wysham, Cavanagh & Arruda, 1994). The debate between alter-globalization activists who argue for the reform of these international institutions and those who demand their abolition has been over-emphasized by scholars who claim – with good reason – that 'if we close down the WTO, there will be no regulation and that will be much worse than the current situation. It will no longer be liberalism but anarchy, the law of the strongest!' (E. Cohen,[16] lecture, 10 December 2004). The necessity of international institutions monitoring trade, finance and the international economy is a matter of unanimity among alter-globalization activists of the way of reason. The debate is actually taking place between those in favour of reforming the current institutions and those who demand that existing structures be dismantled so that regulatory bodies can be established on new foundations. They believe that the current statutes and practices prevent any significant reform. For example, with its 16.77 per cent vote share in the IMF, the United States alone is able to block any reforms contrary to its interests. The 'rupture strategy', however, entails the risk of leaving a void, in the absence of the old institutions. In the same way, much as they favour the dominant countries, the rules of international trade enforced by the WTO nevertheless constitute norms which apply to everyone, including the dominant countries, and may thus be a base for the defence of poorer countries' interests (Randeria, 2007).

Stance towards political actors

Political actors' empowerment with regard to the economic actors is considered as a major objective among the alter-globalization movement. Activists of the way of reason maintain, however, a particularly ambiguous relation with political actors and institutions, who are simultaneously adversaries, objects of pressure, mediators and partners. Four ideal-types of relations between the movement and political actors can be distinguished.

Relations between alter-globalization activists and political actors can be dominated by *confrontation*. Activists denounce, for example, what they call the 'collaboration' of politicians with deregulation of the economy and privatization: 'Political power is decreeing its own incapacity to govern. They are the victims of what they have voted for.'[17] Alter-globalization activists argue that the decisions to liberalize 'often originate with governmental decisions' (Aguiton, 2001: 64), recalling that neoliberal international treaties are negotiated and ratified by the governments of the various signatory countries. According to this statement, 'Adversaries include governments, because leftist governments apply basically the same neoliberal policies as the right' (an Italian activist, WSF, 2002).

Activists have developed *lobbying* activities and political pressure tactics in order to 'convince politicians of the necessity of such measures as the Tobin tax' (ATTAC activist). The call for active citizenship and 'citizens' monitoring' is also part of this strategy: 'Politicans are noticing that all of their activities are being analysed by citizens. This is new! Before they did whatever they wanted and suddenly, they are receiving dozens of emails telling them, "You represent us"' (interview, activist from Global Trade Watch, WSF, 2005).

In other instances, *cooperative* relations can also be established. In certain situations, the expertise of alter-globalization networks can be a valuable asset for governments and politicians:

> They need information! They are disconnected from reality. I receive calls almost every day from people in political parties who want information. I really don't understand how a parliamentarian can fail to be informed on an issue as important as the WTO. That said, all the better, because in this way they are forced to

pay attention to what civil society organizations are thinking about that. (Expert from the Observatoire de la mondialisation, interview, 2000)

A fourth set of relations is thus characterized by *instrumentalization*. Most organizations refuse to align themselves with a political party.[18] However, this does not impede attempts at recuperation of the alter-globalization movement, which seem inherent, particularly in societies dominated by political logics, such as France, Mexico (Zermeño, 2005) and India (Jaffrelot, 2005). Besides, some activists have always been more open to integrating political actors into the WSF, including some of the founders of alter-globalization. Activists of the way of reason argue that 'Elections are not the only way of doing politics. Our project, through debating ideas and contesting power, strives to transform reality, and that is certainly political. But ATTAC does not want to become a party' (P. Khalfa, ATTAC Summer University, 28 August 2004). The WSF Charter explicitly specifies that political parties cannot participate, as such, in the event. Politicians are welcome in their personal capacity, but as listeners and not speakers. However, from the first WSF, important exceptions to this rule were made: notably, for the presidential candidate – and then president – Lula, but also for local elected officials from the organizing city, who greatly benefited from the venue. Alter-globalization debates, gatherings and events have more than once served as platforms for political parties. This was the case, for example, with the Brazilian Workers' Party during the first three WSFs at Porto Alegre. Likewise, the two Indian communist parties were the most visible actors at the 2004 WSF in Mumbai. As we shall see in chapter 10, after 2006, the support of political leaders became increasingly important for some actors of the way of reason, some of whom wished to pull alter-globalization into the orbit of institutional politics, even at the risk of splitting the movement.

A concept of social change

The Tobin tax

Along with the cancellation of third world debt and the abolition of tax havens, a taxation on financial transactions figures among the most emblematic proposals of the alter-globalization movement. They all owe their popularity to three central features: a symbolic significance (the assertion of social agency and of the possibility of regulating the market); 'pedagogical virtue' (they initiate citizens into complex issues from the starting point of a concrete idea); and being a starting point for opening up wider discussion of the Washington Consensus.

The American economist James Tobin first formulated the idea of a tax on financial transactions during a talk in 1972, published in 1974. The idea was later developed in a book published in 1978, three years before the economist was awarded the Nobel Prize, for work unrelated to this tax. According to its inventor, a minimal taxation of financial transactions should encourage greater market stability. It was a matter of 'throwing sand in the cogs of financial markets' (Tobin, 1978, 1997); an expression which lent its name to ATTAC's electronic magazine *Grain of Sand*. James Tobin continued to promote the tax (Tobin, 1997), but kept aloof from the alter-globalization movement and, in particular, from ATTAC[19] (ATTAC, 2002). Many economists have suggested improvements to the 'Tobin tax' (cf. Patomäki, 2000). A set of amendments proposed by P. Spahn (1996) ended up being integrated into alter-globalization demands.

Relaunched by the UNDP in its 1994 Human Development Report, the tax gained international notoriety largely through the efforts of a group of intellectuals around the *Monde Diplomatique* who came together to found ATTAC and inspired the first parliamentary debates on the issue.[20] The 'Tobin-Spahn' tax has known a certain success at the political level and was even adopted by Belgian legislators.[21] The proposal was supported by some heads of state, including Brazilian President Lula, and, in 2009, Gordon Brown. However, even ATTAC's experts recognize that the Tobin tax alone 'could result in a completely empty gesture as holders of capital may find a way of overcoming it by de-territorializing their currency exchange transactions entirely'.[22] In any case, the adoption of this measure would 'diminish the bubble a little, but not change the system' (R. Petrella, interview, 2000). How then to explain the startling trajectory of this measure, forgotten for a quarter of a century?

To its defenders, the attraction of the Tobin tax lies in three of its features. First, activists highlight the *symbolic character* of the measure: 'The Tobin tax is an emblematic measure which exceeds its own content. . . . What is really distressing is the idea that governments could recover part of their power by implementing it' (expert from ATTAC-France). With the Tobin tax, what is really at stake is the assertion of social agency. To activists, this explains the reluctance in adopting such a tax: 'Those who have long sung the praises of neoliberal deregulation find it difficult to admit that recovery of the currency exchange market must happen by means of public regulation, through the institution of a tax' (Ö. Appelvist, ATTAC-Germany, *Grain de Sable* 350, 19 July 2002). As with other technical measures, the Tobin tax as proposed by ATTAC is wedded to mechanisms of citizen control, especially over the management of the resulting funds (see, for example, *Grain de Sable* 350, 19 July 2002).

ATTAC activists also attribute a *'pedagogic virtue'* to the tax: 'The Tobin tax is an extraordinary pedagogical tool to begin to explain the importance of finance' (S. George, European Citizen Congress, 2001); 'The Tobin tax is a simple pedagogical tool to throw neoliberal globalization, in all its aspects, into question. Before being a financial pump for the third world, the Tobin tax is a deadly weapon against "the hegemonic thinking".'[23] Both relevant and symbolic, the tax allows financial mechanisms to be tackled, the issues to be explained, the existence of alternatives to be demonstrated and the political nature of the problem to be exposed: 'the feasibility of the Tobin tax has shown that what is missing is the political will to implement it' (activist from the Raisons d'Agir network, Paris, 2002).

Finally, beyond this fairly simple measure, experts aim to *introduce citizens to broader issues* linked to the relation between political and economic powers. Once this question has been introduced, it allows activists to 'connect the dots: the fact that the political debate on the Tobin tax has happened forces the issue of financial transactions, of the damage caused, of speculation, retirement funds, etc.' (ATTAC activist, 2004).

A *distinctive approach to social change*

Just as in the way of subjectivity, the approach to social change which inspires citizens and experts of the way of reason is constructed in opposition to dreams of Revolution which have, too often, been transformed into totalitarian regimes. Alter-globalization activists see themselves as more pragmatic. However, rather than subjectivity and daily life, citizens and experts of the way of reason focus on abstract measures, institutional regulation and the international level. Against what they consider as an unfair, irrational and democratically deficient system, they propose a host of alternatives, which are not without contradictions. These share eight basic features.

Pragmatic measures over global model

In the way of reason, paths leading to the 'other possible world' are constructed in theory rather than through lived experience. They are the fruit of expertise and translate into abstract, generally universalist, proposals. Detractors of alter-globalization often castigate alter-globalization activists for their incapacity to propose a global alternative. Experts and activists, however, emphasize that 'devotees of perfect systems have never brought anything but difficulties and misfortunes to the world' (ATTAC, 2001b: 43). Instead of a global programme, the manifestos, statements[24] and other alter-globalization platforms consist of a sequence of technical and medium-range measures which are meant to interconnect with other proposals. The most widely referred to are:

- cancellation of the third world debt and honouring development aid commitments;
- regulation of financial markets, notably through the implementation of international taxation;
- mobilizations against free trade agreements and negotiations;
- food sovereignty;
- fair taxation, the end to tax havens and to tax fraud instruments;
- subjecting the rules of international trade to social, cultural and ecological concerns, particularly those which have been adopted by the ILO;
- denunciation of the arms trade and the 'militarization' of strategic regions around the world for the purpose of securing economic interests and natural resources;

- preservation of biodiversity and rejection of life form patenting;
- freedom of movement for people and denunciation of current migration policies;
- tax measures conducive to more equitable resource distribution.

Networks' spaces of expertise elaborate each of these measures in great detail. Reports and books are devoted to the reform of international institutions (Wysham et al., 1994), to alternatives to the WTO (Global Trade Watch, 2006), to the third world debt (Millet & Toussaint, 2005) or to water management as a global public good (Petrella, 2001). Particular emphasis is laid on the technical feasibility of each measure in order to assert that their implementation primarily depends on political will. Alter-globalization experts have achieved a certain success at this level, if the letter sent by French President J. Chirac to the Scientific Council of ATTAC-France is any indication: 'You have demonstrated that the innovative mechanisms to finance the Third World development were technically realistic and economically rational' (5 November 2004).

Technical measures, political meaning and participation

As we have seen concerning the Tobin tax, the purpose and meaning of the measures they propose do not narrowly pertain to economics, but are above all political and symbolic: 'primarily, they indicate that the political is regaining the upper hand' (ATTAC platform). The majority of alter-globalization proposals attempt to combine relatively simple technical measures with citizen participation, generally in the form of monitoring of the proposed mechanisms. Citizen and political permanent monitoring is believed to be the only way to keep the economy under control. The Charter of the World Social Forum strives to oppose 'all totalitarian and reductionist views of economy, development and history and the use of violence as a means of social control by the state' with 'practices of real democracy, participatory democracy' (Article 10). Alter-globalization activists particularly contest the model of development advocated by the World Bank, in which 'the advice of countries from the global south is rarely requested', and maintain that development funds should 'be placed under the authority of public powers but controlled by populations from the global south' (E. Toussaint, European Citizens' Congress, 2001).

Abstraction and economism

A particular feature of the way of reason is the abstract and theoretical manner in which social change is conceptualized starting from expertise, economic calculations and technical measures. Alter-globalization experts and citizens, moreover, often share with their neoliberal adversaries and experts of international institutions a tendency to 'economicism': the reduction of complex reality to a few calculable parameters, essentially resulting from an economic analysis (cf. Scott, 1998). Activists of the way of reason often tend to perceive a common source for all evil: growing inequalities created by neoliberal globalization. This perspective goes as far as to make economic factors the sole source of communalist terrorism and war:[25]

> Bombing Afghanistan would be a catastrophe. Financial crimes should be attacked. . . . Youth turn towards fanaticism because they have no other choice. What must be done is to develop these countries economically and give them a job. (A. Zacharie, September 2001)
> To combat terrorism, they want to restrict our freedoms. On the contrary, what we need is a massive Keynesian programme on a global scale. We must reduce inequalities, which breed terrorism. (S. George, December 2001)

The question of cultural diversity is much less present here than in the way of subjectivity; the communities concerned are viewed through the prism of an abstract and universalizing economism, with all oppressed peoples considered to suffer from the same structural problems as the rest of humanity: 'indigenous peoples are the first victims of debt' (an Ecuadorian during the Genoa Social Forum, 2001); 'women are the worst victims of the changing patterns of global development caused by neo-liberal economical policies' (B. Karat, Indian activist, *The Hindu*, 27 May 2005).

The short and the very long term

The approach to change at play here lies at once in the short and very long terms. The measures elaborated by alter-globalization experts are immediately applicable, but are generally inscribed in social transformations whose results must be evaluated over decades or even generations:

> We are participating in an historical movement, and social changes are made over one or two generations. I don't believe that I will see any big transformations, nor that my activism will result in particular gains where we can say, 'Wow! We won that!' Yes, there are small things, but they are really small in relation to the size of the problem in all its complexity. (Activist from ATTAC-Liège, interview)

A focus on the global scale

As we have seen in chapter 6, the logic of expertise is tied to a top-down vision of change (Scott, 1998; Tilly, 2003), implemented by actors capable of acting at a high level. Activists of the way of reason prioritize the international scale over the national, and the latter over the local. The first reason for this stems from the universalism and degree of abstraction of the measures generally proposed, which, to be effective, must be implemented in broad economic and political regions. A second reason arises from the growing integration and interdependency at the global level (Held, 2007), whether it is the environmental crisis or relations between capital and labour. Finally, experts and entrepreneurs of mobilization, who strongly influence organizations of the way of reason, tend to prioritize the highest geographic levels (see chapter 5).

A more institutional vision

While the way of subjectivity is centred on the construction of alternatives by and for activists themselves, citizens and experts of the way of reason give prominence to political actors and institutions when it comes to the architecture of the 'other possible world'. Political actors prove crucial to the initiation of change and international institutions for its implementation. Economic regulation and the management of international affairs then require the construction of new institutions and reinforcement of some of the existing ones.

The emergence of counter-power

Although it gives policy makers a prominent role, the way of reason is not a quest for elected positions, both because activists believe that the necessary transformations must take place at another level, notably a change in dominant ideas, and because of lessons drawn from previous movements which took this path. Activists believe that political power will transform alterglobalization leaders who acquire it 'just as power corrupted past movements': 'If the movement takes power, money and power will corrupt our leaders. We have to transform the nature of politics! What we need are struggles, constructive actions and a change of values' (an Indian activist, WSF, 2004). The way of reason thus relies on a strategy of counter-power: 'There is a difference of function. Parties are situated on the side of power. Either they hold it, or they strive to hold it. ATTAC wants to construct counter-powers in society so that citizens can reconquer the spaces of freedom that would enable them to influence the course of things' (ATTAC, 2002: 26). The alterglobalization activists' logic of counter-power requires a certain recognition of civil society actors as interlocutors on the part of political actors and institutions,[26] which often demands a substantial lobbying from civil society actors (cf. Massicotte, 2004).

Beyond reform and revolution

The traditional distinction made by movements of the industrial society between 'revolutionary' and 'reformist' approaches loses its relevance for alter-globalization activists. Certainly, some activists remain more radical than others, but all appear to believe that, to eradicate capitalism or to try to 'give it a more human face', there must be a first step of concrete measures with limited significance: the Tobin tax, cancellation of the third world debt or GATS are thus primarily 'lines of attack which enable other questions to be opened' (an activist from Global Trade Watch, WSF, 2003). More fundamentally, the debate between reformist and revolutionary measures has cooled down because this distinction refers to strategies of exercising power, whereas these actors operate according to counter-power logic. Many alter-globalization experts assert that, 'to be revolutionary or anti-capitalist says nothing to me' (A. Zacharie, interview, 2003) ; 'We don't think anymore in terms of revolution or reform but of trans-formation' (a US scholar activists in his sixties, interview, 2009). Consequently, in attempts to understand contemporary move-ments, contrasting reformist and revolutionary attitudes would prove 'more dangerous than useful. It would be a transcription of social struggles in political terms' (Touraine, 1978: 120).

In this context, is the alter-globalization movement then anti-capitalist? This obviously depends on the definition of capitalism. K. Polanyi (2001 [1944]) defined it primarily as the construction of a self-regulating market. In this sense, the alter-globalization movement which struggles to impose social and political regula-tions on the economic system is clearly anti-capitalist. However, it doesn't mean that all alter-globalization activists are in favour of a total change in the economic system. Most recognize some virtue to the market, as long as it is regulated and subsumed to democratic and social concerns. What is at stake is the end of the domination of finance, of profit as the central value, and of rising inequalities, as well as a profound transformation of the relations between the economic and the political; whether or not this dif-ferent society is qualified as capitalist is, for most activists, of little interest.

Conclusion

The way of reason cannot be limited to expertise alone. It is organized around two central elements: expertise (defined as an abstract knowledge on a specific issue) and citizen participation. The entire exercise then consists of articulating these two pillars in each dimension of the movement: the role of experts and that of citizens; technical measures and participation in alternatives; lobbying and popular education; spreading expert knowledge and intellectual autonomy of citizens; the legitimacy of knowledge and that of numbers.

Knowledge, information and expertise (defined as 'technical knowledge of a precise subject or area') are central as they allow citizens to participate in debates on globalization, to critique neoliberal ideology in the name of economic rationality, and to construct alternative policies. The necessity for delegation introduces a fundamental difference between the two trends of alter-globalization. The way of subjectivity is performative, the subject and the object of alter-globalization action are identical: the construction of spaces of experience already belongs to the desired other world. In the way of reason, spaces of expertise aim to produce rational arguments in order to reinforce active citizenship but this 'other world' should not itself be a world of experts.

Relying on these two pillars, actors of the way of reason strive to break the neoliberal hegemony by formulating theoretical critiques around two core values they share with their adversaries: rationality and democracy. The alter-globalization movement has, beyond a doubt, enjoyed a certain success at this level: 'The work of delegitimizing the system is done. No one still believes that we live in the best of worlds. . . . Now everyone knows that markets are not self-regulated' (A. Zacharie, interview, January 2003). A. Minc, a French intellectual and defender of 'happy neoliberal globalization' (Minc, 1997), even published a pamphlet in 2003 in which he expressed his concerns that alter-globalization was becoming the new hegemonic thinking. Several of the movement's main adversaries have been pushed to change their discourse: social themes are so prominent on the website of the World Economic Forum and, to a lesser extent, that of the World Bank, that they sometimes even resemble the website of a Social Forum. With the global financial and economic crisis that started in 2007, some alter-globalization arguments and proposals have been introduced by several of the G-20 leaders (see chapter 10). Beyond the discourses, few have, however, been implemented.

Part 4

Confluence of the Two Paths

8

Tensions and Collaborations

Common problematics

In the previous two parts, we analysed the two paths which lie at the heart of the alter-globalization movement. Each has its own response to the general questions which inspire alter-globalization activists: How to become an actor in the global age? How to organize a movement? How to 'change the world'? For some, the alternatives to neoliberal globalization rely on a transformation of social relations, rooted in everyday life; others focus on a regulation of the economy through technical measures and a democratization of international institutions. The origin and success of the alter-globalization movement lie in its capacity to bring together those who challenge neoliberalism in the name of their subjectivity, oppressed by the consumer society and by the power of transnational companies, and those who challenge it by attacking the irrationality of a hyper-capitalist economy unchained from all social and political regulation. This encounter between two different logics against a common adversary – 'neoliberal globalization' – was present in all the moments in which the alter-globalization movement was symbolically established: the Zapatista uprising; the Seattle mobilizations; the first local and national alter-globalization convergences and Social Forums.

Deeply rooted in local indigenous communities, the *Zapatista uprising* began on the day that the North American Free Trade

Agreement entered into force. In addition to the demand for recognition and autonomy a challenge to the dominant development model and to neoliberal globalization are also constitutive of the movement. The first 'Declaration of Selva Lacondona', one of the founding texts of the movement, published on 2 February 1994, paints the devastation wrought by the neoliberal economy and decries the 'heavy tribute paid by Chiapas to capitalism', the conformism of 'hegemonic thinking' and the pillage of natural resources (EZLN, 1994: 51, 52, 61). Zapatism combines community defence, support for the democratization of Mexico and opposition to global neoliberalism.

The *Seattle mobilization* staged a dramatic meeting of these two trends. It was characterized by a cross-fertilization (Della Porta, 2005) of the logics of the rejection of power-domination, alternative sociabilities and carnivalesque, festive demonstration on one side, with those of the counter-power of lobbying and popular education on the other. Alongside NGO experts and several organizations who had access to the conference centre, exercising various kinds of pressure on government delegations, the streets were occupied by trade unionists as well as black blocs, alter-activists and ecologists who transformed the mobilization into a festive party and a place to express their creativity. Numerous counter-summits later repeated this model, combining the features of the two ways of the alter-globalization movement. Even during the 2001 G-8 counter-summit, between two protests dominated by symbolic and expressive aspects and strong confrontation with the police, the Genoa Social Forum organized a morning of workshops and debates on traditional alter-globalization themes: cancelling third world debt, financial speculation, the welfare state, and so on.

If, as we are claiming, the encounter between subjective and modernizing trends is a structural feature of alter-globalization, it should be evident wherever the movement is at all active. The case studies we carried out amply bore out the hypothesis. In *Nicaragua*, although alter-globalization was only in its early stages, the first meeting of the 'Nicaragua Social Forum' in the town of León, on 5 and 6 July 2003, was marked by the divergences and convergences between these two trends. On one side, participants insisted on the importance of drafting a platform focusing on economic and political issues that needed to be debated in Nicaragua. On the other, activists argued that 'it is most important first of all to get to know ourselves and explain what we are doing locally, how we are resisting in our lives and in our movements' (an activist from Matagalpa). What was essential for the latter was to exchange experiences, develop convivial social relations and root the struggle locally. The Nicaragua Social Forum was born and developed, modestly, out of the meeting of these two trends.

The *Social Forums* are another, particularly strong, incarnation of this meeting of the two logics. They constitute open spaces (Sen & Keraghel, 2004) intended to foster exchange and collaboration among actors belonging to the two alter-globalization trends. Conceptualized by committed intellectuals strongly tied to the way of reason and rather institutionalized, the very first WSF was soon overwhelmed by the creativity of participants from all over the world, the mix of experiences, autonomous spaces and the increasing will to implement alternatives. Most activists consider the informal exchange of activist experience with people from different countries, during attendance at official forum workshops, to be a privilege. The Indian WSF reinforced this expressive aspect with its dances, songs and theatrical performances of the crowd in the alley-ways of the Forum. It also underlined the importance of concrete alternative implementation, including the use of free software. The meeting between the two paths also played out at the level of each individual participant, who shuttled constantly from a technical workshop to the swell of subjectivities in the alley-ways and the exchange of experience with other activists. The Social Forums are thus simultaneously spaces for the elaboration of expertise and for experimentation with another world; for popular education and for exchanges of experience. Conceived on the model of academic colloquiums, the World Social Forums have been overrun by subjectivity and expressive activism from all sides. On its own, the way of reason is not sufficient to explain the World Social Forums or organizations like ATTAC or ReMALC, whose founders clearly wished to associate them with the rational and modernizing trend.

Whatever the intent of their founders, neither ATTAC nor the World Social Forums have been limited to networks of committed intellectuals, nor even to the way of reason. Absent from the founding texts of ATTAC, the subjective aspect is hardly mentioned in the writings and discourses of the main leaders of the organization. But the agendas of local chapters have gone far beyond forums on economic texts, organizing theatre evenings, creative protests, and art exhibits. Moreover, when 7,000 supporters of ATTAC gathered on 19 January 2002 at Le Zénith (Paris), the organization's economic issues were certainly present, but it was the emotionally charged speeches which had the greatest impact on the audience. The stage was then given over to musicians who kept the party going with these ardent defenders of the Tobin tax for three hours. This is far from the studious atmosphere of reading groups and cold technical calculations of the preferred percentage at which to tax financial transactions.

The heuristic distinction on which previous sections of this book rely, between the way of subjectivity and that of reason, should be considered an analytical tool. The two paths run through the spectrum of alter-globalization organizations and activists, though most actors are more closely tied to one or the other trend. Even within those actors used in previous chapters to illustrate one of these logics, the two cannot be totally isolated. While it is certainly true that involvement in alternative social centres such as Barricade is primarily rooted in experience, subjectivity and the local, these activists also mobilized to put pressure on their municipal council to pass a resolution against the GATS, with activists explaining the technical aspects to the local population and elected officials. In the same way, while alter-activist youth prioritize actions and creativity, panels on very abstract topics were organized in their autonomous spaces around the Social Forums. Conversely, expert networks and organizations like ATTAC have developed a convivial and festive aspect to their gatherings, often combining them with cultural events or even direct actions.

The counter-summits, Social Forums, and the many alter-globalization coordinating spaces provide opportunities for alter-globalization activists to mingle and to create the elements of a common identity beyond their diversity. However, presence in the same location and shared reference points offer no more than a context of encounter and do not determine the manner in which the different trends combine, maintain their distance or even confront each other. To what extent do activists of the way of subjectivity and citizens of the way of reason share an interest in the values and practices of the other trend? Is a cross-fertilization process taking place within the alter-globalization movement? Or, conversely, is alter-globalization ruptured between a subjective and expressive revolt on the one hand, and a movement focused on economic measures and the reform of international institutions on the other?

Three main forms of managing the tension between subjectivity and reason within the alter-globalization movement can be differentiated: dichotomization, absorption and cross-fertilization.

Dichotomization: from tension to opposition

When the alter-globalization movement is unable – or can no longer – tie together the paths of subjectivity and reason, the risk of evaporating into the particular and the local or, conversely, into the universal and global increase. The two paths then become autonomous, abandoning the difficult relations which linked them and manifesting a *dichotomized*, ruptured, form of alter-globalization, as isolated historical and cultural movements, united in nothing but a struggle against a common, vaguely defined adversary ('corporate globalization', the 'Washington Consensus', etc.). In this situation, divergences rapidly become ruptures, leading to a delegitimation of the other trend, whose actions are either ignored as useless or perceived as counterproductive and even dangerous for the movement. The lack of continuity or of direct impact on policy makers, for example, can bring leaders of the way of reason to regard spaces of experience and actions expressing subjectivity as marginal: 'It's really nice, but this camp produces nothing concrete', remarked an ATTAC activist after visiting the activist youth camp against the 2003 G-8 summit. For their part, alter-activist youth and anarchists are harsh judges of the approach taken by NGO and WSF leaders: 'In the end, it does nothing but reproduce the system in place'; 'The organisers want to establish themselves as leaders of the European social movements. They want to become partners to negotiate the EU.'[1]

In other cases, the other path is no longer considered a distinct trend of the same movement but as harmful actors impeding the movement's development, even enemies who are criticized with greater vehemence than neoliberal adversaries. During the first protest march against the WTO summit in Cancún, after throwing stones at police, a black bloc began aiming their projectiles at the leaders of organizations who attempted to calm protesters and negotiate with police. They viewed them as 'belonging to the same system as the police and the WTO' (interview with a member of this black bloc). Without going as far, some extreme actors of the way of subjectivity view ATTAC and the NGOs as bodies charged with 'recuperating' the movement, preventing the start of 'real change'.[2] Activists close to anarchist currents are thus generally extremely critical of 'alter-globalization leaders' and the structures – considered very bureaucratic – of the main organizations and of the 'conferences at the end of the world which, in the end, don't result in much' (Catalan activist). Some refuse to participate in the Social Forums which they believe to be 'controlled by a majority of salaried activists working for NGOs subsidized by national and European government agencies. It is the way in which the political class will try to control and destroy this alter/antiglobalization movement.' They thus call for people to 'Drop the ESF, ATTAC and other NGOs: instead prepare for the revolution in your street!' (comment published on Indymedia France, October 2003) and to organize anti-capitalist villages such as the one against the 2003 G-8 summit at Evian and the 'libertarian social forums' held in opposition to the Paris, Malmö and Porto Alegre Social Forums.

Similarly, distrust of activist youth, anarchists and black blocs is strongest where intellectual leaders dominate. At the end of 2001, a leading female intellectual mounted such a virulent crusade against the 'violence of the black blocs' – believing that their actions delegitimized alter-globalization as a whole and in fact served their adversaries – that she provoked the dissolution of the Citizens Coordination against the WTO in Paris. Numerous activists of the way of reason believe that masked protesters 'are not activists, but people who came for a brawl' (ATTAC official during the Nice protests) – even if, in this case, they were very politicized black blocs who participate fully in the alter-globalization movement. Many activists of the way of reason would like to see the movement's organization keeping some clear distance between itself and these groups: 'We must condemn the anarchists. They are not there for the same thing as us!' (ATTAC activist cited in *Le Monde*, 22 July 2001, p. 2). The evening after the main protest at Genoa, learning of the death of a young protester, several activists taking part in an ATTAC-France meeting stated that 'The black blocs were really seeking this. They've got what they were looking for.'

This dichotomization is often accompanied by a sectarianism *within* each of the paths, which quickly transforms divergences into divisions preventing any form of collaboration. The actors best positioned to bring the two paths of alter-globalization together are then cast out of the organizations; this happened, for example, to the webmaster of ATTAC-France, who became closer to various alter-activist networks and was soon fired from the ATTAC headquarters team.

The 2004 European Social Forum in London

The three forms of encounter refer more to ideal-types than concrete reality. However, certain events may approach one form closely. In this way, the European Social Forum held in London (15–17 October 2004) represented a strong polarization of the two paths, all dialogue being impossible between partisans of the two logics.

The importance of the local and national scene in the realization of each international alter-globalization event has already been underlined. English alter-globalization civil society is particularly polarized. Actors close to the way of subjectivity are very active, through small but abundant networks strongly rooted in the way of subjectivity: hundreds of disobedience and alternative resistance groups throughout the country work against the G-8, vivisection or new highways that threaten Britain's forests. These labyrinths of local networks spawned Reclaim the Streets, an alter-activist network which has organized many direct actions relying on theatre and a festive spirit to call forth other social relations and a more convivial world. It helped initiate the first 'global day of resistance' around the G-7 summit in Birmingham in 1998, and has since become known internationally. But England is also home to numerous major international NGOs who joined the alter-globalization movement and the World Social Forums, including Oxfam and Jubilee 2000. Symbolic actions and talks for the cancellation of third world debt were therefore organized around the same summit in Birmingham. In addition to these two trends, two other forces played a determining role in the organization of the ESF in London, marking the event by their determination to hijack it: the Mayor of London, Labour Party rebel Ken Livingstone; and extreme left political groups, notably the Socialist Workers' Party (SWP).

During the first preparatory meetings of the 2004 European Social Forum, discussions between the alternative networks and the more formalized social and political actors were described as 'very tense' by foreign observers. A few months later, all dialogue had become impossible. The two trends confronted each other over radically different visions of organizing the forum. Despite the intervention of four foreign mediators (two Italians and two French), no real dialogue could be established between actors close to the way of subjectivity and the very politicized components who dominated the way of reason. The latter modelled the organization of the ESF after a labour or political gathering; with professionals taking care of logistical aspects, tasks outsourced to private companies (like food and security), agreements negotiated between participating organizations and a pre-eminent place reserved for leaders of the social and political organizations in the 'official' forum panels. In the end, 17,000 people participated; far less than at the two previous ESFs (respectively, 50,000 and 35,000 participants). While at previous ESFs alternative spaces had 'one foot in the forum, one foot out', actors of the way of subjectivity this time preferred to create meeting and discussion spaces entirely 'outside' and often against the 'official' forum. Organized by the 'Wombles', alter-activists, libertarians and networks close to the People's Global Action Network, the main alternative forum, 'Beyond the ESF', attempted to create more horizontal and participatory spaces 'in which local residents and the community will be able to interact, learn and experiment with new ways of exploring our future together' ('Beyond the ESF' flyer). These alternative forums were thus spaces of conviviality, discussion, meeting and implementation of a horizontal and participatory way of organizing. However, all of these initiatives brought together far fewer people than the 'official' forum.

Such a dichotomization of the movement had four main consequences.

First, actors most apt to encourage a liaison between the two poles become less involved in the process. Some large British NGOs including Oxfam, who actively support the World Social Forums, retreated from the organization of the London ESF. The field was thus abandoned to libertarians and creative activists on one side, and the politicians and extreme left activists on the other.

Second, once the networks who objected to the incoherence between practice and the values espoused by the movement were excluded, there was no longer a counter-balance to tendencies leaning towards a hierarchical organization of the 'official' forum. The rather authoritarian nature of decision-making processes, the private security guards charged with expelling those who had not paid registration fees, and the heaps of flyers and notices for workshops which littered the rooms after the crowds left may be taken as examples of this perspective. The alternative networks moreover protested: 'the experts and leaders [who] preach platitudes from their podiums; the food served by chain restaurants who under-pay their employees; no policy for recycling litter; the media centre zapped freeware' (alter-activist who participated in the alternative spaces).

Third, each side perceived only the most extreme aspects of the other. The 'alternatives' viewed the official ESF as the 'headquarters of the campaign for the Mayor of London' or a place 'where all the speeches are pre-fabricated [and from which] nothing interesting can result'. Conversely, the official organizers reduced the alternatives to groups of dangerous *provocateurs* or *window-smashers*. In this context, relations between the two trends of the same movement were transformed into confrontation between enemies. When three young activists from one of the alternative forums attempted to climb onto the stage during the ESF closing march in order to denounce the way in which the Mayor of London and the Socialist Workers' Party had controlled the ESF, organizers immediately called the police, who arrested them before they were able to speak.[3]

Fourth, this dichotomized form of the movement was accompanied by an increased logic of competition among organizations of the official ESF. Strong tensions arose between the main organizers of the official forum and many participating organizations. Each organization was eager to promote its workshops, sell its publications and boost its membership. From a resource mobilization perspective, the 17,000 participants represented an enormous 'activist market' for civil society organizations and small political parties. On the one hand, the important support of the mayor of London, Ken Livingstone, was offset by his seizing control of some aspects of the forum, including the ESF website which was entirely controlled by City Hall. On the other hand, many extreme left parties and groups viewed the event as an opportunity to increase their visibility and recruit new members. At each entrance to the forum, participants were assailed by Trotskyist groups selling their publications and trying to attract new supporters. The Socialist Workers' Party, which had played a major role in advancing the English candidacy for the ESF, was particularly visible – and criticized – throughout the forum. The group 'Revolution' relied on underhanded means to exercise control over the 'Youth Assembly of the ESF', resorting to discourse and practices from an era long put to rest. In a room stacked with their members, having listened to several comments from the floor, three organizers presented different paragraphs from a statement that they had already written. The reading was punctuated by applause and three critical comments from outside activists were roundly booed by the audience. The few 'dissidents' preferred to leave the room before the text was adopted 'unanimously'; it was then presented as the 'youth contribution to the ESF'.

The English alter-globalization movement emerged much divided from this ESF and the behaviour of the political actors, especially the SWP, was denounced by many European activists. Several English organizations were also very critical, admonishing the organizers for their 'excessive verticalism' (release by ATTAC-UK, sent on the ESF list, 30 October 2004). The impact on the ESF of this radical divorce between actors of the way of reason and those of the way of subjectivity was, however, attenuated by a series of factors. The first stems from the relative importance of the European movements and dynamics. Since 2001, the 'European preparatory assemblies' (EPA) have played an important role in organizing the forums (Doerr, 2009). Apart from the political brawls, the forum offered spaces for workshops and popular education activities organized in a relatively autonomous manner by hundreds of European civil society organizations. Moreover, while the delegates of organizations heavily involved in the preparatory assemblies were aware of the conflicts, most of the organizations which participated, foreign activists and Londoners coming to learn more about alter-globalization, only heard echoes of the squabbles. For most participants, the Social Forum remained an *agora* for learning, debate, exchange of experience and strategy, and for meeting other alter-globalists.

Absorption: tension erased by hegemony

In other situations, the configuration of the alter-globalization movement is such that the tension between the two paths disappears under the hegemony of one pole. What remains is a purely expressive or a purely instrumental movement. Like a black hole, whose gravity is so strong that it swallows up all neighbouring stars and the farthest light, a pole or an organization which becomes hegemonic transforms the network, absorbing all nearby organizations and attracting all the attention given to the movement, whether social, political or media coverage. It barely allows actors from the other pole to develop. Empirically, absorption can assume the form of the hegemony of an organization attached to one of the two poles. The competition between movements' organizations can thus lead to a situation of monopoly, where a single organization comes to embody the entire alter-globalization movement. The alter-globalization network then acquires a centre and leaders – those of the dominant organization – while other voices do not find a place or are silenced. This was the case in France, where ATTAC assumed a hegemonic position between 1998 and 2001.

Since its inception, ATTAC-France was able to gather the energies of very diverse organizations and activists around its unifying platform. Thanks to its effectiveness, visibility and 27,000 members, it occupied the centre of the French alter-globalization scene, practically absorbing the whole of French alter-globalization civil society between 1998 and 2001. Almost all French alter-globalization initiatives were closely associated with ATTAC, whose members generally made up more than half of the participants in alter-globalization demonstrations.[4] During this period, in both Belgium and France, 'when social justice networks had to take a position on any question, ATTAC was generally asked to set the tone, so first of all they came to ask us what to think before saying anything at all'[5] (an activist from ATTAC-Liège). The media also focused on the organization, so much so that B. Cassen came to deplore its 'over-mediatization'.[6]

ATTAC was viewed as the sole representative of alter-globalization in France. Even at the end of 2003, acting president J. Nikonoff continued to believe that, 'for many citizens, ATTAC represents and embodies the alter-globalization movement' (General Assembly of ATTAC-France, 30 November 2003). The space left for other protest actors was extremely narrow. Many spaces of expertise which were not connected to ATTAC, such as the Observatoire de la mondialisation, gradually disappeared, while actions and activists of the way of subjectivity were stifled, failing to develop in France as they had elsewhere.

Far from the 'network, without hierarchical structure or geographic centre' written into its international platform, ATTAC restructured the French alter-globalization network from a polyarchic network to a coalition centred in Paris[7] (Wintrebert, 2007) under the 'iron law of oligarchy' found in many social movements (Michels, 1966 [1911]). This hegemonic behaviour of some leaders was the main reason for the failure of the creation of a French Social Forum, which was steadily opposed by ATTAC delegates in convergence meetings.

However, the situation has evolved. Starting in 2003, ATTAC experienced a decline. Critiques of 'ATTAC's hegemonic behaviour' levelled by the 'No Vox' network (illegal migrants, homeless, unemployed, etc.), for example, began to hurt the organization. Other spaces of expertise on alter-globalization topics emerged, either autonomously or within organizations, trade unions and alter-globalization coordinating bodies. The Fondation Copernic and the 'citizens' committees', for example, were central to the alter-globalization debate on the European Constitution in 2005. Actors of the way of subjectivity also began to grow and spread. Among them, the alter-activist youth of Vamos played an important role in the G-8 counter-summit at Evian in 2003. The translators' network Babels also developed in France and reinforced the way of subjectivity in that country. Within ATTAC, local committees gradually assumed greater weight, although they had long been confined to a 'consultative' role. The scandal surrounding ATTAC's internal elections fraud in 2006 thus only reinforced the decline of the organization and the distrust with which its historic leaders were regarded by a growing number of alter-globalists.

Alter-globalization having been identified with this one organization for a long time in France, many citizens and journalists have associated the decline of ATTAC with that of the whole alter-globalization movement, while actors more oriented towards the way of subjectivity generally remain in the shadows or are not considered part of the alter-globalization movement.

Combination: tensions and complementarities

The alter-globalization movement was born, not from a subjective revolt nor from a rational challenge to neoliberalism, but out of the encounter of these two paths. Cross-fertilization should not be confused with a fusion, erasing the differences between the two trends. The opposition and complementarity of these two paths is at the heart of the alter-globalization movement. From this perspective, the tension, which is expressed primarily through conflict and debate among activists and organizations, must not be mistaken for a diversion or deficiency of the alter-globalization movement. On the contrary, it creates a dynamism spurring the movement to adapt to new situations and innovate. Constructive criticism by one of its two constitutive trends is the engine of the movement's evolution. For example, the organization of the World Social Forum, which was initiated mainly by experts of the way of reason, has increasingly come under fire by actors of the way of subjectivity, who, since 2001, have insisted on the value of democratic opening and experimentation with concrete alternatives. These critiques achieved a first victory in the more decentralized way of organizing the fourth and, even more so, fifth World Social Forums, in which actors of the way of subjectivity and 'ordinary citizens' enjoyed much greater space.

WSF 2005: *a will to opening, decentralization and combination*

The fifth World Social Forum was held at Porto Alegre in January 2005. The international political and economic context hardly seemed favourable. The re-election of G. W. Bush in November 2004 was a severe blow from which alter-globalization activists were still reeling and, after the massive mobilization against the war of 15 February 2003, anti-war protests had definitely languished. Many believed that the movement had 'suffocated' and the situation seemed ripe for internal fights and increased institutionalization. The European Social Forum (ESF) in London in October 2004 had been a disappointment. Returning to its stronghold of Porto Alegre, the forum had to deal with the sensitive matter of its own *routinization*. The WSF was targeted by three basic critiques: lack of democracy in the organizing process, particularly within the International Council; the institutionalization of certain bodies and the growing influence of NGOs; and the structural problem of weak integration of the poor and of people of colour (Dawson, 2005). On top of these challenges to the routine and manner of organizing the forum was the additional challenge of numbers. The first four World Social Forums had grown from 15,000 to 50,000 to 100,000 to 120,000 participants. In 2005, 170,000 people participated in the forum; 200,000 protesters marched the streets of Porto Alegre at its opening and some 6,200 journalists covered the event. This massive participation testified to the real success the alter-globalization movement continued to enjoy despite the difficult political and economic context. But given the scale, how to avoid allowing the organizers' central problem from degenerating into one of 'managing the crowds', to borrow the words of a Brazilian organizer in 2003? How to avoid relegating participants to the role of passive spectators? How to avoid a growing institutionalization of the organization?

The founders of the WSF emerged for the most part from international intellectual elites very close to the way of reason.

This logic retained the upper hand throughout the different forums, the first of which strongly resembled alternative academic congresses on a university campus. Since then, calling for greater consistency between the movement's ideals and practices at the forum, people close to the way of subjectivity have criticized the organization of the WSF, demanding that 'the forum also be made a place to experiment with practical alternatives',[8] by promoting the active participation of everyone, respecting the environment and advancing social economy. Starting with the way of subjectivity, criticisms of WSF organizing were relayed all the way up to the International Council: 'the WSF must fulfil two functions: symbolically, it must show a strong resistance to neoliberalism and the World Economic Forum and develop alternatives. . . . But it must also be a place to experiment with alternatives.'[9] The experiences of the Mumbai Forum and the youth camps thus became reference points for experimenting with the use of free software, the promotion of active participation and the involvement of activists in all the organizational and logistical aspects of the forum (see pp. 214–15).

These different factors encouraged organizers of the 2005 WSF to give greater priority to 'implementing a change in concrete practices'. They achieved a better integration of the pole of subjectivity and provided a more active role for hundreds of organizations. Rather than rail against the privatization of education in the private Pontifical Catholic University of Porto Alegre, the main venue of the previous WSF, forum participants held their discussions within the canvas walls of huge tents. Food was sold by small businesses aligned with a solidarity-based economy, and WSF bags were manufactured by organizations active in social reintegration. Free software and alternative technologies were also used. The biggest organizational change was undoubtedly the *decentralization* of the forum and the '*self-organization*' of the entire range of activities, as discussed further in the next chapter. Thus the forum was, to a greater extent than any of its predecessors, a 'terrain of experimentation to invent technical solutions and alternative modes of organization'. A clear limit of this process must nevertheless be mentioned: the proportion of women speakers was much lower than at the 2003 and 2004 forums, both of which had made a concerted effort in this area.

The improved cross-fertilization of the two paths during the 2005 WSF did not result from absorption, in which the differences between the two poles had been reduced. On the contrary, each of the trends was reinforced, more present and better integrated into the WSF dynamic than previously. The fifth WSF in fact had a record number of big international NGOs, who took the opportunity to launch a huge international campaign against hunger. Catholic and Protestant NGOs were also massively present. Their third world development components (such as Jubilee South and the French Catholic Committee against Hunger and for Development) had been involved since the first forums. This time, even the 160 national member organizations of Caritas had all received an email message urging them to participate in the forum. Pax Romana, the World Council of Churches and numerous congregations also attended the forum.

Regarding the way of subjectivity, with 33,000 participants, the youth camp had never been as large. Previously relegated to a spot several kilometres away from the 'official forum', this time the youth camp was located at the centre of the site. Its impact on the entire event constituted one of the major transformations of the 2005 forum. The festive and convivial aspect was certainly present in the camp, but in addition countless discussions were held in the seven 'autonomous spaces' organized by youth of diverse affiliation: Latin American political parties, Brazilian social movements, and international alter-activist networks inspired by Zapatism. In contrast to the London European Social Forum, and while they remained critical of the 'official forum', the activists of these autonomous spaces strove 'not to be excluded from the forum,' maintaining 'one foot inside, one foot outside'. An Argentinian activist from an alter-activist autonomous space expressed a widely shared opinion: 'There are few international meeting spaces in Latin America. Consequently, even for those of us who criticize the forum, it is really necessary.' The 2005 WSF reciprocal will towards openness and dialogue was also illustrated by the participation of International Council members in some of the youth camp discussions.

The relative strength of each pole was even reflected in the topics discussed during the forum. With more than 400 concerts and cultural activities, culture and art were more present than previously – in discussion as well as concerts and exhibits. At the same time, the major campaign at the forum was the 'fight against poverty' launched by big international NGOs. The forum was also characterized by numerous discussions on new information and communication technologies. From alternative information websites to free software, this topic is especially favourable to a cross-fertilization of the two paths, combining legal and technical aspects with the assertion of new forms of cultural expression. More than in the past, this forum brought together two very different views of social change. Rooms were packed to join discussions with philosophers of anti-power, particularly John Holloway; but hundreds also turned out for workshops devoted to reforming international institutions, and the UN in particular. While some swapped experiences, others were talking strategy and seeking effective tactics, especially in mounting political pressure: 'We do political lobbying, we must convince the law makers', summarized Riccardo Petrella in a workshop about access to water. The objective was precise and expressed numerically: 'plugging one and a half billion human beings into the potable water network'.

While the way of reason still dominates the WSF, originally conceived by and for intellectuals, reflection and criticism emanating from the way of subjectivity have had a real impact on the organization of the event and have greatly contributed to its success in spite of the difficulty of the political context. It must be stressed, however, that the three forms of encounter are ideal-types which are not clear-cut in reality. Thus, while the cross-fertilization of the two paths clearly improved, this is not the whole story of the 2005 WSF. Lack of comprehension remained between actors of the two trends, which may occupy the same space without starting a real dialogue. The following conversations, which took place in the same small square within the vast site of the 2005 Forum, illustrate this point. On Thursday, 27 January, several young activists discussed the value of a gigantic banner hanging some 200 metres away, unfurled the previous day by international NGOs in the context of their campaign against poverty. They lamented the 'waste of money' and asked in what way the banner would help poor people. Two days later, in the same location, an organizer of the Belgian Social Forum discussed the utility of the discussions then underway in the autonomous space of the alter-activist youth forum, adjacent to the small square: 'It's an interesting debate, but what use is it? The policy makers aren't there, neither are the journalists who could relay it; and I don't think that it will lead to any concrete strategies. . . . Politicians listen to NGOs and journalists, not youth!' Actors of the two paths can thus successfully collaborate at the same World Social Forum without debating or understanding each other.[10]

The 2007 mobilization against the G-8 in Heiligendamm

At the beginning of June 2007, a week of mobilization against the G-8 in north-east Germany gave alter-globalization activists an unprecedented visibility in public opinion and media in that country. The international mobilization was marked by the enthusiasm of German activists from different generations, as well as their experience in non-violent direct actions and their ability to unite a high degree of efficiency and the horizontal affinity networks that involved thousands in decision-making processes.

The mobilization was characterized by the convergence and reciprocal support of actors from the two paths of alter-globalization. Opened with a march of some 75,000 people in the streets of the neighbouring town of Rostock, the week of protest represented the most important alter-globalization mobilization ever achieved in Germany. Activists from very diverse tendencies participated, from punks to Pax Christi, young members of the socialist party and counter-cultural squatters' groups. In contrast to most alter-globalization events and mobilizations, teenagers between fifteen and twenty years old were numerous. Many of these marched with the black blocs (that gathered more than 3,000 people), adopting the style more as a subculture and identity than a mode of action.

The different paths of alter-globalization had a place in the multiple activities of the counter-summit. Actors close to the way of subjectivity gathered in three camps, where 10,000 youth alter-activists and anarchists debated, took action and lived an alternative experience. The days were devoted to protest, workshops in the camps, and preparation for blockades. Evenings were filled with discussions around the camp fires, film screenings, and songs and dances late into the night. Drawing on the experience of alter-globalization youth camps, which have multiplied since 2002, and supported by the long German tradition of autonomy and organization, the self-organization of the camps combined participation and efficiency, experiments in autonomy and the functional organization of numerous aspects of communal life, from organic food to techno-parties, security, workshops and discussions, cleaning and direct action training.

Citizens and experts of the way of reason organized a large alter-globalization forum in the city centre. Many youth activists attended certain activities of this forum and, conversely, citizens and experts did not fail to show their solidarity with the more direct actions blocking the roads to the seaside resort where the G-8 leaders were meeting. Despite the imposing police set-up, some blockades lasted for more than thirty-six hours. The success of this peaceful action and its essentially symbolic impact were due to the German experience of blocking nuclear convoys and the numerous preparatory meetings to train thousands in carefully defined tactics, as well as the involvement of activists from different generations.

The mutual support and cross-fertilization between the actors of the two paths, however, did not prevent strong tensions from emerging within some German alter-globalization organizations, crystallizing around the question of 'black bloc violence'. The few broken windows and limited confrontations with the police were essentially the work of a small minority of more experienced activists from Europe and particularly Greece. The mobilizations over the following days were marked by resolutely peaceful marches in support of migrants, against war, and in defence of peasant farming. However, the acts of violence sparked a huge debate in the country. The leaders of ATTAC-Germany immediately and firmly condemned them, expressing regret that they had harmed the cause and the image of alter-globalization more than they had advanced it: 'no child in Africa will get more to eat because of stones being thrown at the police'.[11] The black blocs obviously didn't share this point of view: 'We didn't wait for police provocation before attacking. We gathered stones for everyone and then we began. . . . We are in a war against capitalism and the police are their first line of defence' (interview with a Greek activist). This is further evidence that, even when cross-fertilization of the two paths of alter-globalization seems to predominate, the spectre of dichotomization is never far off.

Conclusion

These case studies show that a cross-fertilization of the two paths is not the most frequent form of encounter: the way of reason dominates the alter-globalization movement globally. This path is in fact more compatible with formal organization, which in turn facilitates greater access to material resources, media coverage and influence in alter-globalization international bodies. With the exception of the 2005 and 2009[12] WSFs, NGOs and more institutionalized international organizations have had a far greater influence on World Social Forums than the loose networks of the way of subjectivity. On the other hand, it was the cross-fertilization of the two paths which allowed activists to achieve several of their principal successes: the counter-summits and the fifth World Social Forum.

As for predicting whether the movement is heading towards further cross-fertilization, more propitious to the social movement and the individual subject, or, on the contrary, is moving farther away from it, the diversity and multiple dynamics animating alter-globalization actors invite great caution, even a definitive renunciation of any evolutionary perspective. The alter-globalization movement is not a 'long, quiet river' evolving towards a precise form which gradually materializes. If, at certain times, the encounter between the two trends seems more harmonious, at others it tends towards dichotomization or absorption. Only three months separated the London European Social Forum, marked by a strong dichotomization, and the fifth World Social Forum, which owed its success to an improved dialogue between the two poles. The history of the movement and its continuity do not lie in an evolution from one figure to another, considered superior, but in the permanent tension between these two paths.

9

The Main Debates

Activists of the way of reason and of the way of subjectivity hold different, at times even opposing, visions of social change and movement organization. Taken to the extreme, one side risks degenerating into a rootless cosmopolitanism (Friedman, 1999), falsely universalist; the other into a narrow communalism and localism. One tends towards institutionalization; the other resists this tendency only to, at times, fall into sporadic commitment and ephemeral networks. The first can lose its way in the abstraction of numbers, the second in the incommensurability of experience. Left to itself, the logic of the way of reason can lead to an integration into the institutional and political world, no longer maintaining alter-globalization's ambiguous relations with the political. Conversely, 'pure' subjectivity would lack the concepts and categories to understand a situation otherwise than in terms of experience, leading towards a withdrawal into the local, the communal or into pure hedonism. An overly strong importance attached to self-critique, to participation and to a refusal to delegate can also render all decision-making impossible.

Diversions of the way of reason	Diversions of the way of subjectivity
• Experts remote from citizens	• Activists reject experts
• Efficiency over democracy and participation	• Participation and democracy without attention to effectiveness; populism
• International cut off from the local	• Local cut off from the international
• Institutionalization of the movement	• Very fluid, informal and sporadic networks
• Integration into the political rather than ambivalence	• Rejection of the political rather than ambivalent relations

In each area, the way of reason and the way of subjectivity produce antagonistic diversions. Without the counter-weight of the other trend, they draw apart from each other, eventually rupturing the alter-globalization movement. However, when the actors manage to work together, the tensions between the two paths, expressed principally by reciprocal criticism, allow the movement to avoid the diversions to which each path is prone. Through meetings, alter-globalization activists acquire the experience which enables them to combine participation of the greatest number, central to the way of subjectivity, with the efficiency of decision-making and effectiveness of actions required by the way of reason.

Three issues have emerged as particularly sensitive in the relations between alter-globalization actors: which scale to privilege for action, social movement organization and alternatives; internal organization of the movement; and the concept of social change. These three stumbling blocks constitute both the main sources of debates and controversies among activists and *potential spaces for a combination of the two paths* and for constructive cross-fertilization.

Think local and global, act local and global

Local or global focus?

Activists of the way of subjectivity believe that changing the world begins with the local: 'Facing this cold society, it must be asked: what can I do in my village, in my neighbourhood to change things?' (a Mexican Zapatista supporter, 2003). While they participate heavily in international mobilizations, alter-activist youth insist on 'respect for the local context and the importance of a constant back and forth between the local and the global' (Canadian activist, 2002, WSF). The local level enables them to 'go beyond the big speeches at international conferences' (activist from Vamos) and to act concretely: 'We have an international goal and it is essential to express ourselves in the global movement; but, at the same time, we must act locally. There is lots of work to do at this level; for example, occupations of buildings in the fight against real estate speculation' (young Catalan activist, 2002 WSF).

Activists of the way of reason, on the contrary, believe 'it is increasingly at the global level that things are decided' (an activist from ATTAC), drawing particularly on the examples of the WTO and European Union directives. They consequently promote a top-down concept of change. Globally oriented actors often ignore locally rooted dynamics or consider them merely a step on the way to the main challenge, which is situated at the global level. Local reality is reduced to the point of impact of essentially global processes: 'the problem of child labour in India and Africa is completely interconnected with the problem of employment in Belgium, Wallonia, and Liège. And development will only happen effectively through advances at the level of international organizations' (activist from ATTAC-Liège).

Beyond being global, alter-globalization distinguishes itself by its ability to think, act and develop simultaneously at various levels, from the neighbourhood to the world. Rather than 'think global, act local', alter-globalization activists seek to 'think local and global and to act local and global' (an activist of Barricade, Liège). From reviving local life to the management of a global economy, activists want to 'think problems at the relevant levels and to act at all levels' (*Grain de Sable* 226, 10 April 2001); 'Because neoliberal globalization takes place at many levels, [the] responses also have taken place at different levels' (Feffer, 2002: 17). The Barricade Collective Purchasing Group sees it as a question extending 'from the plate to the WTO': improving daily food by turning to local producers but also addressing the problems of large-scale distribution and agricultural policy, through public education and actions identifying European and global stakes in the issue. Combining various geographical levels in actions, statements and thought remains a constant challenge for alter-globalization activists. While the way of subjectivity focuses on local roots, international connections are crucial for the way of reason.

Narrow localism

Some 'localist' alter-globalization activists consider their neighbourhood or community as the only significant scale for activism. In many cases, local orientation leads to suspicion or even mistrust of all processes and actors that are not directly 'grassroots'. The suspicion may be directed at nationally or internationally organized movements, including alter-globalization convergences. For example, some activists of Barricade considered the Belgian Social Forum events worthless: 'It is like a big mass where everyone feels he has to come and show himself. . . . Nothing really happens here. It is in our towns that we can really make things change.'

Another modality of *localism* leads to the rejection of globalization itself. Social actors of this tendency focus on the defence of their community against the globalization process.[1] This move is exemplified by some libertarian youth activists, who used to take part in alter-globalization demonstrations in Paris; deciding to retire to a country house, they grew vegetables and experienced community life.

However, many locally oriented alter-globalization actors avoid this kind of *localist retreat* and demonstrate a surprising ability to articulate their local struggles within both a national and international framework. This has particularly been the case with some Latin American indigenous movements. The 'universal character' of Zapatism was clearly expressed from the very beginning of the uprising (EZLN, 1994; Le Bot & Marcos, 1997: 203). Indigenous activists consider involvement in the global to be compatible with a strong local dimension: 'resistance to neoliberalism should be led in all spaces and at all levels, local and international, public and private, particularistic and universalistic' (Ceceña, 1997).

From international scholar–activist networks to a global activist elite

As described in chapter 6, greatly interested in global issues, scholar activists and committed intellectuals had established international networks many years before larger alter-globalization gatherings were organized. The International Forum on Globalization was created in 1994, as well as the World Forum for Alternatives, which brings together anti-imperialist intellectuals. A European network of alter-globalization experts and intellectuals was set up in Madrid during the 1995 activist meeting against the World Bank and the IMF summit. In one of the last meetings of this network, before its dissolution into the WSF networking process, over 200 committed intellectuals and experts from all over Europe gathered in Paris on 5 and 6 January 2001. Each of their campaigns was led by a relatively autonomous, multipolar network of committed intellectuals. Such international networks and the personal affinities they created were extremely valuable for the first major international gatherings of the alter-globalization movement:[2] 'We started to know each other and to say that we had to do something. We decided to organize the 'Other Davos'[3] and then the World Social Forums.'[4]

As alter-globalization expanded, international organizational meetings, counter-summits, conferences and Social Forums multiplied. Travelling from one side of the planet to the other became one of the main activities of leaders of networks, NGOs and think tanks. For example, the two Belgian members of the International Council spent less than 100 days in their home country in 2003 and made over ten intercontinental trips the same year. The burgeoning of international meetings thus gave rise to informal but very influential affinity groups of global elite activists[5] that would play a decisive role in many of the major initiatives of the international movement and notably the World Social Forum. At times they have been responsible for highly strategic formal and informal decisions such as the location of the Forum, the main conference speakers, and drafting the Charter of Principles. Similarly, smaller groups of cosmopolitan leaders took initiatives as important as the 'Manifesto of Porto Alegre' and the 'Social Movements and Activists' Assembly'. As R. Nuñes (2005) has shown, 'hyperconnectivity by a select few [led] to concentrating power in undeclared ways'. Many important strategic and political decisions concerning the WSF and the whole international movement have been taken by a few well-connected leaders with restricted representation and loose or non-existent relations to mass movements for which they claim to speak. Immersed in this 'global activism', spending much time in international meetings and hobnobbing more with their international counterparts than with local movements, these cosmopolitan activists may lose touch with grassroots activists in their home countries. In fact, many of these elite activists are not directly connected to any mass or grassroots social movement and sometimes only represent small activist research centres. As in many other sectors of global civil society, many alter-globalization leaders are neither designated by nor accountable to their organization's members (Chandhoke, 2002: 48).

Until mid-2004, the crucial prerequisite for joining the International Council (IC) of the WSF was not being a large movement or waging a significant struggle against global capital but being an 'international network', even though many of these 'international networks' had a very restricted social base. Even some of the main organizers of Continental Social Forums had been kept out of the IC for not being sufficiently internationalized networks. The capacity to connect with affinity groups of cosmopolitan activists was hence crucial not only for those who wanted to take part, even modestly, in the future development of the international movement but also for those who sought the recognition accorded by an IC membership in the arena of national civil society. As described in Chapter 6, individual committed intellectuals and scholar–activists are more likely to develop such connections than grassroots movement activists, indigenous activists or unemployed workers.

The IC was initially built around a group of Brazilian activist leaders and some French connections. These two countries as well as the rest of Western Europe remained over-represented among the influential movement elite. Some committed intellectuals and a few civil society leaders from the global south have also joined these cosmopolitan networks. Among them, some Indian and Malian activists played a major role in the organization of the WSF in their home countries. Nevertheless, in most cases, these forum organizers seemed much closer to their European counterparts than to grassroots activists from their own countries. For example, Aminata Traore, former Malian minister of culture and one of the most cosmopolitan of African activists, was the key actor in the Bamako 2006 Polycentric WSF organizational process.

This elite group of alter-globalization activists should not be considered homogeneous: strong controversies and disagreements animate the international global justice sphere. These are not only disagreements over strategies or distinct political orientations but also power struggles and inter-personal conflicts.[6] The IC was notably animated by recurrent debates between a more politically oriented line, which wants the forum to take political positions and coordinate actions, and those who think the forum itself should not adopt political statements but yield the possibility of such initiatives to its participants (cf. Sen & Kumar, 2007; Whitaker, 2004). However, both share a similar, top-down vision of the organizational process of the movement and an overall emphasis on the global level, which clearly distinguishes these groups from activists of the way of subjectivity.

Bridging the gap: multilayered actors

The gap between the two ways of alter-globalization widens when alter-globalization actors become entirely focused on a single scale to the neglect of others. On the one hand, there is the risk of activists becoming mired in a narrow localism, closed identity or communalism that struggles *against globalization*, while the alter-globalization movement is struggling for *another* globalization. On the other, cosmopolitan elites risk merging with experts of international institutions as members of a new global class (Friedman, 1999).

When cross-fertilization predominates, actors and alter-globalization convergences at different levels support and reciprocally stimulate each other. Local and national activists' networks of the host country have played a major role in each of these meetings. In turn, the World Social Forum inspired a myriad of national and local convergences. Alter-globalization activists benefit from the wide media coverage of the World Forums, and endeavour to bring its energy home to their local organizations: the numerous talks in many countries around the world to report back from the WSF often concluded by highlighting the importance of implementing ideas acquired at Porto Alegre or Mumbai at the local level. In a similar vein, the objective of the Mesoamerican Forum was 'promoting and supporting experiences of struggle throughout the region without claiming to substitute for local and national organizations' (Fundación Humbold, 2002: 8).

The multiplication of meetings and events at an international level has strengthened the process of the constitution of an alter-globalization cosmopolitan elite that gained an unprecedented influence over the alter-globalization movement. However, the World Social Forum process also provided new opportunities for encounter and interactions between these two categories of activists, in significant ways.

World Social Forums have offered local activists from all over the world opportunities to meet, share their experience and network. Since 2003, the No Vox network has gathered together French illegal migrants, Indian dalits, Brazilian landless farmers and homeless movements, and Argentinian unemployed *piqueteros*. This has enabled it to frame their local struggles in a wider perspective and to connect them to a larger movement. As an Argentinian *piquetero* summarized, 'We are here to make our revolt part of the global movement, to contribute to the movement and to learn from it' (WSF, 2003). For many activists, the WSF also represents a unique experience of global consciousness: 'For the first time in my life, I perceive myself as taking part in something truly global' (an Indian activist, WSF, 2004). Indeed, the WSF has allowed many local activists to access the global level in their claims, experience and networks. Such international meetings have tended to counter myopic tendencies that can emerge in local struggles. The WSF also provides local activists with an international platform, which can help them make their claims and messages heard not only internationally but also within their national spaces. For example, the 2007 WSF in Nairobi allowed Kenyan and other African homosexual rights activists to make their cause visible to their local and national audience at an unprecedented level.

While the WSF process propelled local and national activists into global civil society, it also generated a renewed interest amongst cosmopolitan activists in national and local movements in their home countries, which they had previously neglected. This has especially been the case in the third world solidarity and development sector, whose actors and networks found renewed interest in the political and social contexts of their homelands through the national and local Social Forums processes. Some of them have become key actors in both local and national alter-globalization convergences. In Austria, the national Social Forum was initiated by the director of a research centre on Latin America, a long-time globetrotter involved in the international movement. Likewise, the Catholic Committee against Hunger and for Development (CCFD) has become one of the leading actors of the French alter-globalization convergence (see Dreano, 2004; Agrikoliansky, Fillieule & Mayer, 2005).

A Belgian activist research centre built around a travelling scholar–activist, the *Tricontinental Centre* was formerly exclusively dedicated to the global south and anti-imperialist struggles. The centre has been deeply involved in the international alter-globalization movement since its early beginnings. Since 2002, the Tricontinental Centre has become involved in the Belgian Social Forum and in numerous local forums, increasing its activities in Belgium as never before. The main French-speaking Belgian development NGO network followed a similar path. It played a major role in the launch of the Belgian Social Forum in 2002 and 2003 and hired some of the most productive young intellectuals of the alter-globalization national scene. In addition to its development campaigns in the global south, which remain the main focus of the organization, it has set up several new projects and campaigns in Belgium. A similar evolution has been observed at the local level. Once Oxfam's national and international networks got heavily involved in the World Social Forum, its local chapter in Liège decided to join the city's alter-globalization convergence. It developed new contacts with local civil society actors that it had formerly ignored: 'Before, we had very little contact with activist sectors in Liège. Now, with the local Social Forum, we know what everyone is doing and we try to see when and how to support their initiatives' (an employee of Oxfam-Liège, 2003). Without abandoning its international solidarity commitments, Oxfam-Liège became an actor embedded in the dynamic local civil society.

The WSF process has provided both an easier and broader access to an international scale to local actors and a renewed interest in local and national actors and struggles amongst many cosmopolitan activists. Both of these dynamics have been crucial in limiting the distance between movements active at the local level and travelling elites, and in avoiding the antagonistic diversions of a retreat into the local, on the one side, or domination by cosmopolitan elites far removed from local struggles on the other.

The movement-internal organization

Horizontal vs vertical networks

The organization of the movement is unquestionably one of the major stumbling blocks and the focus of countless internal criticisms and debates. Activists of the way of subjectivity consider alter-globalization movements and events to be laboratories in which experiments in organizing practices coherent with the values of the movement must be conducted. They consequently devote a lot of energy to organizing their networks in a 'democratic, horizontal and participatory' manner (Wainwright, 2005). They greatly distrust 'bloated structures' which do not allow 'horizontal, informal and convivial' relations to be maintained within the movement and constantly denounce the leadership maintained by a few organizations in the Social Forums and by some cosmopolitan leaders within these organizations. Moreover, activists of the way of subjectivity do not share the idea that their organization should grow and gather more members in order to transcend the local, moving upward to the national and then to the international. As we explained in part 2, rather than incorporate more members and other localities, they would like their movement to 'swarm' – that is, to encourage the creation of similar autonomous spaces, networks, social centres and initiatives in other communities, neighbourhoods and cities: 'We don't seek to build one big organization but many, many small organizations which all remain locally rooted and keep their specificities' (a local Social Forum activist in France).

On the other hand, citizens and experts of the way of reason are also organized into networks but believe some delegation of responsibilities to be necessary to ensure a well-organized and effective movement, whether in preparing forums and other large mobilizations or in putting forth clear messages to citizens, public, the media and policy makers. The ideal of participation by the greatest number comes into collision with the need for efficiency in meetings, when time is short and decisions must be made. The efforts to improve internal democracy and the openness of decision-making processes slow and make more complex the answers to problems in a changing context (Sikkink, 2002: 312). There have been occasions at some of the Social Movement Assemblies at the WSF and the preparatory meetings for the ESF (EPA) when 100 activists have spoken in turn, without the assembly being able to arrive at a clear decision. However, preparing a forum for tens of thousands of people requires a more permanent administration and a decision-making body. Closed and informal groups are then substituted for the assemblies: 'We are forced to create, at night, closed working groups – it would therefore be better to create a real working group at the European level instead of only General Assemblies' (a coordinator of the ESF process, after the EPA in Istanbul, 2004). Therefore, activists of the way of reason furthermore consider some of the governing bodies of the movement – the Board of ATTAC-France, the International Council or the Brazilian and Indian secretariats – to be 'poles of stability in a movement where everything is unstable' (B. Cassen, French alter-globalization coalition meeting, 27 April 2004). Such bodies must certainly be pluralist, but also, and primarily, effective, which makes – according to this way of thinking – a certain structure or even institutionalization necessary. This logic favours a top-down construction of the movement. In response to critics who decry the incoherence between practice and the declared values of the movement, some alter-globalization leaders justify it in the name of efficiency – even their stays in five-star hotels in Porto Alegre: 'Where else can we find rooms for press conferences and meetings, day and night? . . . That is where we meet among ourselves but also with politicians and journalists' (B. Cassen, WSF, 2003).

Thus two concepts of organizing the movement coexist within alter-globalization. On one side, structures are reinforced and even institutionalized for the sake of efficiency. On the other, there is a will to avoid overburdening the movement with structure in order to avoid stifling its dynamism, adaptability and innovative potential, as well as to prevent hierarchies from forming.

Way of subjectivity	Way of reason
– Participation of all in decisions	– Effectiveness
– Bottom-up	– Top-down
– Swarming of autonomous local movements	– Need for national/global decision-making bodies
– Validating the informal	– Institutionalization (structure)

In some cases, such as the process of organizing the European Social Forum in London in 2004, this coexistence engenders vehement and sterile denunciations: some are accused of betraying the movement by imposing their decisions on grassroots activists in scarcely democratic ways; others of failing to go beyond sporadic events and achieve results. However, as the WSF 2005 illustrates, cross-fertilizations and cooperation between these two visions can result in efficient organizations and successful events. The way of reason is no more opposed to internal democracy[7] than the way of subjectivity is to being efficient; they simply assign different priorities to these values. Criticisms launched by activists of each path may thus be constructive, enabling them to avoid antagonistic diversions.

The tension between these two approaches exists at all levels: within the International Council of the WSF, within ATTAC-France – where the two ideas about organization clashed during the 2006 internal election campaigns – as well as in the discourse and desires of individual activists. 'There shouldn't be very institutionalized, well-established structures. . . . But of course we also need some structures in order to work' (a young activist of ATTAC-Germany: Hurrelmann & Albert, 2002: 315). The internal tension lent to the alter-globalization movement by the coexistence of the two paths and the permanent vigilance each side maintains regarding the other have helped it to avoid the classical evolution of social movement towards institutionalized organizations (Kriesi, 1993). During its first fifteen years, the alter-globalization movement has not consistently evolved towards greater institutionalization. An ever precarious, unstable and unsatisfying balance between fluidity and structure has been maintained, creating the image of permanent tension between two visions of the convergence: one prioritizing efficiency and delegation (though far less institutionalized than large international NGOs); the other, a more informal and horizontal logic. The interactions of the two and resulting tensions generate many of the movement's transformations.

The attractions of institutionalization

In some cases, the pull towards greater efficiency gains the upper hand and profoundly modifies the structure of local networks. A more institutionalized organization of the movement or of some of its actors helps the perpetuation and the development of some of its activities. But it also means accountability on predetermined projects, generally making the movement less innovative and less 'alternative' according to a process which has 'tamed' (Kaldor, 2003) generations of social movements.

Between 2003 and 2005, the alter-globalization network in Liège was affected by the assimilation of several actors of the way of subjectivity by more institutionalized actors who have historically dominated Belgian civil society. These latter chiefly include two large trade unions, Christian and socialist respectively, which joined the alter-globalization movement very early on. Besides, a part of the state budget for development aid is, moreover, distributed among hundreds of NGOs and development education organizations which have heavily influenced local alter-globalization and recruited some of its most dynamic young activists. Finally, there are several subsidy programmes to which organizations have recourse, particularly for projects framed as social integration and popular education. While the institutionalized actors, and especially the trade unions, provided the Belgian alter-globalization network with the means necessary to develop in the first years, the situation also lent itself to absorption of the way of subjectivity by institutionalized structures able to hire activists. This process is notably evident in the individual trajectories of a few of the most innovative activists close to the way of subjectivity in Liège. A dozen of them, who were in their early thirties, were offered employment in a union, an NGO or through access to grant money. Another young founder of the local alter-globalization coordinating body, active in libertarian and alter-activist networks, was invited to participate in the electoral list of the Green party. Once elected, however, her mandate and political activities increasingly took priority and transformed her activist commitment. But the Liège case also shows that there was nothing inevitable in this evolution. Alongside these now more institutionalized organizations, new creative and expressive initiatives sprang up, such as the festive Euro Mayday parades, a samba group, illegal occupations of buildings to create social and cultural centres, and several alternative, convivial spaces in working-class neighbourhoods.

The 2005 WSF experience: towards an open forum

The 2005 WSF organization process offers a case study of a successful *cross-fertilization* in which activists from the two trends of the movement have inspired each other by their values and practices. The Social Forums have worked as 'open spaces' that put international leaders in contact with the more horizontal and participatory values and visions of the forum held by grassroots activists. Increasing questioning and criticism of the organization of the forum, as well as concrete alternative practices, led the International Council to adopt deep changes to the WSF, especially in 2005.

In many aspects, the 2001 WSF looked like an academic congress, with well-known intellectuals and academics monopolizing the large panels and even most of the smaller workshops. Nevertheless, organizers and cosmopolitan activists were overwhelmed by the crowd and its enthusiasm. Many participants quickly began contesting the organization of the WSF and used the open space it provided to build alternative and more participatory workshops and meetings.

During the 2002 and 2003 WSFs, young activists organized the Intergaláctika Laboratory of Disobedience, a participatory forum for sharing experiences among resistance movements from around the world. Radically opposed to the hierarchical character of the WSF, they engaged in a festive demonstration and a direct action against the WSF VIP lounge with the slogan 'We are all VIPs.' This action resulted in forum organizers renouncing the VIP lounge for subsequent Social Forums. More generally, it challenged movement leaders about WSF hierarchy and elitism. After the strong critiques of the 2003 WSF (see chapter 5), IC members progressively became more open to ideas and suggestions of how to make the organization of the forum more coherent with the values it defended: waste recycling, solidarity economy, more active participation, etc. The 2004 Mumbai WSF, the international youth camp and the international activist interpreters' network, Babels, constituted spaces of experimentation for such alternatives, repeatedly asking the IC to adopt horizontal and participatory practices for the whole forum.[8] In January 2004, the message was largely accepted and even relayed by various founding members of the IC: 'the sons and daughters of Porto Alegre are not here. . . . We have to change the methodology of the Forums. We need a democratic dialogue with Continental Social Forums, especially between the World Social Forum and the Asiatic Social Forum and the European Social Forum.'[9]

Finding a new way to organize the 2005 WSF became a major challenge. Allowing its 170,000 participants to take a more active role in meetings and debates was not an easy task. Massive panels or lectures with an audience of 10,000 disappeared from the programme. Indeed, WSF organizers did not hold a single panel, in this way giving more importance to the thousands of workshops organized by participating organizations. Instead of massive crowds listening to famed intellectuals, hundreds of tents were set up to host smaller and more participatory events. After introductory speeches, the assembly was often split into smaller groups, giving each person the opportunity to express their own opinion.

While the rising institutionalization of the WSF could have paralysed its 2005 occurrence, the cooperation and dialogue between activists of the two paths opened the forum to actors from the way of subjectivity. The bottom-up dynamics gave the event a new and refreshing momentum. This tendency came to counter-balance the trend towards institutionalization favoured by the organizational requirements of such a gigantic event.

Nevertheless, even the 2005 WSF reality was not always the 'total self-organization' and '100% horizontal process' that J. Miola, the 'WSF *executive manager*' (*sic* – my italics) (*Libération*,

1 February 2005), claimed it was. The Forum was, for example, the venue for the Porto Alegre Manifesto, written by nineteen intellectuals without consultation of other participants (see pp. 150–1).

The WSF is in fact a double-sided process. It has increased the influence of international leaders over the movement, in conformity with Michels' (1966) 'iron law of oligarchy' within social movements. However, it has also propelled grassroots activists to the global level and helped spread alter-activists' horizontal values and practices at this level. Their interactions resulted in some *cross-fertilization* that transformed both tendencies: global leaders have become more aware of the importance of internal openness and democracy while networked subjective activists are more open to collaboration with the organizers of the WSF. Dialogue between these two trends can result in more participatory – but still efficient – meetings and to a better balance between local and global claims, strategies and events.

Rethinking social change

The logics of counter-power and anti-power – the logics associated with the two different paths – can be analysed along five dimensions:

	Way of subjectivity	Way of reason
Direction of change:	From below / 'Swarming'	Top down
Organization and change:	Coherence of means and ends	Efficiency
Pragmatism:	Concrete, local experience	Technical measures
Stance towards power:	Anti-power	Counter-power
Institutions:	Protecting autonomy	Regulating the economy

Divergences over the right level and direction of social change and over the role of organizations in the movement have already been touched on in the previous sections. The way of subjectivity privileges change from below – starting with the local, with small groups and everyday life – which spreads through emulation: 'swarming'. More attuned to universalism and the global, activists of the way of reason seek to impose global measures in order to change modes of regulation, especially over the international economy. The next three sections will focus on pragmatism, the stance towards power, and institutions, the last three dimensions in the chart.

Pragmatic idealism and the rejection of the general model

To alter-globalization activists, the journey from Seattle to Porto Alegre symbolizes the transition from a phase dominated by opposition to neoliberalism to another mainly dedicated to the elaboration of alternatives: 'This year, we are here to make proposals. The critical analysis has already been made. We know what we don't want. Now we have to say what we do want' (B. Cassen, January 2002).

Almost a decade later, no universal alternative and no general programme have emerged. This absence can be interpreted in two ways. An analysis based on traditional models of social change and centred on institutional politics would frame it as the failure of a hetereogenous and still immature movement: 'These movements are still emergent and the alternatives only partial. Internal criticisms of the system are expressed ever more strongly, but they have nothing comparable to what Keynesian ideas represented during the middle of the last century' (Aguiton, 2001: 62). It may also be recalled that an entire century elapsed between the initial blossoming of the labour movement and the development of a universal alternative model.

On the other hand, the absence of a universal alternative is embraced by activists who view it as the rejection of a totalizing ideology and of the notion of a planned revolution, the Soviet system being the archetype: 'We are purveyors of alternatives. But for the moment, I don't see anyone with a universal alternative. And this is a good thing. The wealth lies there!' (Barricade activist); 'The very absence of a manifesto is the movement's strength' (comment posted on Guardian.co.uk, 15 May 2008); 'This idea of having different opinions and a single practice must end. . . . To resist is to build millions of practices, nodes of resistance which don't get trapped by the real world which expects us to be serious spectators of our own lives' (Benasayag & Sztulwark, 2000: 161).

From this perspective, the absence of a universal alternative and general models does not refer to a deficiency of the movement, but constitutes an instrinsic and constitutive feature of alter-globalization. Activists of the way of reason and of the way of subjectivity in fact emphasize that 'devotees of perfect systems have never brought anything but difficulties and misfortunes to the world' (ATTAC, 2001b: 43). As N. Klein stressed (talk at the 2002 WSF), 'the challenge to the movement does not lie in finding a vision but in resisting the desire to choose one too quickly'. The sociologist F. Khosrokhavar (1996: 95) also points out that 'many new forms of mobilization will only be effective if they refuse the temptation to defend a utopia, that is, another totality as the way of managing society'.

The end of the twentieth century and its modern concept of progress and revolution also brings to an end a period that drained many revolutionary dreams from which activists woke up only to realize that their emancipatory revolution had become an oppressive regime. Alter-globalization activists believe that a pre-established plan does not and cannot exist, any more than a 'prefabricated model' can: 'To me, one of the main defects of the communists, particularly in the USSR, was that they believed Marxist philosophy was like an Ikea kit; something that could be used just about everywhere with the same model, with the same pieces of furniture, with the same stuff. . . . But it is not true, such a model doesn't exist' (a French activist). Neither the participatory budget of Porto Alegre, nor the Zapatista experience represent models: 'Zapatismo seems to be a model which has had particular success and from which everyone seems to have a lot to learn. But it is in no sense a universally applicable model. Each place must find its model. The experiences of others can help, but importing a model wholesale can never work' (a *piquetero*). As theorized by M. Benasayag and D. Sztulwark (2000: 29), 'There is no social model which represents the concretization of the desire for liberty and emancipation. . . . The only thing that exists are multiple acts of liberation.' Alter-globalization activists call on a multiplicity of alternatives in order to create 'a world in which many worlds fit'.

Their activism is not structured around a revolution or messianic visions, but from the starting point of concrete and limited projects,[10] which, together, should lead to a different society. From the perspective of the way of reason, a 'project' would be a regulatory measure, for example to regulate financial speculation, which is then gathered together in platforms and other alter-globalization points of consensus.[11] In the way of subjectivity, 'projects' refer to the creation of spaces of experience and alternative practices. While these will only affect a limited number of people, their impact on the lives of these people is immediate. In contrast, projects of the way of reason have a far less direct impact but are generally universal in scope and aim to benefit a much larger population.

The absence of teleology, resulting from the crisis of modernity (de Munck, 1999), clearly distinguishes alter-globalization activists from the labour movement, which appealed to Progress and History. Far from 'The Revolution' and the long wait for a 'generalized crisis of capitalism,'[12] alter-globalization activists opt for a *'pragmatic idealism'*: 'The "revolution" means nothing to me. What must be done is to change what we can, starting with concrete things' (coordinator of the Belgian Social Forum); 'Trying to precisely define the other world makes no sense. With our ideals, we have to try to see what we can do concretely' (alter-activist from Barcelona, 2004). Their struggle is inscribed in a more pragmatic perspective, non-dogmatic and non-teleological, which sees itself as more reflective and consequently less inclined to ideological sectarianism. To the alter-globalization movement, which was constructed in opposition to proclamations of the end of history – both neoliberal and Soviet – questioning and internal critique are fundamental: 'Our not-knowing is also the not-knowing of those who understand that not-knowing is part of the revolutionary process. We have lost all certainty, but the openness of certainty is central to revolution. We ask not only because we do not know the way (we do not), but also because asking the way *is part of the revolutionary process* itself' (Holloway, 2002: 215; see also Shukaitis & Graeber, 2007).

Nothing equivalent to the meta-ideology of the Revolution unites alter-globalization activists who assert that 'the path is made by walking' (Zapatista saying) or 'that it is through a succession of small, concrete steps that we will manage to change things' (ATTAC-Liège activist). The will to debate and the openness to diversity thus seem central. But if the era of pre-determined recipes is over, how to avoid succumbing to a post-modern dispersion into disparate projects, unrelated to any general perspective?

Alter-globalization pragmatic idealism questions the opposition between reformists and revolutionaries, and challenges those who remain rooted in classical revolutionary ideologies. Holders of the latter, however, view this rejection of a programme as a reformist position, even 'poetic', and regard the distance that alter-globalization activists maintain from political power as a 'victory of neoliberalism'. Thus, A. Boron (2003) believes that theories of anti-power are 'fully compatible with dominant neoliberal discourse'.

In the face of power

The twentieth century has shown that even liberation, decolonization and revolutionary movements can quickly transform into forces of oppression (Hobsbawm, 1994). J. Holloway (2002: 29), one of the influential thinkers of the way of subjectivity, draws a bitter lesson:

> For over a hundred years, the revolutionary enthusiasm of young people has been channelled into building the party or into learning to shoot guns, for over a hundred years the dreams of those who have wanted a world fit for humanity have been bureaucratised and militarised, all for the sake of winning state power for a government that could then be accused of 'betraying' the movement that put it there.

The first global movement since the fall of the Berlin Wall, alter-globalization was built in the wake of and in opposition to the strategies of change which begin by seizing political power. At the dawn of the twenty-first century, alter-globalization activists believe that we should lay aside plans to take the Winter Palace, and move forward with logics of counter-power, concrete alternatives and specific projects. Following the path of new social movements that have emerged since the 1960s, alter-globalization opposes, to those who maintain that it is illusory to change the world and transform society through the conquest of state power (e.g. Boron,[13] 2003), that 'it is [also] illusory to hope for change by means of a central power if it is not imposed from everywhere' (website of Vamos, 2003). Even committed intellectuals close to progressive state leaders stress that 'Nobody believes that change can be produced in the short-term, by a simple political revolution' (Houtart, 2001: 9).

Many alter-globalization activists have experienced a huge disappointment once left-wing leaders came to power. They claim, for example, that 'The Jospin [left-wing] government privatized in France more than any government of the right' (activist from ATTAC-France) and that 'Lula applies the policy of the international financial institutions to the letter' (ATTAC-Brazil activist, WSF, 2005). A year after his election, comments were particularly harsh about President Obama among activists at the second USSF.

Rather than building political parties, alter-globalization activists put their efforts into constructing spaces allowing participation of the greatest number – locally for some, internationally for others. Both trends in the alter-globalization movement also stress the foremost importance of the fight over ideas, the struggle against the hegemony of neoliberal ideology. Asserting that 'it is first and foremost a fight in our heads and minds against the logic of capitalism in which we are steeped' (young *piqueteros*, interview 2003), activists of the way of subjectivity echo the words of B. Cassen who stressed that 'the daily work of ATTAC is to exterminate the neoliberal virus in our heads' (talk in Paris, March 2003).

For activists of the way of reason, it is a matter of counter-balancing the influence of other – political or economic – actors in political decisions, according to the logic of counter-power close to Montesquieu. Activists of the way of subjectivity have rather adopted a conception inspired by Foucault that has notably been developed by intellectuals close to the movement (such as M. Benasayag, J. Holloway, M. Hardt, A. Negri, etc.). The aim is to create spaces of experience and other social relations following the logic of 'anti-power' or the fight against 'power-domination'. Between the diversions of the former, which lead to an integration into the institutional political sphere, and those of the latter, which can lead to a total rejection of political actors, the permanent tension between the two paths holds alter-globalization in a posture of critical distance from political actors. It enables alter-globalization activists to combine a will to engage in the political sphere with a rejection of traditional forms of political engagement.

However, activists of the way of reason maintain an ambiguous relationship with political leaders. While they aim to develop counter-power, in an attempt to influence political actors with the quality of their arguments and 'citizen monitoring', they also defend the power of policy makers to make decisions against economic actors. Thus, as a new generation of leftist leaders has come to power in Latin America, the most 'political' tendency of the way of reason has assumed greater importance, as chapter 10 will show. Besides, the forceful return of state intervention in the economic domain following the global economic crisis has considerably increased this tendency.

Institutions: a stumbling block

The stance towards institutions appears to be another point of divergence between the two paths of alter-globalization. While some 'reclaim the streets' as collective public spaces, others 'reclaim the state' (Wainwright, 2009) as a major tool for progressive policies and social justice.

Activists of the way of subjectivity are generally distrustful of institutions which embody, in their eyes, a 'top-down', state-centred approach to political life which they reject. They seek to construct spaces of experience outside institutions. Many activist groups have developed a monolithic and often very simplified view of institutions and the state, which they consider proxies of their capitalist and neoliberal adversaries. They may thus develop a strong rejection of all intervention by institutions and all dialogue with political and institutional actors. Citizens of the way of reason, on the other hand, accord a central place to institutions, whether to defend them against the hold of markets or to enable a better regulation. The reinforcement of some international institutions – such as the UN – and the creation of new ones – particularly in the area of international law and the environment – are among their flagship campaigns.

However, each of the two paths has developed more complex and often ambiguous relations towards national and international institutions. These institutions in fact function simultaneously as adversaries and partners of the movement, which denounces them at the same time as it demands their recognition and the establishment of new rights. On the issue of international economic institutions, activists of the way of reason consider there to be 'too much IMF and not enough regulation' (workshop on international institutions, WSF 2005). While all agree on the need for international regulation, some believe that this requires the dissolution of the current bodies (see p. 167). The danger of this strategy is that it weakens existing institutions in a somewhat utopian hope of founding new ones. This was notably illustrated with the opposition to the European Constitutional Treaty. It raised massive alter-globalization mobilizations throughout the continent. However, once the Constitution project had failed, it didn't mean that a more progressive vision of Europe would take the lead. On the contrary, it first led to some paralysis of the EU institutions and then to the adoption of a less ambitious but no more progressive treaty by the state leaders. Moreover, the potential role of existing institutions in strengthening democracy is often underestimated by activists. A social movement scholar and a leading activist in the US Social Forum, J. Smith (2008: 228) argues that 'To re-embed the global economy within a global society, social movements must focus on strengthening the institutions that can support a global human rights culture.' She thus advocates that 'social movements must approach political institutions as potential allies in their struggle'.

In the way of subjectivity, the stance towards institutions is also much more ambiguous than what appears in activists' discourses. The radical discourse of a complete rejection of the state and its institutions is thus frequently contradicted by actions and concrete practices. Virulent anti-state discourse ('They are puppets! They do nothing but apply programmes decided in Washington.': interview with a demonstrator, 2003) and the assertion of a will to develop autonomous neighbourhoods did not prevent many radical *piqueteros* groups from demonstrating to claim a broader access to the state social benefit. For Argentinian *piqueteros,* as elsewhere, the state was in turns the instrument of an exacerbated neoliberalism and a bulwark against globalization; a key actor in the fight against poverty and in the repression of popular movements.

The Zapatista movement represents a major exception, having managed to build long-term autonomy without state support. However, the fact that improvement of material conditions in the communities remains limited, or in any case falls short of hopes held by the rebels at the time of the uprising, also illustrates the limits of local autonomy unsupported by national institutions. Local organization can considerably improve the quality of life of the residents affected, but cannot in itself counter the deterioration of social rights and of a citizenship that remains tied to nation-states (Davis, 2007: ch. 3). State institutions can go beyond some of the limitations of local spaces and codify social benefits into law.

In addition, the reconstruction of institutions represents a central issue for autonomous communities. In the Zapatista zones, this is especially true of the organization of local democracy, justice (López Bárcenas, 2005) and teaching methods which integrate indigenous languages and 'culturally relevant innovations in education' (Gutiérrez Narváez, 2006). While embedded within highly unstable regions in crisis, these spaces of experience achieve a stability and a reappropriation of social, cultural and political institutions hitherto regarded as external and hostile. These new institutions attempt a better adaptation to the specific needs and reality of the communities, bearing alternative values and subject to decisions made at assemblies of the people affected.

Participation at the heart of alternatives

The two ways of alter-globalization are articulated around the central aim of fostering participation. Whether close to the way of reason or that of subjectivity, all alter-globalization activists believe that 'representative democracy alone is not enough': 'We can vote once every four years . . . and then for four years we cannot participate in any decision, and then, after four years, all we can say is "super" or else "stop, no way". I don't consider this to be democracy. . . . Democracy is when everyone can participate in decisions' (a young activist from ATTAC-Germany, in Hurrelmann & Albert, 2002: 318). To alter-globalization activists, the great challenge is thus to 'reconquer spaces lost by democracy to the financial sphere' (ATTAC platform).

From the viewpoint of the way of subjectivity, N. Klein (WSF 2002) emphasized the 'thousands of alternatives of the movement, in which political participation prevents the reduction of the political to a policy from and by specialists', while various anarchist trends have long stressed the importance of participatory organization, particularly through workers' and consumers' assemblies (Dupuis-Déri, 2004; Graeber, 2002). It is also within this demand for participation that Subcomandante Marcos locates the *raison d'être* of Zapatism: 'All these claims stem from the absence of legal spaces of participation for us – the indigenous people of Chiapas and all Mexicans – in national political life (EZLN, 1994: 101). Similarly, facing ecological problems, the landless peasants and Pan-Amazonian Social Forums favour solutions based on 'sustainable, popular and participatory land management' by its inhabitants.

To actors of the way of reason, this translates into an insistence on 'public monitoring by citizens', which is central to many alternatives. Alter-globalization activists demand that 'the main socioeconomic choices, investment priorities, fundamental orientations on production and distribution, [be] democratically debated and established by the population itself and not by pseudo "laws of the market"' (M. Löwy and F. Betto, WSF 2002). Alter-globalilzation activists advocate a model of justice close to the deliberative democracy of Habermas (1984) and N. Fraser's (1997) 'parity of participation': because interpretations and judgement can never be eliminated from decision-making processes, a just decision requires nothing less than full and free participation by all parties concerned. This dialogical process should eventually privilege the best arguments. In addition, as D. Held (2010: ch. 6) states, 'increased participation, the prioritization of social justice and a focus on sustainability are not just critical values for a better world, but core operating principles for effective global governance'.

Participation and debate are also promoted within the move-ment. At the WSF 'assemblies of the social movements', just as during the preparation of the ESF, meetings are organized in ways which allow the maximum number of people to express their opinions and be actively involved. This ideal is never perfectly realized (Pleyers, 2004) but as S. Hodkinson (2003: 36) notes, the fact that alter-globalization activists do not agree with each other about responses and strategies towards neoliberalism 'seems to be less important than the will to openly discuss the restric-tions faced'.

The central place given to participation distinguishes alter-globalization from – and places it in opposition to – the vanguard Perspectives developed by numerous revolutionary movements of industrial society. At the core of alter-globalization alternatives and organization principles, participation is inscribed within a will to give the central place to citizens, displacing purely systemic logics, whether embodied by a model of inflexible planning, the invisible hand of the market or the internal contradictions of capitalism.

At the heart of the alternatives proposed and of internal criti-cisms, grassroots and citizens' participation appears to be a central value of alter-globalization, a major issue with adversaries of the movement, and the cornerstone of the concept of change: 'My ideal society is one in which things are discussed more fully, with more participation in decisions, . . . and with little distance between leaders and those who are led' (activist of ATTAC-Germany; Hurrelmann & Albert, 2002: 319). Globalization tends to move certain centres of political decision-making farther away from citizens, establishing these centres at a supranational level. However, the two paths of alter-globalization have shown that globalization also offers new opportunities and opens new spaces to citizen participation, whether within the global debates on international institutions, active participation in neighbourhoods and the transformation of daily tasks, or new forms of participa-tion created by virtual spaces.

Conclusion

The full potential of the alter-globalization movement is achieved in the combination and complementarities of its two ways. It then becomes a matter of seeking to combine a better mode of regulation and personal transformation, global institutions and daily actions. Nevertheless, despite the common foundations and shared central values (participation, questioning of the traditional concept of revolution, and pragmatic idealism), for the most part, alter-globalization alternatives are elaborated inside each of the two paths: economic and legal measures on one side; predilection for local change inscribed within everyday life on the other.

Building viable alternatives based on new solidarities and new regulations, anchored in the global age instead of the nation-state, represents a major challenge of our time. Willing to face it, alter-globalization activists refuse preconceived, universal, alternative plans. They rather seek to develop, through trial and error, a multiplicity of alternatives articulated around one of the two paths and the will to promote citizen participation in all fields. It remains to be seen to what extent this reflexivity and the hesitations of these experiments will prove efficient, given the urgency of current global challenges.

10

Towards a Post-Washington Consensus Alter-Globalization

Reconfigurations

The end of the Washington Consensus

The global financial and economic crisis that started in 2007 has provided a *theatricalization* of a global ideological shift that started a few years earlier: the end of the three-decade hegemony of the Washington Consensus (Held, 2005; Touraine, 2007; Stiglitz 2008). The rise of financial speculation on the global market in the 1990s and 2000s led not to a more accurate distribution of investment but to the worst financial crisis since 1929. After the collapse of Lehman Brothers, no one contested that markets and the financial sector need more regulation.

Several major alter-globalization arguments have in fact reached far beyond the movement's supporters and political divisions. In the 1990s, opening up a country to international trade was seen as the only path to greater economic growth. By 2008, many state leaders, among them French President Nicolas Sarkozy and Indian Prime Minister M. Singh, openly declared that they would 'refuse to sacrifice hundreds of thousands of agricultural jobs on the altar of neoliberalism' (*Le Monde*, 22 July 2008). Barack Obama's administration had promised to take concrete measures against international banks, including UBS, which offered US citizens opportunities to evade tax through tax havens, and the then UK prime minister Gordon Brown was looking for allies to help him implement a Tobin tax on financial transactions as well as a special tax on banks. The G-20 has largely replaced the G-8. While it doesn't give voice to the poorest countries, it nevertheless offers a more global perspective than the G-8 and puts greater emphasis on the regulation of the global economy. Its promise to limit tax havens addresses a major concern of alter-globalization activists. Other important proposals are on the table, notably the creation of a new global reserve system, proposed by China and supported by Russia, Brazil, South Africa and South Korea, as well as by the United Nations Conference on Trade and Development (UNCTAD, 2009) and the 2009 'Stiglitz report'.

The legitimacy of, and need for, state intervention in the economy was claimed by the alter-globalization movement in opposition to neoliberal thinkers who considered the market to be a more rational actor (see pp. 157–63). In 2008, even former Brazilian President F. H. Cardoso, once a major target of alter-globalization activists, stated that 'There are very few countries that adopted neoliberal prescriptions and have not completely collapsed like Argentina. Countries that managed to globalize successfully did so by maintaining state decision-making capacity over economic matters.'[1] Since the summer of 2008, the state has regained the legitimacy of intervening in economic matters and has again been accepted as a key economic actor (Bernardi, 2008).

It could be expected that this 'ideological victory' would increase the enthusiasm of alter-globalization activists. However, at a time when prominent world leaders share core alter-globalization ideas and when targeted international institutions have been widely delegitimized, losing much of their influence, the future of the organizations and events that have symbolized alter-globalization seemed uncertain. In Western Europe, major activist networks – such as the Movimiento de Resistancia Global in Barcelona, ATTAC and most local Social Forums – have disappeared or declined. ATTAC-France's internal election fraud in June 2006 accelerated the downfall of alter-globalization in one of its oldest regional bastions. In 2007, ATTAC-France could count on the support of less than 10,000 members, compared to 27,000 five years earlier. Alter-globalization is also much less dynamic in Italy; the time when dozens of Social Forums were active throughout the country seems very distant. While 300,000 people demonstrated against the G-8 in Genoa in 2001, there were only 10,000 eight years later in Aquila, near Rome. In Mexico, Zapatism has lost its pre-2001 dynamism; at the national and international level, Marcos' speeches have sometimes lost their innovative thoughts, at times even resembling old, far-left ideas.[2] The 2007 WSF in Nairobi welcomed three times fewer participants than the two previous forums, in Porto Alegre and Mumbai. The large events which launched alter-globalization onto the front pages of the newspapers, particularly the World Social Forums and international counter-summits, no longer benefit from the attraction of novelty and corresponding media- tization. Even the global financial and economic crisis only gener- ated limited mobilizations: 'With the strong crisis of 2008, when people were losing their houses, the result of the neoliberal poli- cies was clear. We should have been able to mobilize massively at that time' (an American activist, 2010).

Rather than the end of alter-globalization suggested by some European analysts,[3] significant empirical evidence suggests, however, that the global movement has instead undergone a deep transformation, consisting of four sets of changes. The first has already been much discussed: paradoxically, the alter- globalization movement has had a hard time adapting to the end of the Washington Consensus era it helped to bring about and to the shifts in the international ideological, political and economic context. As R. Zibechi (2006) and F. Polet (2008) note: the coming to power of progressive candidates with a strong popular support and the crisis of the Washington Consensus gave birth to a starker global scenario, in which a series of evolutions pos- sibly meets some of the expectations of the alter-globalization movement, though without gaining the support of all of its com- ponents (see pp. 237–9).

The second transformation relates to the geography of the movement. Alter-globalization organizations have lost impetus in several of the movement's historic strongholds; at the same time, the global movement has undergone a considerable geographic expansion since 2004.

Third, the process of cross-fertilization between the two paths has brought the organizational model of many alter-globalization actors under critical scrutiny; vertical organizations were particularly challenged during this period. The risk is, however, that the movement may actually break down or disappear because of the emphasis on decentralization and suspicion of authority.

These shifts have resulted in a deep reconfiguration of alter-globalization around three axes, which form the fourth set of changes. The first results from an intense involvement of actors of the way of subjectivity in local and daily life. The second extends the expert and citizen logic of specialized networks, which have become the neurological centres of the Social Forums. The third emerges from the growing place assumed by the 'political' current; relying notably on the success alter-globalization ideas have lately enjoyed with progressive governments, especially in Latin America.

A *new geography*

While it has experienced a decline in some of its Western European strongholds, alter-globalization has met with new success in strategic and highly symbolic regions. North America has turned into the most dynamic region for Social Forums. A Canadian Social Forum was held in Calgary in May 2009 and a Quebec Social Forum in October of the same year. In Mexico, the 2008 national Social Forum, working within a highly divided local civil society, initiated a new convergence (Pleyers, 2010). The first US Social Forum, held in 2007 in Atlanta, gathered together over 10,000 activists from a broad range of civil society organizations, diverse backgrounds, and different social and political sympathies (NGOs, local movements, alternative liberals, anarchist networks). For five days, many issues were discussed: war and repression; environmental questions; migrant struggles; women; Native Americans; workers; and even survivors of Hurricane Katrina (Smith, Juris & the Social Forum Research Collective, 2008; Milani & de Freitas, 2007). The second US Social Forum gathered over 15,000 in Detroit in June 2010, among which there were an outstanding number of activists from minorities.

The movement of Seattle and Porto Alegre has often been criticized for failing to take root in Africa, a continent activists consider to be 'the worst victim of neoliberal globalization'. Yet over sixty national or regional Social Forums have been held across Africa since 2005. Bamako, the capital of Mali, hosted one of the three World Social Forum meetings in 2006; the 2007 WSF in Nairobi was attended by 50,000 people and contributed to the creation of national Social Forums in neighbouring Tanzania, Uganda and Congo. The 2011 World Social Forum in Dakar should strengthen this tendency. Anti-privatization movements are very active in South Africa (Ballard, Habib & Valodia, 2006). The Social Forum dynamic is also strong in the Maghreb. In January 2008, 1,200 Moroccans and 100 foreigners gathered for three days in Morocco, among them many youth and women. The dynamic Social Forum process in the Maghreb also gives the movement an opportunity to raise and discuss questions relevant to the Arab and Muslim world that had previously only been tackled superficially among alter-globalization forums.

While not as strong as in 2001 and 2003, an alter-globalization mobilization continues in Europe. In Germany, 80,000 people protested against the G-8 in June 2007, and 50,000 gathered in April 2009 to press the leaders of the G-20 in London to adopt an ambitious programme of international regulation. In the host city, some 30,000 participated in the same protest in April 2009. The European Social Forum process has, moreover, been very active in supporting movements in the east, including in Poland, Ukraine and especially Turkey. The 2010 Continental Forum was actually held in Istanbul.

However, it is above all Latin America which continues to raise the hopes of many alter-globalization activists. There is still a great deal of enthusiasm for the Social Forum process in Brazil, as demonstrated by initiatives in about fifty Brazilian cities during the global week of mobilization around the 2008 WSF, and by the 130,000 participants in the 2009 WSF in Bélem.

In Asia, there are alliances between indigenous communities, peasants, green activists, NGOs and scholar–activists against privatization and projects that will take the land out of the peasants' hands. However, the relations between these various actors are not always easy, notably when the state plays on their divergences (Aditjondro, 2007). The global peasant network Via Campesina is now based in Djakarta. It unites millions of small farmers in South and South-East Asia (Wright, 2008). In

Indonesia, India, Thailand, South Korea and numerous countries of South-East Asia, peasant movements have led the resistance to neoliberal policies, and demonstrations are regularly conducted against the WTO for the cancellation of the third world debt and for food sovereignty.

With the transition to a global age marked by a consciousness of limited world resources, exacerbated by growing demographic pressure and strong economic growth in some of the region's countries, Asian peasants must defend their lands against businesses increasingly covetous of natural resources (Srikant, 2009) and Gulf countries that have started buying land to ensure their food supplies. At the same time, hunger riots struck the continent in 2008. The establishment of new city–country relations, to ensure affordable food for city-dwellers and decent wages for peasants, is thus one of the most interesting axes developed by the Asian movements.

South Korean trade unions and peasant movements have, for many years, been at the forefront of alter-globalization struggles. They led the charge against the WTO during the 2003 mobilizations in Cancún, and have since regularly organized massive protests and alter-globalization forums. South Korean students' networks are also very committed towards global issues, including global warming. (Park, 2009: 456–7). In China, the main sectors that are critical of globalization belong to anti-globalization, or anti-western, nationalist currents (Loong-Yu, 2006). Alter-globalization activists have, however, a growing interest in Chinese civil society actors, as attested by the multiplication of texts about this country on mailing lists and in alter-globalization reviews. They are particularly attuned to the situation and mobilizations of workers in the 'world's factory' and to struggles for democracy which, notably, take place on the internet. Western activists also closely follow the positions taken by the Chinese government on the environment, and on economic relaunch and development programmes. They appreciated, for example, its proposal for a more stable monetary system based on an international reserve during the London G-20 in April 2009.

Many analysts of the movement remain stuck in the initial geography of alter-globalization; they look for the movement in places where it is no longer based. By concluding hastily that the movement is declining, they ignore the fact that it relies on diverse actors from a broad range of backgrounds and that the movement has its own rhythm in each city, country and region. Alter-globalization and the Social Forums process have progressively expanded to new regions, where activists undergo a different set of experiences and thereby develop new dynamics. Less active in Western Europe, the movement has become more global than it was at the beginning of the 2000s. The downside of this geographic expansion is that greater diversity in the movement increases the difficulties of coordination and of agreeing common guidelines.

Evolving forms of activism

As chapter 9 showed, the idea of putting the values of participation and democracy into practice within the movements' events and organizations has been progressively integrated by activists and then leaders of the way of reason. This process of cross-fertilization of the two paths intensified after 2006, thereby furthering criticism and emancipation of hierarchical forms of organization. In the WSF International Council, as in many other alter-globalization networks, a lot of energy has been devoted to discussing and rethinking the organization of the movement and the preparatory process of its main events in order to reconcile openness, flat hierarchy and democracy with the requisite efficiency. The European Social Forum created a dynamic working group that gathered various times in 2006 and 2007 to discuss and remodel the organization of the ESF networks and assemblies.

The transition of an organizational model centred on historic leaders and intellectuals to a more decentralized and participatory movement had dramatic consequences for some organizations that formerly most strongly embodied the alter-globalization movement. As chapter 6 showed, the confrontation was particularly vigorous within ATTAC-France. While it had always adopted a more collegial and decentralized structure, ATTAC-Germany had its own shake-up in 2007. Most founding members resigned from the national coordination committee. In France as in Germany, ATTAC evolved towards a more collegial, less hierarchical, more decentralized structure, with a younger steering committee (two members of ATTAC-Germany's new national committee were 24 and 26 years old), more feminine (A. Trouvé, the new co-chair of ATTAC-France, was a 27-year-old woman) and more open to new themes, including sustainable development. Although dynamic actions have resulted, the organization has not recovered the breadth and strength it enjoyed until 2003.

The promotion of a more horizontal and networked movement as well as the valorization of personal autonomy have also favoured a greater detachment of activists from civil society organizations. In previous models of commitment, individual activists were often considered as tools in the strategy of mass organization (Ion 997). Alter-globalization has reversed the logic: civil society organizations constitute tools through which individual citizens access information, meet like-minded people and get resources to implement projects and actions. The internet favoured this evolution by offering means of staying connected and well informed without belonging to any specific organization. With the 'revolution of 2.0 citizenship', a growing amount of activism (Brecher, Costello & Smith, 2009) and citizen participation (Toscano, 2010; M. Thompson, 2009) plays out directly on the web. Anyone with a web connection can post texts and comments that may be read around the world. As a Californian activist explains, 'These tools are allowing us to leverage a collective body of knowledge and glean from it best practices and models for alternatives ways of making.'[4] The web was, however, only one among several factors in this deep transformation of contemporary political engagement, which include a general decrease in older forms of collective identity, solidarity and activism (McDonald, 2006; Aguiton & Cardon, 2007; Ion, 1997). The movement may thus appear at times more of an 'opinion movement' than a clearly identified social movement.

In many ways, the evolution of the 'Generation of Seattle' illustrates a wider transformation of alter-globalization. As the young alter-activists became adults with kids and demanding jobs, their commitment to activism has undergone dramatic changes, both in the time dedicated to protest actions ('In October 2008, they organized a demonstration at Wall Street, with 5,000 people. But I had so much work that I couldn't even join them') and in its style ('10 years ago, we were more radicals. Many of us became professors and you can't slogan anymore as you did 10 years ago'[5]). They usually keep informed about alter-globalization main events and challenges, some adopt alternative consumption patterns, others occasionally march in a demonstration, but very few can still afford to spend one week at a counter-summit or discussing the way a decision process may become more horizontal and participatory. These changing patterns in their activism don't mean they all threw away their values and political culture as they became parents and skilled professionals. They may actually represent the alter-globalization movement's best hope for a lasting impact in at least three fundamental ways.

First, D. McAdam's studies (1989) have shown how intense experience of political activism during one's youth transforms social identity and political beliefs in fundamental ways, with lasting effects on vote patterns and daily life practices. Strong experience of global events and meeting with people from around the world also durably transform one's world vision.

Second, many (former) alter-activists now occupy professional positions with higher responsibilities where they may actually have a much greater influence. When three organizers of the 1999 and 2001 protests in Seattle and Quebec met at the 2010 New York Left Forum, they were working, respectively, at the Rockefeller Foundation, as the editor of a magazine and as an assistant professor. Similarly, the initiators of the Parisian network Vamos became teachers, assistant professors, researchers,[6] and lawyers, or work in trade unions and civil society organizations. Two of them have taken editorial responsibilities – one in a left-wing journal and one in a magazine.[7]

Third, this generation may also be the best able to combine the two ways of the alter-globalization movement. As young activists, they were deeply rooted in the way of subjectivity. Now active in more institutional civil society organizations or in the education sector, they are often closer to the way of reason. Many insist, however, on maintaining some of their alter-activist practices in their professional environment, for example by fostering more horizontal relationships in schools or among third sector organizations. Besides, as they acquire some distance from their former experience, they are also the best able to acknowledge both the importance and the limits of alter-activism and to underline the complementarity of expressive activism with NGOs and actors of the way of reason:

After the success of Seattle, the question that came was 'So what?'. We were not able to go to something more concrete, like a change in the law. Larger NGOs, like Public Citizens and Global Exchange, occupied the space in the media. They were able to articulate the failure of the WTO with concrete demands. We, as radical activists, we were not able to do it.

The most fruitful outcomes of the generation of Seattle and Genoa – and, beyond, of the whole alter-globalization movement – may thus be yet to come.

Towards concrete outcomes

Neoliberal ideology is under attack from all sides, including from political leaders. However, alter-globalization activists believe that concrete policies have not really changed: 'the privatization of public services and certain neoliberal policies still receive support, particularly from the Barroso [European] Commission' (an activist from Friends of the Earth UK, 2009). However, activists call attention to the huge gap between the promises and speeches of the G-20 and the measures actually implemented. Tax havens were presented as a major target of the G-20 leaders, but action against these strategic spaces of a deregulated global economy remains limited. In April 2009, the London G-20 summit decided to shore up the IMF by tripling its budget (from $250 billion to $750 billion) in order to help stabilize the economy and the markets. Alter-globalization activists questioned: 'Being the source of many problems, it is curious how the G-20 and the IMF can project themselves as a solution too' (interview after the London G-20, April 2009). The international agreement on the necessity of reinforcing internal democracy and increasing representation of emerging countries in the institution resulted only in a modest reform, bearing on 5 per cent of the votes. Moreover, while the G-20 brings together the leaders of two-thirds of the world's population, it hardly gives voice to the poorest countries. Several alter-globalization leaders have thus called for the UN to become the central organizing body in this global crisis.

Likewise, while partisans of more equitable models of development have some reasons to celebrate the repeated failure of WTO trade negotiations since 2003, they should remain cautious. First of all, the motivation of the large emerging countries (China, Brazil, South Africa, India) who joined together during these negotiations was not to challenge free trade but to reinforce it, by demanding wider access to northern markets for their agribusiness industries. As Via Campesina has repeatedly stated, such an opening of the market will hardly benefit small producers in the global south.[8] Second, although it has slowed the process of trade liberalization, the WTO failure has not prevented bilateral free trade agreements from being signed, such as those between the European Union and Mexico and between the United States and Central American countries. Such agreements offer less protection and less capacity for negotiation to the weaker countries.

While celebrating the fact that states have recovered a greater role in the management of the economy, alter-globalization activists criticize the fact that the 'measures taken by governments against the crisis have tended to support the actors who, in part, originated the crisis, particularly through plans to save the banks' (an English activist protesting against the G-20 summit in London, 2 April 2009); 'The only preoccupation of the US government is to go back to "business as usual" and to start again as before the crisis. They are convinced that the system will recover soon and they don't talk about reform' (an activist in Boston, 2010). Activists deplore the absence of measures sufficient to avoid the recurrence of a similar crisis: 'In the absence of effective measures against financial speculation, [current measures to address the crisis] will contribute to creating new bubbles – the one on the American treasury bonds is swelling before our eyes. And financial history teaches us that bubbles always end up bursting' (Zacharie, 2009).

The peak of the financial crisis was hardly past before the traders' bonus system was back in action. While most activists had great hope that the major economic and financial crisis would lead to profound changes in the system, they were soon disillusioned (Caruso, 2010). Like Boaventura de Sousa Santos (2009), one of the leading figures of alter-globalization in this new phase, many activists thus wonder: 'Some people say "Neoliberalism has come to an end." But we don't know what that really means – if it has really come to an end, then what is after that? In any case – whatever it is, it's not very hopeful, but it is clear that it is not going to be the same type of free trade orgy that used to be the case in the past.'

At the 2009 WSF in Bélem, activists drew two conclusions out of this statement. First, 'None of the opportunities for [social transformation] will come out of the crisis by themselves, without interventions' (WSF IC report, October 2009). The 1997 Asian crisis hardly slowed speculation. The economic crisis, with the end of the Washington Consensus, represents an opportunity for the alter-globalization movement because it attests to the limitations of the neoliberal model and the importance of some of the critiques advanced by alter-globalization. Nevertheless, *however large it is, the crisis in itself will not generate social change. The latter will depend on the capacity of social movements to bring out the questions pose' by the historic situation and to advance alternative political visions and economic rationality.* During the year following the crash of Lehman Brothers, the alter-globalization movement did not have that capacity, but the battle is far from over.

The second conclusion now shared by all alter-globalization activists is that the *time has come to focus on concrete alternative outcomes.* Ten years after the famous slogan on a wall of Seattle: 'We are winning' – activists state that 'We won't win the struggle by ideology itself. We need concrete outcomes. People often enter the movement with very concrete demands' (an organizer of the 2007 and 2010 US Social Forums). However, while clear opposition to the Washington Consensus and massive demonstrations provided both media coverage and causes to unite the movement, alter-globalization activists are far more divergent when it comes to the implementation of alternative policies. The movement has been reconfigured around three distinct tracks. The way of subjectivity has greatly developed, re-focusing the activities of many movements on the local level and daily life. The way of reason is more divided. On one side, many thematic networks have been created. They bring together experts and citizens around a less mediatized logic, which has nevertheless proven effective on certain issues. On the other side, the political victories of progressive and charismatic leaders in Latin America have bolstered the more political tendency of this path. Many activists have lent support to these progressive regimes and political parties, in line with positions defended by several intellectuals involved in the way of reason.

A focus on the local level and alternative consumption

In both north and south, in cities and countrysides, two modes of renewed interest in the local and in daily practices have become widespread. The first turns to the construction of more self-reliant communities; the second to practices of alternative consumption. Lived experience, reinforcement of convivial social relations and experiments with concrete alternatives are at the heart of these initiatives, which clearly share the logic of action and values of the way of subjectivity.

Neo-localism

In the Americas (Hocquengem, 2009) as in India (Srikant, 2009), numerous indigenous peoples' movements place local organization at the core of their struggles. The post-2003 evolution of Zapatism is a good illustration of this trend (see pp. 61–5). Urban movements are also seeking to 'reappropriate' local spaces (a neighbourhood or an alternative community centre) to build concrete autonomies and live in another way: 'Through collective processes, we can create spaces that allow us not only to live but develop our creativity as human beings. We create a space where another form of living is possible' (youth during the first Mexican Social Forum, 2008).

This aspiration to build a world based on local communities that are much more self-reliant also became widespread in western countries' movements, especially in Australia, the USA and the UK. Broad citizen networks maintain that 'Relocalization provides us with an opportunity to gradually extend our freedom, creativity and richness in how we live economically, socially, culturally and spiritually. It could also help us to reduce humanity's impact on the Earth' (Global Trade Watch, 2006: 38). These 'relocalization movements' develop a wide range of local experiments aimed at reducing consumption and producing locally, building community resilience as a response to climate change and a way to preserve and promote local knowledge and culture (Hess, 2009).

The tendency towards a communalist withdrawal, raised in chapter 2, is undeniably present in some of these movements. However, most 'Relocalization Networks' insist that 'relocalization would not necessitate putting an end to international trade or isolating ourselves from the world, but rather encouraging and reinvigorating local communities to be self-sufficient and strong' (Global Trade Watch, 2006: 38). These networks echo the alter-globalization dynamic in that they allow citizens to take charge of their own lives and experiment with practical alternatives by 'acting locally on global issues'. Concerned citizens 'have decided to take action for themselves rather than wait for further debate or to wait even longer for business and government to take action'.[9]

Alternative consumption

The way of subjectivity has encouraged a sensitivity to the significance of everyday life. All over the world, grassroots movements are developing forms of critical, local and convivial consumption (Leonini & Sassatelli, 2008; Pleyers, 2011). This has sometimes even eclipsed other forms of alter-globalization involvement: numerous activists and social centres in Italy, which were at the heart of the large alter-globalization mobilizations a few years ago, now focus on neighbourhood life, cultural exhibits, and alternative consumption networks (Rebughini & Famiglietti, 2008; Toscano, 2011).

Alternative food networks such as Teikei (community-supported agriculture) in Japan, the 'Community Supported Agriculture' networks in the USA and the UK, and local 'consum'actors groups' have become widespread in recent years. Most of them are actually 'self-help' groups whose aim is to provide quality local food to consumer groups and secure outcomes for local farmers (Maye & Kirwan, 2010; Seyfang, 2009: ch. 5). However, groups who emerged from the alter-globalization movement tie these concrete practices of consumption to a broader social transformation 'from below'. They reject the model of a consumer society based on 'anonymous and inhuman supermarkets', question food policies and support small organic farmers. Most of these alternative food networks gather a limited number of families, often around twenty, and seek to develop strong and convivial social relations among their members. Activists from the Brooklyn Food Coalition or the international Slow Food Movement indeed consider food practices to be at the heart of major societal challenges: public health issues (diabetes, obesity, etc.), lack of access to healthy food in poorer neighbourhoods (the 'urban food deserts'), fostering convivial relatinships among communities (e.g. with collective gardens or shared meals), global warming (Lappe, 2010) and a struggle against the domination of global corporations and industrial farms. Behind this alternative consumption lies the question of a radically different society. In the words of I. Illich (1973: 28), it is a matter of 'moving from productivity to conviviality'. This conviviality and stronger local social fabric are now at the centre of a multitude of 'new convivial urban movements', ranging from 'critical masses' of bicycles, to promoting the use of bicycles in cities, to city-gardeners who create small, green areas in corners of the city to promote 'convivial and beautiful public spaces' (interview, London, 2009).

Alongside other movements which have developed around alternative consumption, networks for 'convivial degrowth' and 'voluntary simplicity' (De Bouver, 2009) seek to implement a lifestyle that puts less of a strain on natural resources, reduces waste and develops convivial relationships. These activists try to fight 'hyper-consumerism' by decreasing their own consumption. They prioritize reuse of objects, recycling, bicycles and public transport.

The limitations and diversions of the way of subjectivity evoked in chapters 2 and 4 are, however, even more present in these very individualized modes of involvement. In some cases it leads to the disintegration of the alter-globalization movement or its dissolution into depoliticized 'self-help' groups, more personal considerations of health or the quality of produce replacing the sense of opposition to neoliberalism and consumer society (Seyfang, 2009).

Citizens' and experts' advocacy networks

Another stream of the movement believes that concrete outcomes will be achieved through efficient single-issue networks able to develop coherent arguments and effective advocacy, rather than mass assemblies and demonstrations around global summits. On this basis, energy previously devoted to global and continental Social Forums[10] has largely shifted towards thematic networks. With the rising demand that Social Forums should not only be spaces of discussion but also lead to concrete actions and campaigns, issue-based networks have often become the most dynamic actors of Social Forums. The latter have become opportunities for the networks to meet for a few days, hold their general assemblies, establish agendas for the coming year and exchange experience of recent local and national struggles. At the Malmö European Social Forum in 2008, three new continental networks were launched to oppose privatization of public goods and services, around the themes of water, public transport and health care. They joined numerous other European networks already active around issues such as education, 'tax justice' and transnational corporations. Prominent global environmental coalitions, such as 'Climate Justice Action', have also been founded during Social Forums.

These networks are less well known to the public and less covered by the press than organizations like ATTAC or Focus on the Global South once were. It does not prevent them from often being more effective, for two basic reasons. First, the quality of discussion and arguments at meetings tends to be considerably improved, since participants have increasingly specialized in the issue and come to know each other.[11] Second, the less formalized character of these networks and the fact that they are less covered by the press encourage a more pragmatic approach towards policy makers and efficient advocacy. Numerous networks include civil servants (from ministries of finance in the Tax Justice Network, or from municipalities in the network defending the public management of water) and even some local elected officials. Moreover, some governments, notably those of Ecuador and India, appeal to alter-globalization expertise to assess the country's debt management or to take part as official delegates in international trade negotiations.

Networks for a sustainable public management of water are a good illustration of this new dynamic within the alter-globalization movement. The topic has enjoyed growing prominence among activists from all continents. Alter-globalization forums have helped local groups build continental networks in the fight against privatization of the management of water. The African network was created during the 2007 WSF in Nairobi, largely thanks to the dynamism of South African struggles in this area (Ballard et al., 2006). Indigenous movements have been particularly active within the Inter-American Water Activists Network which struggles for the protection and collective management of water. Their position, however, is distinct from that of urban-dwellers in that they promote 'community management' – which does not necessarily pass through the public sector.

In Europe, the fight against water privatization is particularly significant in Turkey, where dozens of local committees have organized against the ambitious privatization of river water which has been sold to private corporations with a 49-year lease. In Italy, where there are local networks in more than 300 municipalities. The issue of water has already been taken up in various local Social Forums, notably in Florence and Berlin. However, it wasn't until 2008, in the European Social Forum in Malmö, that the European Public Water Network was officially launched by about 100 activists coming from fifteen countries. They adopted a manifesto calling for the 'sustainable, public and participatory management of water'. Zealous opponents of privatization, they maintain, however, that 'it is not about giving public authorities a blank cheque for water management'; 'public monitoring' by citizens is promoted as an essential element, as is collaboration between citizen users, elected officials, and workers in this sector, who 'must be fully integrated in our water seminars'.[12] Through the protection of water, these activists also seek to raise the broader issue of global public good commodification, to oppose global corporations and to support public services.

A wide diversity of actors has joined to these water networks: citizen users, bureaucrats, some elected officials, unions, alter-globalization expert networks, local Social Forums and, where the movement is more organized, national topical convergences such as the 'Italian Water Movements' coalition. Several well-known intellectuals are also associated with this issue, including

Susan George and Ricardo Petrella. However, unlike committed intellectuals among alter-globalization organizations at the beginning of the 2000s, they often remain outside the organizational processes of these networks. The European network relies for the most part on five 'network facilitators' from different countries, chosen during the network's general assembly. A larger group of 'coordinators' is open to everyone 'that commits herself to spending time on this question over the next year' (GA, Malmö 2008). While 'water justice activist' networks are generally reliant on practices of the way of reason, the values of the way of subjectivity are also felt, notably in the will to develop 'an open and horizontal network' and to maintain local organizing at its heart.

Although it gets little media attention, this network has already proven its efficiency, notably by contributing to the decision taken by the city of Paris in December 2008 to re-municipalize its water distribution, which had been managed previously by private corporations. For weeks and months prior to this decision, activists and experts from networks in Germany, Britain and Montpellier travelled to the French capital to participate in lobbying actions and forums organized by the local network for the 'remunicipalization' of water. European activists organized an important counter-summit to the fifth World Water Forum, held in Istanbul in March 2009, to denounce the domination of this Forum by transnational companies (cf. Pigeon et al., 2009).

The growing interest of alter-globalization networks in water can be explained by two main factors. First, water is at the nexus of a series of issues which have gained in importance: preservation of natural resources, global common goods, struggles against privatization, defence of public services, and citizen participation in the management of public goods. Second, the topic of water corresponds particularly well to the features of the way of reason. Very concrete alternatives exist and alter-globalization activists intend to show, empirically and theoretically, 'the greater rationality of public management of water relative to its privatization' (a French civil servant, GA in Malmö). The water issue is equally appreciated for its 'pedagogical virtue': starting from this issue, which affects all citizens in their daily life, questions are raised about public policies and neoliberalism. With the idea of citizen monitoring over elected officials and public services, the full issue of citizen participation is raised by the alternative model of water management.

Supporting progressive regimes

Strengthening state agency in social, environmental and economic matters has always been a major objective for activists close to the way of reason (see chapter 7). Now that the global economic crisis has lent new legitimacy to state intervention in the economy, and with the rise to power of several progressive leaders, especially in the Americas, a third trend of the alter-globalization movement believes that the time has come to support the efforts of progressive political leaders to implement alternative policies. They consider the state to be the fundamental lever of social change. At the national level, it allows public policies and progressive economic policies to be adopted, and the wave of privatization to be stopped and even reversed with the nationalization of natural resource extraction companies, as in Venezuela and Bolivia. At the international level, coalitions of progressive states are able to implement new regional projects and institutions, such as the 'Bank of the South' that has replaced the IMF in several South American countries. Coalition of states also have the power to block the progress of trade liberalization, as they have within the WTO.

The rise to power of progressive and charismatic leaders in several Latin American countries marked an important evolution in the 2000s. The leftist presidents of Brazil, Venezuela, Bolivia, Ecuador and Paraguay participated in the World Social Forum in Bélem in 2009. Certain alter-globalization ideas have actually been taken up by several Latin American heads of state, although none of these can be identified with the movement. With the Bank of the South, its strong opposition to the Free Trade Area of the Americas and its anti-imperialist discourses, Hugo Chavez has seduced many alter-globalization activists, particularly among intellectuals of a generation previously involved in anti-imperialist struggles. They even decided to hold one of the three 2006 WSF events in Caracas. A few years earlier, alter-globalization activists pinned their hopes above all on the election to the Brazilian presidency of Lula, who had, after all, participated in each World Social Forum in Brazil. They were nevertheless disappointed by Lula's policies. This tendency is also present in the United States, where the impetus generated by the first national Social Forum in 2007 was largely redirected towards Senator Obama's extensive presidential campaign, eventually followed by widespread disappointment among alter-globalization activists.

The 'political' tendency has always existed within the alter-globalization movement. It has, however, gained impetus since 2005. Some of the main leaders of the organizations which shaped the movement between 1997 and 2005 even called for a 'post-alterglobalization' firmly anchored in political struggles (Cassen & Ventura, 2008). They support the idea of a 'permanent front of political parties, social movements and international networks'[13] and call the movements to join Hugo Chavez' initiative for a Fifth International, conceived as 'a tool for the convergence towards actions and the elaborations of an alternative model'. Walden Bello[14] calls the movement to follow the recommendations Chavez made during the WSF in Caracas: 'Up to now, we have adopted a "counter-power" strategy. We, the social and political movements, must occupy positions of power at the local, national and regional level.' The Brazilian intellectual Emir Sader even considers the cause of the 'failure of the WSF' to be its 'incapacity to link itself with progressive governments'.[15]

As stated in chapter 4, it is thus hardly astonishing to find alter-globalization intellectuals who emerged from the anti-imperialist currents of the 1970s turning towards progressive heads of state in the global south, hoping for a 'new Bandung'[16] (Sen & Kumar, 2007). However, even alter-globalization experts who had previously kept their distance from the political sphere are now running for election. During the 2009 European elections, the founder and ex-leader of ATTAC-Germany, Sven Giegold, joined the German Green Party; the alter-globalization expert Raoul-Marc Jennar joined the French far-left New Anticapitalist Party; and José Bové became one of the main figures of the French party 'Europe Écologie'. All hoped to continue their activism and take some alter-globalization arguments to the European Parliament. Should this development be interpreted as a sign of the movement's decline? Or, on the contrary, is it an acknowledgement of the movement's importance on the part of the political parties who enlisted these activists? Either way, it is clear that a process of absorption into the sphere of institutional politics – a classic phenomenon in the evolution of social movements (Klandermans, Roefs and Olivier, 1998) – operates among certain currents of alter-globalization, bringing both risks and new potential to the alter-globalization movement.

By moving closer to political leaders, alter-globalization activists may lose their autonomy. The position the movement took on Hugo Chavez and other state leaders has raised long debates. Taking a step back, Boaventura de Sousa Santos (2009) analyses: 'What happened in that situation was that the International Council [of the WSF] could not do an in-depth analysis of the situation there, and it is never going to do that.' As stated in chapter 7, another risk lies in the delegation of the decision-making power to state leaders, while the alter-globalization movement's aim was precisely to favour broader citizen participation in decision-making processes and less vertical political practices. On the other hand, a closer relationship with heads of state and progressive parties could, at the same time, allow activists to have greater influence over important decisions and to become more effective – thanks particularly to a certain political realism of their new partners: 'The problem is that the movement is big but diverse: everyone shouts in a different direction. If we manage to agree on one target for this year, it would give us a lot of strength' (Bolivia's ambassador to the UN, Left Forum, New York, 2010).

While wishing to maintain autonomy and a certain distance, plenty of alter-globalization activists view alliances with progressive political leaders on strategic issues favourably (Ponniah, 2005). This is particularly true of activists of the way of reason, but is also the case with some actors who are closer to the way of subjectivity. In this way, indigenous movements strongly supported Bolivian President Evo Morales' initiatives during the climate summit in Copenhagen. B. de Sousa Santos, though generally wary of the potential for the instrumentalization of alter-globalization actors, also believes that the search for a 'new articulation between political parties and movements' is a major current issue. But is it possible to find a balance between complementarity and autonomy? As we shall see, experiences related to environmental issues are of interest on this question. Will we see the same type of coalition for a Tobin tax on financial transactions, for which several European leaders have shown support?

It would in any case be a mistake to pit 'movements' against the 'state' and 'activists' against 'political leaders'. The boundaries between these two worlds have become somewhat blurred. At many large international summits, some members of national delegations are drawn from civil society rather than from the ranks of elected officials or the civil service. Experts from the alter-globalization network numbered among the Indian and Malaysian delegates to the WTO summit at Cancún, and representatives of indigenous movements participated in the Bolivian delegation to the UN summit in Copenhagen. We have also highlighted the involvement of local elected officials in thematic alter-globalization networks, such as around public water management. Some Latin American state presidents have a social movement background or regularly attend alter-globalization forums. In some cases, they even initiate dynamics very similar to Social Forums and the global civil society repertoire, as is the case with Evo Morales' conference on climate change that gathered social movements, NGOs, political parties and state presidents in Cochabamba in April 2010.

A return to pre-alterglobalization?

Alter-globalization has entered a new phase, more focused on obtaining concrete results than on struggling over ideas. Each of the three trends emerging from this reconfiguration has transformatory potential and could lead to the implementation of alter-globalization alternatives on the local, national and global scales. However, they are also marked by a tendency to return to more traditional models of action, political cultures and concepts of social change, which the two paths of alter-globalization claimed to have moved beyond. This is particularly clear of the most political tendency, which is inscribed within a very classic repertoire and institutionalization process (Kriesi, 1996). Several aspects of the so-called 'post-alterglobalization' recall 'pre-alterglobalization' political cultures: in the principal actors (for the most part, coming from the anti-imperialist movements of the 1970s); in the often very vertical practices of organizing; and in the way social change is conceived – much less about encouraging citizen participation than about changes 'from above' through the agency of progressive, national political leaders.

The statement could be similar concerning *thematic networks*, reminiscent of the transnational advocacy networks which had their heyday in global civil society in the 1990s (Keck & Sikkink, 1998). For sure, the majority of alter-globalization networks continue to distinguish themselves by the importance they assign to citizen participation and by their involvement in a much larger movement against neoliberalism. However, while issue-based campaigns have sometimes been successful, the aftermath of the 2008–9 global crisis has underlined the weakness of the appeal to a more global change. The promotion of the latter had been a distinctive characteristic of the alter-globalization movement, in contrast with many 1990s NGOs and global civil society campaigns focused on single issues. The *retreat into the local* is also not without echoes of widespread practices among the 1970s movements, particularly in counter-cultural circles. Emphasizing the limits of punctual global events and gatherings, many alter-globalization activists have turned to local movements, for example networks against gentrification or for alternative consumption. In some cases, the global scope and the link with international Social Forums was lost while grassroots activists focused only on local and domestic concerns: 'Global spectacle was something important at a time but it can't do it all. Many of us went back to local organizing, to build something from the bottom. But then it became so local that it was often as if the rest of the world didn't exist' (an activist from Montreal, 2010).

In each of the three new directions, risks of a return to 'pre-alterglobalization' clearly exist. However, each of these trends offers opportunities for new alliances between activists of the way of subjectivity and others closer to the way of reason – for example, through the integration of numerous 'Seattle generation' alter-activists into more institutionalized civil society organizations or through new forms of alliance between social movements and political actors on the question of climate change. Moreover, several recent Social Forums have been very successful in articulating struggles and actors locally and globally. Amazonian indigenous movements influenced the Bélem forum and have assumed a major role in alter-globalization downstream of that meeting. The articulation of local struggles with a global movement and global issues was also a major goal of the second USSF.

Climate justice

In the previous section, we highlighted the fact that the 2009 WSF in Bélem served as an opportunity to re-adjust alter-globalization strategies in the face of the economic and financial global crisis. The Forum also confirmed the major importance of environmental issues in the alter-globalization movement. At the 2009 Forum, indigenous movements lent the issue a new momentum. Their conception of development centred on 'living well' ('buen vivir') was adopted by the activists attending the forum, and by the entire alter-globalization movement when those activists shared their experience and ideas from Bélem with fellow activists in their home countries. The concept of 'living well' is meant to provide an alternative vision of development, opposed to the modern idea of progress, economic growth dogmatism and mass consumption.[17] Moreover, their insistence on the 'sacredness of Mother Earth' has placed indigenous movements at the forefront of the struggle against climate change.

The mobilizations around the UN Summit on Climate Change in December 2009 in Copenhagen, and the international forums that followed, provided another illustration of the rising concern for environmental issues in the alter-globalization movement. Along with civil society actors specifically dedicated to environmental issues (and who had often attended some Social Forums), the wide diversity of alter-globalization actors was represented in the Danish capital: Friends of the Earth, ATTACs, NGOs, black blocs, trade union delegates, engaged artists, charismatic figures such as José Bové, and, ten years after the Seattle event, a new generation of young activists lived an intense experience of global activism: 'the spirit, the conviction and enthusiasm that made that demo and other moments in Copenhagen so magic'.[18] The counter-summit brought together civil society coalitions and activists based mostly in the north with major movements of the global south (Via Campesina farmers from all continents, indigenous peoples and dozens of delegates from activist networks).

In Copenhagen, a wide array of the climate justice movement borrows the forms and repertoires of action of the alter-globalization movement: the counter-summit and its expert panels; festive and colourful protests; performances of direct actions; and 'climate camps', which represent a continuation of the alter-activist youth camps, to a large extent adopting their modes of organization, their concern with concrete alternative experiments, and their thirst for experience.

The two paths of alter-globalization thus intertwined at Copenhagen. The 'Klimaforum' offered dozens of talks, often very technical, where experts and activists discussed precise topics. It was animated, for the most part, by global networks of NGOs and actors rooted in the way of reason, such as Climate Justice Now and Our World Is Not for Sale. All around and throughout the city re-baptized 'Hopenhagen', venues were planned to encourage convivial meetings and exchanges of experience, around a table with some organic food. Concerts, theatre performances and cultural activities contributed to a festive atmosphere and strengthened the 'pleasure of being there'. The diverse modalities of the way of subjectivity were also particularly well represented by indigenous movements, old People's Global Action activists and, above all, innumerable affinity groups of alter-activist youth and anarchists, often involved in the Climate Justice Action network or the climate camps.

More profoundly, the continuity of the movement is marked by the assertion of the same will to be an actor in global challenges and debates, as well as by the fact that the two paths of alter-globalization also animate the climate justice movement and have found new combinations in this struggle. Against global warming, just as against neoliberal policies, activists sought to re-assert their capacity to act as citizens in the face of decisions taken at the highest levels. This central meaning was everywhere proclaimed in Copenhagen: 'The 850 of us in this train believe that citizen mobilizations can change things and are necessary because political decisions are very much insufficient in relation to the urgency of climate change' (a spokesperson for the train which brought French and Belgian activists to Copenhagen); 'It's time for our diverse people's movements to unite and reclaim the power to shape our future. We are beginning this process with the people's assembly. We will join together all the voices that have been excluded' (a spokesperson for Climate Justice Action[19]). Copenhagen thus offered a new theatricalization of the central conflict waged by alter-globalization activists for more than fifteen years. As was the case in Seattle in December 1999, world citizens, indigenous people and committed experts opposed in Copenhagen a 'corporate-and-market-driven system being propped up by governments responsible for the crisis';[20] 'When dealing with climate change, the voices that are heard are transnational companies' lobbies, the US, the EU and a few emerging countries of the G-20' (a Mexican activist, interview, 2010). The attitude of the American president particularly incensed activists: 'Obama announced, "Now, we have a deal", only after negotiating with Brazil and China and while most countries hadn't had the opportunity even to see the text' (an activist at the Left Forum, New York, 2010).

Besides demands and denunciations, two core features of the alter-globalization movement were encountered in Copenhagen – the will to open new spaces for debate on questions reserved for experts and policy makers, and the desire to complement criticism with alternative proposals: 'The governments of the elite have no solutions to offer, but the climate justice movement has provided strong vision and clear alternatives.'[21] While activists of the way of subjectivity argued for reducing consumption, engineers focused on developing green technologies, and economists demanded that wealthy countries acknowledge their 'climate debt' and proposed innovative mechanisms to integrate the cost of waste treatment into company accounts and consumer goods. Indigenous and farmers' movements of the global south, who suffer most from environmental degradation, have been struggling for years for food sovereignty, energy sovereignty and a different conception of development based on 'living well'.

Beyond the Copenhagen mobilization, the logics of action, political cultures and conceptions of change of each of the two paths animate coalitions, campaigns and networks for 'climate justice'. Different parts of this chapter have already underlined the importance of indigenous movements and their conceptions of ecology, the success of movements for 'relocalization' and the considerable interest in critical consumption and voluntary simplicity among alter-globalization activists. By fostering the use of bicycles, switching off the lights or changing consumption habits, everyone can play an active part in the preservation of natural resources in their daily life.

The way of reason is equally well represented. Scientists and experts have been the front-runners in the emergence of climate change as a major challenge since the mid-2000s. The Nobel Prize-winning Intergovernmental Panel on Climate Change (IPCC) is only one among many examples. One can also find NGOs and more institutionalized actors of global civil society; a multitude of thematic networks, sometimes stemming from alter-globalization forums (e.g. water networks and Climate Justice Now); economists; those who support the initiatives of progressive regimes; and, most of all, a large number of 'ordinary citizens', concerned about the future of the planet.

While alter-globalization actors now accord a major importance to climate change, they conceive these issues and construct alternatives according to logics of action marked out by the ways of reason and of subjectivity. They keep turning the debate to question the dominant economic model: 'Let's mobilize for another kind of development. The energy, climate and food crises cannot be solved without rethinking the model of development' (president of ATTAC-France in Libération, 15 November 2008).

Unsurprisingly, alter-globalization intellectuals and experts generally develop an institutional and economic vision of global warming: 'It requires an immediate financial commitment from Northern countries and it requires institutions and internal regulations in the medium-term' (Oxfam-Belgium spokesman, interview 2009). According to the same logic which led them from poverty to inequalities and to the denunciation of policies which strengthen the latter (see p. 154), they dropped the expression 'global warming' in favour of the discursive regime of 'climate justice', a framing that highlights political responsibilities, supports demands for new rights and allows the denunciation of a major injustice of the global age: 'It is essentially the North that polluted, and it is now the inhabitants of the South who are paying a high price' (an activist in London, interview). While they give greater importance to ecological questions, the experts of the way of reason have not left behind their economicism (Friends of the Earth and ATTAC demand, for example, 'that rich countries reimburse poor countries for the ecological debt'), nor their focus on social inequality ('Climate change is very much connected with highly unequal capitalism': an American activist, Left Forum, 2010), or their demand for deep reform of the economic system ('If we want to avoid increasing climate change, we need to change the economic system': F. Houtart, talk at the University of Louvain, 2009). They thus join actors of the way of subjectivity – particularly around the indigenous movements' idea of 'living well' – in emphasizing the necessity of rethinking the model of development: 'We want to participate in another model of development, based on social needs and responsibility for ecological damage' (Belgian trade union activist, on his way to Copenhagen).

With 'climate justice', activists also aim to raise issues of global governance. They stress the urgency for international regulations and denounce the disproportionate weight of northern countries and a few emerging countries in the negotiations. They thus chose to support initiatives taken by some progressive Latin American governments. Many positions taken on the climate justice initiatives actually confirm the redefinition of relations underway between alter-globalization activists and political leaders; all with risks for movement autonomy, but also with a potential for greater impact on global decisions. On climate change, even more than on other issues, the boundaries between social movements, political parties and some progressive political leaders have become blurred. It was more than a symbol for government delegations from Bolivia, Venezuela and Tuvalu to leave the UN Conference temporarily to join the Peoples' Assembly in Copenhagen. On the other hand, the 'Indigenous Environmental Network' clearly stated: 'We marched out in support of our brother, President Evo Morales of Bolivia, and his demand that the rights of Mother Earth be recognized in the negotiating text here in Copenhagen.'[22] With his proclaimed objective to 'build a worldwide movement for life and for mother earth' and 'Peoples' World Conference on Climate Change and the Rights of Mother Earth' held in Cochabamba in April 2010, Evo Morales further crossed divisions by borrowing from the repertoire of action of global civil society and Social Forums.

25,000 people from 147 countries gathered in Cochabamba, for a conference with a strong indigenous peoples' participation. The meeting was similar to Social Forums in many aspects: expert workshops that developed technical alternatives and discussed the appropriate percentage for the reduction of greenhouse gases; activists sharing local experiences and concrete steps towards a greener and a fairer world; dances; a few discourses by political leaders; and even the organization of an autonomous counter-forum that criticized the lack of commitment to environmental policies shown by Evo Morales and other progressive state leaders. The four days of the conference were mostly dedicated to the collective elaboration of seventeen thematic platforms, with analysis of and concrete proposals about global warming. The final document was then presented to the UN Secretary-General as the official contribution of Bolivia to the climate change negotiations. The document was not accepted by the UN Secretary. The Cochabamba Climate Conference nevertheless marked a new step in the alliance of civil society activists coming from all over the world with some progressive leaders, based on a collective deliberation process and elaboration of alternative proposals on a specific issue.

Conclusion

The alter-globalization movement emerged some fifteen years ago and has ever since been presented as suffocated, even buried, on more than one occasion. This was particularly the case after September 11, 2001. The continued development of the movement and the success of some of its mobilizations after this conjuncture attested to a maturity of this movement, now inscribed in the socio-political landscape in the medium and long term. After 2006, in Europe, the alter-globalization movement was again perceived as moribund by many analysts, while some of the activist leaders who had helped found it issued a call to move into 'post-alterglobalization'. If it was slow to address the impact of the financial and economic crisis, the alter-globalization movement has progressively regained momentum. The 2009 WSF was attended by 130,000 activists, climate camps have become widespread and forty-two international Social Forums have been organized in 2010. The climate justice mobilizations and forums in Copenhagen and Cochabamba also gave an impetus to activists. In the meantime, the aftermath of the global financial and economical crisis has validated many of the alter-globalization movement's positions.

As we have underlined throughout this book, it is worth focusing the analysis on the alter-globalization movement as a global historic actor rather than on the concrete civil society organizations which embody it at times (see p. 11). Those who have identified the movement too immediately with one or other of its organizations (such as ATTAC-France) or specific charismatic figures have regularly perceived a decline in the movement at every setback suffered by these actors. Over the past few years, alter-globalization has undergone a profound reconfiguration, in its geography, mode of engagement, organization and new major issues. In an era shaped less by neoliberalism than by its crisis, the movement has become less visible in the media but more global and has given way to other forms of action, which seek concrete outcomes through local consumption, citizen advocacy and policies advanced by progressive leaders. It has also moved to integrate environmental issues as a major concern, relating them both to the consequences of three decades of neoliberal globalization and to an urgent need for cultural change and alternative conception of development.

The economic and financial crisis represents both an opportunity and a challenge. It certainly corroborates many of alter-globalization's analyses. Nevertheless, no matter how large it is, a crisis in itself cannot unleash social transformation and trigger the emergence of a new society. This relies on the existence of social actors capable of bringing the underlying questions in this historic crisis to the fore, and of outlining the contours of broad policy directions for the years ahead. Alter-globalization activists did not have that capacity in the two years that followed the subprime crisis and probably lost a major opportunity to bring the world leaders to implement their alternative and more regulated vision of globalization and markets. But the battle is far from over. An escape from the crises of economy, sustainability and governance is a huge task that may last a generation.

Conclusion

Recent Social Forums, counter-summits and campaigns show us that alter-globalization remains very dynamic in various parts of the world. The movement has, however, undergone major transformations. Almost two decades after its first stirrings, alter-globalization has partly undergone a similar process to Green and feminist movements before it. Stages of early intellectual leadership with passionate supporters have been followed by more pragmatic changes into everyday life, public opinion and, in a few cases, some impact on political leaders. Alter-globalization's most recent developments around consumption and environmental issues directly affect the wider population – such as water distribution and climate change. It has become less exuberant, and less visible in the media, but not necessarily less efficient. In the decade after Seattle, it has actually made major contributions to the changes of our time. Among the most structural ones, we may list the end of the Washington Consensus, the fostering of a global debate and global citizenship, experimentation of two paths for social agency in the global age, the strengthening of global consciousness and, most importantly, the reaffirmation of the possibility for citizens and civil society to become influential actors in the global age.

First of all, alter-globalization contributed to a major historical shift: *the end of 30 years dominated by the Washington Consensus.* In the mid-1990s, neoliberal ideology and trade liberalization were widely described as an 'inevitable progress' (e.g. Minc, 1997). Fifteen years later, few people still believed that the self-regulated market would lead to financial stability and a decrease in poverty. Many of the international institutions that supervised international trade liberalization and encouraged southern countries to adopt neoliberal policies are now discredited. The WTO has experienced a series of setbacks. South American governments even buried the Free Trade Area of the Americas project, and the 2008–9 global crisis has shown that many of alter-globalization's analyses and predictions were correct. On the climate change issue, innovative alliances are set up between global activists, indigenous people and some progressive governments. Many of alter-globalization's ideas are now shared, in large part, by public opinion, while some have become consensual themes in the discourses of many G-20 leaders.

The battle is, however, far from over as the change in ideology has still had little impact on concrete policies. We are reminded daily of the importance of global regulations and global challenges that require international cooperation (Held, 2007). The 2007 food crisis and the consequences of the economic crisis and of climate change have underlined the fact that economic inequalities (Wade, 2007) and global social justice remain major issues. With climate change and the economic crises at hand, and as banks have been saved with massive state interventions but little reform of the system, alter-globalization activists are particularly concerned that a return to the previous financial and economics practices and policies will lead to an even deeper crisis.

A second major contribution lies in the active role alter-globalization activists took in opening up debates hitherto restricted to international experts. This challenge goes far beyond trade and economic policies. It represents a valuable contribution to *fostering global democracy and citizenship*. By promoting citizen debates on local and global issues and economic policies, by demanding new global regulations and by gathering activists from all over the world, the alter-globalization movement has contributed to strengthening a global public space and a more active citizenship at local, national, continental and global levels. By its vigilance regarding international institutions and governments' actions and by proposing alternative policies, it has fostered the emergence of counter-powers in the global arena, setting up fundamental mechanisms for contemporary democracies (Rosanvallon, 2006). However, here again, much remains to be done. The difficulties world leaders have faced in reaching an agreement on climate change, in spite of major public concerns about this issue, illustrate the limits of citizens' influence on current global governance. Ten years after Seattle, the UN summit in Copenhagen offered a new *theatricalization* of the opposition between citizens, activists and committed intellectuals pushing global concerns and world political leaders entrenched in a conference centre that was defended like a fortress under siege.

Global democracy and citizenship remain, for the most part, to be invented. Their forms and paths will be very different from the models we know in the nation-state frameworks (Held, 2004). The challenge is thus not to build a global state and a global government but to find ways for citizens, civil society, elected political leaders and international institutions all to take part in decisions that will affect their common future.

The two paths of the alter-globalization movement conduct useful experiments from this perspective, *exploring ways of complementing representative democracy*, building *new ways of social change in the global age*. The exploration of both paths by alter-globalization activists is valuable experimentation from this viewpoint. The way of subjectivity has especially highlighted the importance of starting from below and of transforming one's own practices, even in response to global challenges such as human aspects of economic relationships, global democracy and climate change. For its part, the way of reason has insisted that economic and political decisions cannot be left to a few experts in international institutions and advocacy networks. Citizens should thus acquire knowledge, particularly in the areas of economics and law, in order fully to take part in global debates. Taken together, the two paths offer concrete ways forward for a multi-dimensional approach to building a global society that simultaneously acknowledges the key role of self-transformation, local communities, citizen activism, national policies and international institutions.

Considering the two paths explored by the alter-globalization movement as useful experimentation means that analysing their inherent limits is at least as important as underlining their successes and breakthroughs. The limits and illusions of changing the world 'from below' and without institutional support have become more striking. For example, the recent evolution of Mexican society offers a clear illustration that, as innovative as they may be, multiple local autonomous communities and spaces of experiences are unable to impede the strengthening of free market policies in the country and a strong decline in most Mexican living standards. On the other hand, a committed intellectual vertical conception of social change may foster strong leadership that actually threatens citizens' active participation. As we have shown, the combination of the way of reason and the way of subjectivity often allows these limits and excesses to be balanced. In the wake of successive encounters within the Social Forums, dialogues were opened and processes of cross-fertilization initiated. For example, a growing number of experts and alter-globalization activists close to the way of reason now insist on the complementarities of the two paths in bringing about social change. G. Massiah, an expert-activist, concluded his synthesis of the 20-month-long open discussion on the reconfiguration of the World Social Forum, with the following words: 'Obviously, one cannot claim to change the world without developing change in behaviour, including one's own, but, on the other hand, one cannot claim that the question of transforming the world can be reduced to a matter of individual transformation' (ESF, 2008, Malmö). The modalities and the strength of the combination of the two ways vary considerably among the actors of the movement and their successive meetings. After a period characterized by taking some distance from the two paths in their quest for concrete outcomes, and by a strengthening of trends that are closer to political leaders, signs of new articulations between the two ways have become more visible, particularly around the climate justice issue.

Having emerged a few years after the fall of the Berlin Wall, alter-globalization may be considered as the first truly 'global movement', both because it gathered grassroots citizens from the north and from the global south, and because it has raised some of the major challenges of the coming global age. Along with INGOs, committed intellectuals and civil society organizations that had already become increasingly international (Kaldor,

2003), grassroots actors from the north and from the global south have played a key role in this movement since its early beginning. This has particularly been the case with small farmers and indigenous movements which have been key actors in several of the founding events, including the Zapatista uprising and the Asian farmers' mobilizations against the GATT. Their forms of activism and their poetical discourses have become a major source of inspiration for activists in the north and in the south. Their global networks are unrivalled, with Via Campesina uniting over a million farmers and becoming a central actor in global protests and Social Forums. With the issue of climate justice, both small farmers and indigenous movements are once again at the forefront of the global struggle, not only because they are particularly threatened by global warming, but also because they have developed some of the most inspiring alternatives regarding this issue. Previously considered as anachronistic left-overs of a pre-modern era that would eventually disappear with the modernization process, small farmers and indigenous peoples are now at the forefront of a global debate around rethinking our development model, in a world that is less characterized by its perpetual expansion and growth than by the limitedness of the earth and of its natural resources.

In a deeper perspective, what makes alter-globalization a fundamentally global movement is its ability to connect personal concerns and global challenges (Wieviorka, 2005; Touraine, 2007), activists' subjectivity and the sense of their own globality. Through mobilizing for global causes, meeting activists from all over the world and taking part in world forums and global events, these activists have acquired a cosmopolitan perspective (Beck, 2006) and a broader sense of the global challenge which fosters global citizenship. The long-term subjective impact of global activism experience may thus be even more important than its objective outcomes on the course of globalization.

In all these dimensions, alter-globalization has been both an outcome and an actor of the major cultural and historical shift that leads us to a global age (Albrow, 1996). This new era has brought its uncertainties, its fences and its injustices but also some new opportunities. Alter-globalization activists have been able to grasp some of them and to point to this age's major challenges better than any other social actor. They have thus opened the way for new waves of social movements, whether or not they chose to register their movement under the broad banner of alter-globalization. The path to a more democratic global governance and a more equal and sustainable share of our planet remains long. However, alter-globalization battles and its quest for alternatives have left a central message which fundamentally altered the global landscape: contrary to what was proclaimed in the 1990s, social and political agency has not disappeared under the crushing weight of globalizing markets; it is possible for states, the civil society, local communities and citizens to become actors in the global age.

Notes

Introduction

1 Association pour la Taxation des Transactions financières pour l'Aide aux Citoyens; in English: 'Association for the Taxation of Financial Transactions for the Benefit of Citizens'.

2 For example, the article by V. Quintana, 'Globalifóxicos', *La Jornada*, 9 Aug. 2003, p. 9.

3 The *New York Times* editorialist Thomas Friedman was among the first ones to develop this idea in the 19 September 2001 edition. On 26 September 2001, *Financial Times* columnist Martin Wolf labelled the movement 'violent anarchists' – those who blame the attacks on the 'US promotion of global capitalism'. Meanwhile, Silvio Berlusconi, who faced intense criticisms over the policing of the Genoa protests in July 2001, put the alter-globalization movement in the same category as the perpetrators of the 11 September attacks (*Guardian*, 29 Sept. 2001).

4 A. E. Ceceña is a Mexican scholar and activist, close to the Zapatista movement, and a member of the Continental Social Alliance, a pan-American alter-globalization network.

5 Speech of President Sarkozy on 'the measures taken to sustain the economy', Argonay, 23 Oct. 2008.

6 See the *Guardian*, 13 Dec. 2009; 12 March 2010.

7 A wide range of students of social movements have recently compelled us to pay greater heed to the social movement's culture, its imaginaries, meanings and significance (Jasper, 2007b; Alvarez, Dagnino & Escobar, 1998; Goodwin, Jasper & Polletta, 2001), as

well as activists' experience and reflexivity (Dubet, 1994; McDonald, 2006).

8 Cf. Touraine (1978). This move arises from an attempt to synthesize reality which resembles a Weberian ideal-type in its 'will to a reduction of complexity and to a principle of selection of facts' (Coenen-Huther, 2003) with 'a deliberate accentuation of certain features of the object under consideration' (Weber 1995[1922]: 91). As Weber notes (1995: 290), 'the fact that none of these ideal-types we have discussed are historically present in a "pure" state cannot prevent a conceptual fixation as pure as possible'.

9 For more detail on methodology and field research data, see pp. •• and ••.

1   The Will to Become an Actor

1 See Forrester (1996) and Assayag's (2005) interesting case studies on South Indian farmers' suicides.

2 ATTAC-France online magazine. It came out twice a week and reached over 60,000 people between 2001 and 2004. Similar newsletters are published in several languages by national chapters of ATTAC, notably in Germany, Argentina, the UK or Japan.

3 Latin Americans add the *coup d'état* by Pinochet in 1973.

4 E. Cohen is a French economist close to Pascal Lamy, the WTO director since 2005.

5 For the latter, this version of events had the notable advantage of attributing the failure to an external actor and partly concealing the importance of tensions within the organization. See, for example, 'WTO boss: protesters harm the poor', BBC News, 1 Dec. 1999, http://news.bbc.co.uk/2/hi/business/544543.stm.

6 Two of the main slogans used by ATTAC.

7 Studies of the values of young Germans over the past five decades show a declining influence of post-materialist values in recent years (Hurrelmann & Albert, 2002). This evolution could be linked to the socialization of new generations within successive economic crises since 1970. R. Inglehart (1977) in fact explained the growing attraction of post-materialist values by the socialization of generations that grew up in a postwar context of social and economic progress.

8 Interview with a Belgian NGO leader who is very active in alter-globalization.

9 This is, for example, the case for Oxfam at the international level and the CCFD (Comité Catholique contre la Faim et pour le Développement) in France.

10   A delegate of the Ecuadorian indigenous coalition CONAIE, 2002 WSF; see also Ceceña (2001b).
11   F. Betto and M. Löwy, in a text presented at a plenary session of the 2002 WSF.
12   The model is *idealized* in the sense that it embellishes the reality created during meetings, and *ideal* because the idealization represents the full achievement of all the values present in alter-globalization utopias, particularly in terms of respect for difference.
13   This is one of the chief criticisms that alter-globalization activists level at the WTO, whose decision-making process is also consensual.
14   Specific analysis of each of these meetings and protests as well as an overview of the alter-globalization dynamics and components in France and Belgium have been published in Pleyers (2007).

2   The Experience of Another World

1   J. Holloway is an activist sociologist, close to Zapatism. His book *Change the World Without Taking Power* (2002) has become a reference for activists of the way of subjectivity.
2   A youth participating in the alternative camp against the G-8 meeting in Evian (France), 2003.
3   An activist during a meeting of the French alter-globalization coalition 'Conseil d'Initiative Français' (French Initiative Committee), 2004.
4   A *piquetero* from the Movimiento de Liberación Territorial, Buenos Aires, 2003. The concept of social change related to this 'prefigurative' engagement will be developed in ch. 4.
5   Following the literal meaning of the word 'autonomy': establishing one's own norms.
6   Many of these spaces of experience are inscribed within locations which must be protected against incursions by state forces. In Chiapas, the Zapatista Army (EZLN) remains crucial to protecting the autonomous communities, which face regular paramilitary actions.
7   Some of these spaces continue and reinvent a long tradition that can be associated particularly with the counter-cultural movements of the 1970s (cf. Lotringer & Marazzi, 2007).
8   Email from the Toronto chapter of Reclaim the Streets, quoted by Klein (2002a: 323)
9   These radio stations have recently become widespread in Italy, Mexico, Venezuela and India (Pavarala & Malik, 2007).
10   From autonomous protest movements to the World Bank (1997–2000) and numerous social scientists, a strong consensus has

emerged over the past decade about the importance of local social fabric in reducing social exclusion, improving the quality of life of community members, and permitting them to influence political decisions at the local level.

11 An organizer of the 'social movement assemblies' of the 2002 European Social Forum.

12 Contribution to a meeting of the French Initiative Committee, 2004.

13 Extract from *Les dirigeants face au changement* (Leaders in the Face of Change) (Paris: Éditions du huitième jour, 2003) – italics added. This text, reproduced on many alter-globalization websites, particularly outraged young activists.

14 However, most activists in this way of subjectivity seek to combine political involvement with a certain realization of themselves in a professional career, notably in third sector organization or as teachers.

15 According to the organizing committee, final press conference of the WSF 2005.

16 The following chapter will examine this group more closely.

17 'Plan B has started already, join the battle of joy' in the leaflet 'Voices of Resistance from Occupied London', 2007.

18 One of the organizers of the three-day 'School of the Cybermandais', Liège, 2003.

19 An activist involved in the 1999 mobilization process in Seattle, at the New Left Forum 2010.

20 An activist involved in the 2001 mobilization in Quebec City, 2010.

21 Drawing on M. Wieviorka (2003), by 'diversion' we refer to a distancing of actors from initial meanings and objectives of a movement due to the increasing strength of one logic of action (e.g. the aspiration to lived experience) that was previously constrained by the tensions with other logics of action and by the prevalence of the movement's original goals and central values (e.g. expressive activism as a way to become an actor in the global age and to oppose neoliberal globalization, and not as an experience in itself). This concept may also be related both to R. Merton's 'displacement of goals' and C. Tilly's (2004: 155–7) 'scenarios for social movements' development'.

22 Quoted by A. Martins in 'A trip to Planet Mumbai', www.forum-socialmundial.org.br.

3 From the Mountains of Chiapas to Urban Neighbourhoods

1 EZLN: Ejercito Zapatista de Liberación Nacional, Zapatista Army of National Liberation.

2   These relations have deteriorated since December 2008, following authoritarian and sectarian developments within the Zapatista Commandant committee.

3   This value is central for numerous indigenous movements: 'We are human beings and we want to be considered as such' explained a Mapuche delegate to the 2002 WSF.

4   Similarly, the national indigenous organization of Colombia demanded of the state, 'respect and guarantee of the legitimate rights of indigenous communities to cultural, social, political and economic self-determination, to their land, culture, traditional authorities, to their own forms of organization and development and to education conforming to interests and necessities' (Padilla, 2000: 220).

5   CGRI: Comité General Revolucionario Indígena (Indigenous Revolutionary Committee).

6   A Zapatista activist during the first 'Encounter with the Peoples of the World'.

7   This section is based on an ethnographic study carried out in 2003 and 2004, a series of interviews and meetings with different active members of the group. M. Louviaux (2003) also supplied historical context for the cultural centre as well as an analysis of the Collective Purchasing Group. Quoted text without other reference is drawn from comments made by members of Barricade during meetings and interviews between February 2003 and February 2004.

8   Barricade document dated 1996, quoted by Louviaux (2003: 13).

9   An analysis of these categories of young activists as well as previous versions of two sections of this part have been published in Pleyers (2004, 2005) and Juris & Pleyers (2009). I thank Jeff Juris for his valuable contribution, our long discussions and his friendship.

10 We will return to this point in the analysis of the 2005 WSF in ch. 9.

11 Similarly, in 2007 A. Trouvé, a 27-year-old woman, active in a student chapter of ATTAC that used to be very critical of the hierarchical management of ATTAC itself, became the new co-president of ATTAC-France.

12 For example, numerous youth participated in such actions, organized by Via Campesina, during the 2002 WSF.

13 The proclaimed objective of Vamos' website is thus to 'help build our actions, make them known, and allow us to colllectively review them through constructive criticism'.

14 In Liège, the fleeting School of the Cybermandais broadcast on FM, while pirate radios have multiplied in Mexico. Free radio was

also central to youth camp activities during the WSF in Bamako, January 2006.

15 'The movement for Global Resistance has died . . . Let the Party begin', e-mail sent on the electronic list of the ESF on 27 January 2003.

16 An activist during a youth assembly organized to prepare the mobilization in Cancún: Mexico City, 23 Aug. 2003.

17 The No Border camp's 'Manual of inter-barrio geopolitics'.

18 It is important to remember that all young people are not alter-activists and all alter-activists are not young people. However, alter-activists are *more likely* to be young.

4   Expressive Movements and Anti-Power

1 This concept has been defined as 'episodic, public, collective inter-action among makers of claims and their objects when (a) at least one government is a claimant, an object of claims, or a party to the claims and (b) the claims would, if realized, affect the interests of at least one of the claimants' (McAdam, Tarrow & Tilly, 2001: 5). It aims primarily at crossing the borders between institutional and non-institutional politics.

2 Leaflet presenting an autonomous youth space at the European Social Forum in Paris.

3 This is a strong version of Jasper's (2007b) 'extension dilemma'.

4 Feminist activists and theorists had an important influence on the alter-globalization movement on this issue. In the early 1970s, feminist theorists already had very similar discourses: 'We cannot wait for the revolution before we change our lives, for surely chang-ing our lives now is part of the revolutionary process' (Wortis & Rabinowitz, 1972: 129–30). See also Lamoureux (2004) and Rebick (2009).

5 J. Holloway, M. Benasayag and the main theoreticians of this trend generally use the term 'counter-power'. As they underline (Holloway, 2002; Aubenas & Benasayag, 2002; Benasayag, Brand & Gonzalez, 2001; Hardt & Negri, 2000: 489), it is power-over that must be fought and not the capacity to act.

6 Network created in 1997 and active on all continents.

7 They later added opposition to the 2003 war, against which several feminist movements, especially 'Women in Black', were very active.

8 Extract from document 'Pour une analyse sexuée de la mondialisa-tion (Towards a gender analysis of globalization)', available (in French) at www.local.attac.org/paris14/FM/doc-attac-14/interventions-ag-st-brieuc.html (accessed May 2007).

9   As A. Touraine (1978, 2000) argues, it is in conflict with an adversary that social movements are built and attain historicity. Without the pole of opposition, there is no intermediary between identity and the 'totality' (the global social change supported by a social movement).

10 A worker from the 'occupied and recuperated' Bruckman factory, interview, February 2003.

5   Expertise for Another World

1   In what follows, 'citizen' will refer to this category of grassroots activist of the way of reason, who is tied to the value of knowledge and concerned with reforming modalities of political participation.

2   'Popular education' refers to education (through workshops, panel discussions, flyers, pamphlets) organized by civil society organizations or institutions to sensitize and educate people about questions that are of broad public interest.

3   They represented anti-war collectives as well as several of the main alter-globalization networks such as Focus on the Global South, the Italian Social Forum and the World March of Women.

4   Extract from the definition provided by the *Encyclopaedia Universalis*.

5   As was the case, for example, of the Democratic Citizens' Movement (Mexico) and of the Nicaraguan Centre for Human Rights.

6   In the rational-legal model, the legitimacy of the expert rests on her scientific competence, assimilated to the possession of an objectivity capable of guiding political action for the common good (Restier-Melleray, 1990).

7   Conference at the University of Paris VIII, April 2002.

8   In an informal interview, a member of the ATTAC-France national committee calculated the number of members to be around 10,000 at the beginning of 2007.

9   In Spanish: Red Mexicana de Acción Frente al Libre Comercio.

10 A former EU commissioner from Italy. He has been involved in several alter-globalization networks.

11 Informative Report no. 326 (2000–1), by J. Bourdin, Senate of the French Republic, p. 27–8. www.senat.fr/rap/r00-326/r00-3261. pdf.

12 Corporate Europe Observatory (2006) estimates that more than 15,000 lobbyists are working in the European sector of Brussels.

13　The American press flaunted a strong unanimity, often going to the point of assuming partisanship. It wasn't until a year after the official end of the offensive in Iraq that the first *mea culpa* on this question appeared in some media outlets. During the summer of 2004, the *New York Times,* for example, published several articles and editorials criticizing its own war coverage.

14　Alternative newspapers and magazines have played a major role in the emergence of many organizations of the way of reason, such as ATTAC.

15　These alternative media generally reproduce the classic format of mass communication: a few 'experts' mass-spreading information to largely passive receptors. The alter-activists' media differ on this point.

16　The removal of the person responsible for this magazine by the president of ATTAC deeply affected its quality and its periodicity, which became random by the end of 2003.

17　This is the explanation of the fourth 'paradox' of ch. 1, which presents a discourse opposed to those 'who speak on behalf of others' and another which accepted that those 'who work hard' could be 'put in front'.

18　Similarly, E. Durkheim (2002 [1898]: 18) considered that, 'on a question on which I cannot speak with a full knowledge of the facts, it costs my intellectual independence nothing to follow a more competent opinion'.

19　E. Cohen is a French economist close to Pascal Lamy, who has been Director-General of the WTO since 2005.

20　As E. Durkheim underlined (2002 [1898]: 17), individualism, 'this cult of man, has its first dogma in the autonomy of reason, and its first ritual in free thought. . . . Individualism is not without a certain intellectualism because freedom of thought is the first freedom.'

6　Citizens, Experts and Intellectuals

1　Several questionnaire studies have attempted to pin down the profile of participants in alter-globalization gatherings. While recognizing the limits of such methods in a population which defies strict definition and has proven to be extremely fluid, we rely on these for more detailed data on this question (Agrikoliansky & Sommier, 2005; Reese et al., 2008). For the purposes of ATTAC, we rely chiefly on the questionnaire study carried out in France under the direction of P. Cours-Salies (2002) and on the exploratory study of ATTAC-Liège activists that we carried out in 2000. The two studies led to very similar results.

2   'Citizen movements' which appeared on all continents in the 1980s and 1990s (Kaldor, 2003: 50–77; Tamayo, 1999; Roma, 2001) contributed to the birth of alter-globalization. This wave of citizen movements spawned few sustainable organizations but some elements of its new political culture and engagement have been inherited by the alter-globalization movement.

3   R. Boudon (2004) shows that the production of intellectuals is subject to arbitration by diverse audiences with very different expectations and criteria for judgement; the chief of these being the scientific community, affected groups and opinion.

4   For example, this is how the 'Transnational Institute' (a member of the International Council) defines itself.

5   A leading activist of the 'International Network of Technicians, Experts and Researchers' (AITEC), European Citizens' Conference, 2001.

6   Interview with an Asian network employee, 2003.

7   During a meeting of the French national alter-globalization coordination network, 27 Apr. 2004.

8   An activist-researcher from the French Globalization Observatory, interviewed in 2000.

9   The case of Arnaud Zacharie, already cited, provides an excellent example. A volunteer at the creation of ATTAC-Liège, he was hired four months later as a researcher at the Committee for the Abolition of Third World Debt (CATWD) and became the head of research at the Centre National de Coopération au Développement, a coalition of eighty NGOs, three years later.

10 This is not the case in other countries. ATTAC-Germany and ATTAC-Belgium were built on the basis of local committees and retain a very decentralized structure. ATTAC-Belgium's local committees keep 75 per cent of membership dues, for example.

11 We should note that the absence of election and clear mandate, as well as a certain co-optation, are also features of affinity groups which take care of organizing events in the way of subjectivity. Activists of the way of subjectivity try to compensate partially for these deficiencies by opening meetings and trying to integrate as many activists as possible in decision-making processes.

7   Reason, Democracy and Counter-Power

1   A Marxist sociologist and intellectual leader of CLACSO, a wide Latin American network of research centres with close ties to social movements, and a member of the WSF International Council.

2 The denunciation of the irrationality of the economy and the call for human-centred development were already central to critiques formulated by the anti-colonial third world solidarity movement (cf. Poncelet, 1994; Amin, 1973), which alter-globalization took up.

3 An expert from the US 'Share The World's Resources' (STWR) network, WSF, 2005.

4 Some aspects of these plans took on board alter-globalization critiques of 'Structural Adjustment Plans', which dominated World Bank policy in the 1990s.

5 Cited by the daily *La Nación*, Buenos Aires, 17 Apr. 2002, p. 3.

6 According to a report by the World Bank and data from the Istituto Nacional de Estadistica y Geografía (Mexico) published in *La Jornada*, 1 Dec. 2002.

7 E. Duflo, 'Mondialisation: la peur justifiée des ouvriers', *Libération*, Monday, 13 May 2002.

8 The ATTAC online magazine has been published in different languages with different content and with a fully independent editorial board in each country. The Spanish *Grano de Arena* has been coordinated by Latin American activists.

9 On this question, alter-globalization activists follow on the heels of several previous trends: from partisans of sustainable development (Milani, 2009) to Marx-leaning analysts (Wallerstein, 1999 & 2004; Gadisseur, 1998; Amin, 2001: 29–30) and globalization thinkers (Giddens, 1990; Held, 2004).

10 See, for example, C. Harman, Market madness, *Socialist Review*, Oct. 2009: www.socialistreview.org.uk/article.php?articlenumber=10546, accessed 1 June 2010.

11 C. and M. Kielburger from the network Global Voice, 'How the Iraq war's $2 trillion cost to U.S. could have been spent', *The Star*, 21 Jan. 2008: www.thestar.com/columnists/article/295870, accessed 1 June 2010.

12 General Agreement on Tariffs and Trade (GATT), which gave birth to the WTO.

13 M. Weber (1963: 144–5) showed that, in the sixteenth century, it was already because of a princely tendency towards dilettantism that management of public finances was entrusted to career bureaucrats: 'In the end, the private counsellor generally prevails over the non-specialized Minister in carrying out his will. . . . The main instrument of the superiority of bureaucratic administration is specialized knowledge, whose absolute necessity is determined by modern *techne* (technical knowledge) and the goods-producing economy.' Four centuries later, it was in response to the same

tendency of elected politicians that the independence of central banks and the broad autonomy which European bureaucrats enjoy in major international negotiations were proclaimed.

14 Workshops on UN reform, for example, enjoyed enormous success at the 2005 World Social Forum.

15 In November 2003, the Paris ESF was deeply influenced by the growth of the European Union to the east. Six months before the official entry of ten new countries into the EU, Polish, Hungarian and Czech activists came to the forum to share their struggles and integrate into networks which had hitherto primarily involved actors from the west of the continent. The 2010 European Social Forum took place in Turkey.

16 A French economist close to Pascal Lamy, the WTO director since 2005.

17 A French trade unionist during the CCC-OMC meeting in Paris, March 2001.

18 The distance from political parties is also mentioned in the platform of ATTAC, as in founding texts of numerous organizations, such as the ReMALC in Mexico.

19 While I. Ramonet proposed an 'Association pour la Taxe Tobin d'Aide aux Citoyens – ATTAC' in December 1997, this tax was but one of numerous points in ATTAC-France's platform. It was not even among the seven objectives of the international platform of ATTAC, elaborated on 11 and 12 December 1998, in which there was a more general reference to wanting to 'impede international speculation'.

20 R. Boudon (1989: 123) demonstrates that an idea or a theory can become influential, not by virtue of its intrinsic qualities but 'when it attracts the positive attention of specific groups of intellectuals'.

21 However, the Belgian law will only be enforced when similar measures are adopted by the other Euro-zone countries.

22 M. Harribey, *Capitalisme financier et taxe Tobin*, www.france.attac.org/spip.php?article163, 5 Sept. 1999. M. Harribey has been ATTAC-France co-president since 2006.

23 P. Tartakovsky quoted by O. Toscer, 'Tobin des Bois à l'assaut des spéculateurs', *Le Nouvel Observateur* 1923, 13 Sept. 2001.

24 For this part, we have analysed thirty-five of the most significant documents published by the alter-globalization movement, including social movement declarations from the World and European Social Forums, the ATTAC-International platform, the Porto Alegre Manifesto (2005) and the Bamako Appeal (2006).

25   J. Nikonoff's text after the tsunami in Asia offered a striking illustration.

26   The logic is very different from that of the anti-power espoused by alter-activist youth who do not recognize governments 'as legitimate interlocutors'.

8   Tensions and Collaborations

1   Dutch activist in 'Who controlled the Florence ESF?', http://web. inter.nl.net/users/Pail.Treanor/esf.html, quoted by Juris (2005: 266).

2   These terms arose during discussion with 'Wombles' activists in Whitechapel, London, 2007.

3   Throughout the week of the ESF, the police were highly visible around some of the autonomous forums.

4   For example, this was the case within the alter-globalization demonstration during the European summit in Nice in December 2001.

5   This comment, moreover, illustrates the importance of the delegation of expertise.

6   Colloquium, 'ATTAC, ses militants et leurs motivations', Paris, 24 May 2002.

7   As we have previously shown, this has never been the only logic of ATTAC-France, but it was clearly dominant before 2006.

8   An activist from Babels, a network of activist volunteer translators, during the meeting of the International Council in Mumbai, 2004.

9   Report by C. Aguiton of discussions during the International Council meeting in April 2004.

10   Chapter 9 will provide an analysis of further aspects of the organization of this 2005 WSF and some illustration of the limited but real cross-fertilization that took place on this occasion (see pp. 194–8).

11   Peter Wahl, one of the founders of ATTAC-Germany, in 'Anmerkungen zur Gewaltdebatte nach dem G8' ('Comments on the debate on violence after the G8'): email sent on 21 June 2007 on the 'G8 Protest' mailing-list.

12   Chapter 10 will develop some insights into the 2009 WSF.

9   The Main Debates

1   Since the 1990s, globalization has produced numerous currents leading to a retreat into the local, communalism, and ethnic or

nationalist withdrawal (Barber, 1996; Castells, 1997). These actors do not belong to alter-globalization but constitute an anti-globalization movement: communalist movements that 'call defensively to their community and its consensus against an outside enemy' (Touraine, 1984: 160).

2   B. Cassen's book (2003) gives a very personal view of the role affinity groups played in the process of forming the alter-globalization movement and the WSF.

3   An international counter-summit held in Switzerland in 1999; cf. Houtart & Polet (2001 [1999]).

4   E. Toussaint, lecture in Louvain-la-Neuve, 2006. Eric Toussaint is the founder of the Belgian-based Committee for the Abolition of the Third-World Debt. With the rise of the alter-globalization movement, he became a busy globe-trotter and has developed his network in Africa, Asia and Latin America.

5   They constitute a 'cosmopolitan' elite in the sense given to this word by J. Friedman (1999: 396). Drawing on S. Tarrow (2005), we could also talk about an 'un-rooted cosmopolitans'.

6   See, for example, Cassen (2003).

7   Organizations challenged over their own lack of internal democracy can nevertheless take up the cause in other contexts. For example, ATTAC-France strongly criticized the lack of democracy in the French national alter-globalization coalition (CIF) in 2004.

8   Moreover, the European Social Forum was considered a more transparent counter-model.

9   L. Gabriel during the IC meeting in Mumbai, January 2004.

10 This validation of projects over long-term objectives is isomorphic with the new culture of capitalism (Boltanski & Chiapello, 2005 [1999]; Sennett, 2006).

11 For example, a project could be to have the Tobin tax adopted by the national Parliament or developing an argument for the cancellation of third world debt.

12 According to this conception, one would wait for the moment when the system's contradictions bring about its inevitable end, or lead to a general uprising. While most alter-globalization activists are strongly resistant to this idea, some long-time committed intellectuals who now participate in alter-globalization maintain similar positions. I. Wallerstein (2004) thus believes that 'our historical system will not last much longer. I believe that it is in its final structural crisis, in a chaotic transition to another system, a transition that will only last another 25 to 50 years maximum.' During a seminar at the École des Hautes Études en Sciences

Sociales, Paris, on 23 April 2005, he added, 'I have studied these phenomena sufficiently to know that it is not the alter-globalization movement or any social movement which will bring down capitalism. It is a matter of systemic contradictions.'

13 A Marxist intellectual based in Buenos Aires. He claims that 'to abandon the project of conquering power reflects not only a political capitulation to the bourgeoisie but also the flaws of a theoretical conception which fails to grasp the significance of the phenomenon of social power'. He recalls that Lenin demonstrated the full importance of power and that the 'conversion of the proletarian class into the dominant class is indispensable. . . . With power, the conquerors can transform their interests into law and construct a normative and institutional framework' (Boron, 2003). While rare, such positions remain in networks close to alter-globalization.

10 Towards a Post-Washington Consensus Alter-globalization

1 Lecture held at the Institute for Political Studies, Paris, 12 June 2008; see also Cardoso (2008) and Held & McGrew (2007: 220).

2 For example, on 4 April 2006, Marcos paid a long tribute to Lenin during his speech in Morelia.

3 See, for example, L. Brooks, 'Spirit of the Wombles', *Guardian*, 15 May 2008; Fougier (2008); Brand (2005).

4 S. Tay, 'Looking back on 2008', The Relocalization Network, 17 Dec. 2008: http://old.relocalize.net/looking_back_on_2008, accessed 1 June 2010.

5 Respectively, a Canadian and a US activist who took part in the organization process of the 1999 and 2001 mobilizations in Seattle and Quebec City: Left Forum, New York.

6 (Former) alter-activist social scientists may also impact the evolution of their academic discipline. For example, in anthropology, they have fostered a renewed interest in the epistemological debate on the relation between research and activism by discussing 'research activist' positions and contributions (see Juris & Khasnabish, forthcoming; Osterweil & Chesters, 2007). Economics also constitutes a particularly challenging field in this perspective, as the dominant paradigm has come under harsh criticism after the global crisis.

7 This trend is even stronger among youth activists closer to the way of reason. Many have been hired by civil society organizations, become teachers and professors, or work in political organizations.

For example, Arnaud Zacharie became the head of the French-speaking Belgian consortium of development NGOs. His opinion and his writings are considered by politicians across party lines.

8 See, for example, 'Position Via Campesina Cancún', 2 Sept. 2003, http://viacampesina.org/en/index.php?option=com_content&view=article&id=385:position-via-campesina-cancun&catid=24:10-years-of-wto-is-enough&Itemid=35. acessed 1 April 2010.

9 R. Grayson, 'Relocalisation – acting locally on global issues', Online opinion (Australia), 27 Feb. 2007: www.onlineopinion.com.au/view.asp?article=5538, accessed 1 June 2010.

10 Thematic Social Forums have multiplied, such as those devoted to Amazonia in 2005, to migration in September 2008 in Madrid, to *maquiladoras* (assembly-line factories) in June 2009 in northern Mexico or to education in 2010 in Ramalah.

11 As we saw in chapter 5, efficiency in civil society networks which are based on expertise relies on specialization.

12 Comments made during the Water Network Assembly, European Social Forum, 2008.

13 E. Toussaint, *Au dela du Forum Social Mondial, la Cinquième Internationale*, www.cadtm.org/Interview-d-Eric-Toussaint-Au-dela, accessed 13 Feb. 2010.

14 Walden Bello (2007) *The World Social Forum at the Crossroads*, www.zcommunications.org/the-world-social-forum-at-the-cross-roads-by-walden-bello, accessed 1 June 2010.

15 Seminar '10 years of WSF', Porto Alegre, Jan. 2010. Quoted in R. Zibechi, 'Décimo Foro Social Mundial: síntomas de decadencia': www.observatoriodelacrisis.org/. . ./decimo-foro-social-mundial-sintomas-de-decadencia, accessed 1 June 2010.

It can be noted that, while committed intellectuals concerned with bringing the movement closer to political leaders have decided that the Social Forums have become useless, more than 120,000 people participated in the WSF in Bélem in January 2009, and 15,000 at the USSF in June 2010. Many activists stress the importance of the movement's autonomy from political parties and leaders. Even during the 2006 WSF in Caracas, some activists organized an 'autonomous forum' and adopted a critical attitude towards Chavez' policies. In the way of reason, just as in the way of sub-jectivity, plenty of activists still assert their distance from political actors. They do not necessarily consider progressive political leaders as opponents, but they maintain their distance, emphasizing that 'there is no such thing as an alter-globalization activist taking power' (a demonstrator during the G-20 protests in London, 2009).

16 In 1955, the Conference of Bandung assembled leaders from Asian and African countries in order to promote economic and cultural cooperation among them and to oppose colonialism. It raised the hope of a third way, between western capitalism and Soviet communism.

17 Cf. *The Concept of 'Living Well'*, www.boliviaun.org/cms/?page_id=621, accessed 20 April 2010.

18 Olivier de Marcellus (a Swiss activist and one of the founders of People's Global Action who attended the Copenhagen mobilizations), *Reclaimng Power in Copenhagen*, January 2010: www.commoner.org.uk/?p=88.

19 Quoted in A. Petermann & O. Langelle, 'What really happened in Copenhagen?', *Z Magazine*, 1 Feb. 2010.

20 Ibid.

21 Climate Justice Now, Final Statement after Copenhagen, www.climate-justice-now.org/cjn-final-statement-in-copenhagen, accessed on 17 April 2010.

22 Quoted in A. Petermann & O. Langelle, 'The iron fist of the market versus iron in the soul of the social movements', *Z Magazine*, 1 Feb. 2010.

Bibliography

Aditjondro, G. J. (2007) Indonesia: paddling through increasingly treacherous and neoliberal waters, in F. Polet, ed., *The State of Resistance: Popular Struggles in the Global South*, London: Zed Books, 186–91.

Agrikoliansky, E., Fillieule, O. and Mayer, N. (2005) *L'altermondialisme en France: la longue histoire d'une nouvelle cause*, Paris: Flammarion.

Agrikoliansky, E. and Sommier, I. (2005) *Radiographie du mouvement altermondialiste*, Paris: La dispute.

Aguiton, C. (2001) *Le monde nous appartient*, Paris: Plon.

Aguiton, C. and Cardon, D. (2007) The strength of weak cooperation: an attempt to understand the meaning of Web 2.0, *Communications and Strategies*, 65, 51–65.

Albert, M. (2004) WSF: where to now? in J. Sen, A. Anand, A. Escobar and P. Waterman, eds., *World Social Forum Challenging Empires*, New Delhi: Viveka Foundation, 323–8.

Albrow, M. (1996) *The Global Age*, Cambridge: Polity Press.

Albrow, M. (2007) Situating global social relations, in I. Rossi, ed., *Frontiers of Globalization Research: Theoretical and Methodological Approaches*, New York: Springer, 317–32.

Albrow, M., Eade, John, Washbourne, N. and Durrschmidt, J. (1994) The impact of globalization on sociological concepts: community, culture and milieu, *Innovation*, 7(4), 371–89.

Albrow, M. and Glasius, M. (2007) Democracy and the possibility of a global public sphere, in M. Albrow, M. Kaldor, M. Glasius and Anheier, H., eds., *Global Civil Society 2007/8*, London: Sage, 1–18.

Alternatives Sud (2005) *Mouvements et pouvoirs de gauche en Amérique latine*, Paris: Syllepse.

Altvater, E. (1997) Markt und Demokratie in Zeiten von Globalisierung und ökologischer Krise, in E. Altvater, A. Brunnengräber, M. Haake and H. Walk, Vernetzt und verstrickt, Bochum: Westphalisches Dampfboot, 241–8.

Alvarez, S., Dagnino, E. and Escobar, A., eds. (1998) *Cultures of Politics, Politics of Cultures*, Boulder: Westview Press.

Alvarez Garín, R. (1998) *La estela de Tlatelolco*, Mexico: Itaca.

Amin, S. (1973) *Le développement inégal*, Paris: Minuit.

Amin, S. (2001) Quelles alternatives à la dimension destructrice de l'accumulation du capital? *Alternatives Sud*, 7(2), 27–50.

Anderson, P. (1999) *Neoliberalismo: balance provisorio*, Buenos Aires: Clacso/Eudoba.

Animat, E. (2002) Surmounting the challenges of globalization, *Finance & Development*, 1–4.

Antentas, J. M., Egirun, J. and Romero, M., eds. (2003) *Porto Alegre se mueve*, Madrid: Catarata.

Aquino, A. (2010) *Entre le mouvement social et l'expérience migratoire: les enfants des luttes indiennes s'en vont au Nord*, doctoral thesis, Paris: EHESS.

Arnett, J. (2004) *Emerging Adulthood: The Winding Road from Late Teens through the Twenties*, Oxford: Oxford University Press.

Arroyo Picard, A., Calderón Salazar, J., García Suárez, M. and Peñaloza Méndez, A, eds. (2002) *Area de libre commercio de las Américas: análisis y alternativas*, Mexico: Instituto de estudios de la Revolución Democrática.

Assayag, J. (2005) Seeds of wrath, in J. Assayag and C. Fuller, eds., *Globalizing India: Perspectives from Below*, London: Anthem Press, 65–87.

ATTAC (2000a) *Une économie au service de l'homme*, Paris: Mille et une nuits.

ATTAC (2000b) *Tout sur ATTAC*, Paris: Mille et une nuits.

ATTAC (2001a) *Enquête au coeur des multinationales*, Paris: Mille et une nuits.

ATTAC (2001b) *Penser global, agir local*, Paris: Mille et une nuits.

ATTAC (2002) *Tout sur ATTAC 2002*, Paris: Mille et une nuits.

ATTAC (2004a) *Le développement a-t-il un avenir?* Paris: Mille et une nuits.

ATTAC (2004b) *L'empire de la guerre permanente: Etats-Unis et mondialisation*, Paris: Mille et une nuits.

Aubenas, F. and Benasayag, M. (2002) *Résister, c'est créer*, Paris: La Découverte.

Baechler, J. (1995) *Le capitalisme. I: Les origines*, Paris: Gallimard.

Bajoit, G. (2003) *Le changement social*, Paris: A. Colin.

Bajoit, G., Houtart, F. and Duterme, B. (2007) *Amérique Latine: à gauche toute?* Charleroi: Couleurs Livre.

Ballard, R., Habib, A. and Valodia, I. (2006) *Voices of Protest: Social Movements in Post-Apartheid South Africa*, Durban: University of KwaZulu-Natal Press.

Bandy, J. and Smith, J., eds. (2005) *Coalitions across Borders*, Lanham: Rowman and Littlefield.

Barber, B. (1996) *Jihad versus McWorld*, New York: Ballantine Books.

Barro, R. (1986) Recent developments in the theory of rules versus discretion, *The Economic Journal*, 5(96), 23–37.

Bartra, A. (2009) Los campesinos contra el ogro omiso: meandros del movimiento rural en el último cuarto de siglo, in F. Mestries, G. Pleyers and S. Zermeño, eds., *Los movimientos sociales: de lo local a lo global*, Barcelona: Anthropos, 154–63.

Bauman, Z. (2000) *Liquid Modernity*, Cambridge: Polity Press.

Beaudet, P., Canet, R. and Massicotte, M. J. (2010) *L'altermondialisme, un état des lieux*, Montreal: Ecosociété.

Beauvoir, S. de (1954) *Les mandarins*, Paris: Hermes.

Beck, U. (1992) [1986] *Risk Society*, London: Sage.

Beck, U. (2005) [2002] *Power in the Global Age*, Cambridge: Polity Press.

Beck, U. (2006) *Cosmopolitan Vision*, Cambridge: Polity Press.

Beck, U., Giddens, A. and Lash, S. (1996) *Reflexive Modernity*, Cambridge: Polity Press.

Bekkers, R. (2001) *Participation in Voluntary Associations: Resources, Personality, or Both?* Proceedings of the 5th Conference of the European Sociological Association, Helsinki.

Benasayag, M., Brand, U., Gonzalez, H., Holloway, J., Mattini, L., Negri, T. and Colectivo Situaciones (2001) *Contrapoder: una introducción*, Buenos Aires: De mano en mano.

Benasayag, M. and Sztulwark, D. (2000) *Du contre-pouvoir*, Paris: La Découverte.

Benhabib, S. (2002) *The Claims of Cultures: Equality and Diversity in the Global Era*, Princeton: Princeton University Press.

Bennett, L. (2005) Social movements beyond borders: understanding two eras of transnational activism, in D. Della Porta and S. Tarrow, eds., *Transnational Protest and Global Activism*, Lanham: Rowman and Littlefield, 203–26.

Bennett, W. (2003) Communicating global activism, *Information, Communication and Society* 6, 143–68.

Bernardi, B. (2008) October 2008: the return of the State? *La vie des Idées*, www.laviedesidees.fr/October-2008-the-return-of-the.html, accessed 1 June 2010.

Bey, H. (2003) [1991] *TAZ: The Temporary Autonomous Zone, Ontological Anarchy, Poetic Terrorism*, 2nd edition, New York: Autonomedia.

Bizberg, I. (2003) L'ALENA: inégalités et démocratie, *Cahier de recherche* 03/02 (Montreal: Institut d'Études Internationales de Montréal).

Blossfeld, H. P., Klijzing, E., Mills, M. and Kurz, K., eds. (2005) *Globalization, Uncertainty and Youth in Society*, London: Routledge.

Boltanski, L. and Chiapello, E. (2005) [1999] *The New Spirit of Capitalism*, London: Verso.

Boron, A. (2003) Poder, 'contrapoder' y 'antipoder', *Revista Chiapas* 15, 143–62.

Boudon, R. (1989) [1986] *Analysis of Ideology*, Cambridge: Polity Press.

Boudon, R. (1998) Social mechanisms without black boxes, in P. Hedström and R. Swedberg, eds., *Social Mechanisms: An Analytical Approach to Social Theory*, Cambridge: Cambridge University Press, 172–203.

Boudon, R. (2004) *Pourquoi les intellectuels n'aiment pas le libéralisme*, Paris: Odile Jacob.

Bourdieu, P. (1984) [1979] *Distinction*, London: Routledge.

Bourdieu, P. (1998) *Contre-feux*, Paris: Liber – Raisons d'Agir.

Bourdieu, P. (2001) *Contre-feux 2*, Paris: Liber – Raisons d'Agir.

Brand, U. (2005) *Gegen-Hegemonie: Perspektiven globalisierungskritischer Strategien*. Hamburg: VSA

Brecher, J., Costello, T. and Smith, B. (2002) *Globalization from Below: The Power of Solidarity*, Cambridge, MA: South End Press.

Brecher, J., Costello, T. and Smith, B. (2009) Social movements 2.0, globalization from below: the power of solidarity, *The Nation*, 15 Jan. www.thenation.com/article/social-movements-20, accessed 1 June 2010.

Capise (2008) *Viento de guerra*, San Cristobal de Las Casas: Centro de Análisis Político e Investigaciones Sociales y Económicas A.C. www.capise.org.mx/files/Vientos%20de%20Guerra.doc, accessed 17 April 2010.

Cardon, D. and Granjon, F. (2003) Peut-on se libérer des formats médiatiques? Le mouvement alter-mondialisation et l'Internet, *Mouvements*, 25, 67–73.

Cardoso, F. H. (2008) A surprising world, *International Journal of Communication* 2, 472–514.

Carlsen, L., Wise, T. and Salazar, H. (2003) *Enfrentando la globalización*, Mexico, DF: Porrúa.

Caruso, G. (2010) Excitement to depression: social movements and civil society activists in the crisis, paper presented at the World Congress of Sociology (RC 47), Göteborg.

Cassen, B. (2003) *Tout a commencé à Porto Alegre*, Paris: Mille et une nuits.

Cassen B. and Ventura, C. (2008) Which alter-globalism after the 'end of neo-liberalism'? 18 Sept.www.cetri.be/spip.php?article838&var _recherche=Cassen&lang=en.

Castel, R. (2003) [1995] *From Manual Workers to Wage Laborers: Transformation of the Social Question*, New Brunswick, NJ: Transaction.

Castells, M. (1996–8) *The Age of Information*, 3 vols., Oxford: Blackwell.

CATWD (2004) *Le droit international, un instrument de lutte*, Paris: Syllepse.

Ceceña, A. E. (1997) Neoliberalismo e insubordinación, *Revista Chiapas* 4, 33–44.

Ceceña, A. E. (2001a) Por la humanidad y contra el neoliberalismo: líneas centrales del discurso zapatista, in J. Seoane and E. Taddei, eds., *Resistencias mundiales: de Seattle a Porto Alegre*, Buenos Aires: CLACSO, 131–40.

Ceceña, A. E. (2001b) La marcha de la dignidad indígena, in G. Michel and F. Escárzaga, eds., *Sobre la marcha*, Mexico: UAM – Rizoma, 161–78.

Ceceña, A. E. and Sader, E., eds. (2003) *La guerra infinita: hegemonía y terror mundial*, Buenos Aires: CLACSO.

Cefaï, D. (2007) *Pourquoi se mobilise-t-on?* Paris: La Découverte.

Chandhoke, N. (2002) The limits of global civil society, in M. Glasius, M. Kaldor and H. Anheier, eds., *Global Civil Society 2002*, Oxford: Oxford University Press, 35–53.

Charle, C. (2001) Intellectuals: history of the concept, in *International Encyclopedia of Social and Behavioral Sciences*, London: Elsevier, vol. XI, 7627–31.

Chomsky, N. (2003). *Hegemony or Survival: America's Quest for Global Dominance*. New York: Metropolitan Books.

Cockburn, A., St. Clair, J. and Sekula, A. (2000) *Five Days that Shook the World*, London: Verso.

Coenen-Huther, J. (2003) Le type idéal comme instrument de la recherche sociologique, *Revue Française de Sociologie*, 44(3), 531–47.

Cohen, D. (2004) *La mondialisation et ses ennemis*, Paris: Hachette.

Cohen, E. (2001) *L'ordre économique mondial*, Paris: Fayard.

Colectivo Situaciones (2002) *19 y 20: apuntes para el nuevo protagonismo social*, Buenos Aires: De mano en mano.

Conway, J. (2008) Space, place, and difference / axes of new politics at the World Social Forum: before and after Nairobi, *Sociology Without Borders*, 3(1), 48–70.

Cooney, P. (2008) Dos décadas de neoliberalismo en México: resultados y retos, *Novos Cadernos*, 11(2), 15–42.

Corporate Europe Observatory (2006) Lobby Planet. Brussels: The EU Quarter, Brussels: *Corporate Europe Observatory*, http://archive. corporateeurope.org/docs/lobbycracy/lobbyplanet.pdf accessed 1 June 2010.

Cours-Salies, P. (2002) *ATTAC. Qui sont ses adhérents? Que veulent-ils? Une enquête à partir de l'analyse de 1000 questionnaire*, Paris: Le Fil d'Ariane – Institut d'études européennes.

Crozier, M. and Friedberg, E. (1980) [1977] *Actors and Systems*, Chicago: University of Chicago Press.

Davis, M. (2007) *Le stade Dubai du capitalisme*, Paris: La Découverte.

Dawson, M. (2005) Who is resisting globalisation? Questioning the diversity of global social movements, paper presented at the conference 'Encounter in Open Space 1', Picada Café, RGS, Brazil, 21–24 January.

De Bouver, E. (2009) *La simplicité volontaire*, Charleroi: Couleurs Livre.

De Munck, J. (1999) *L'institution sociale de l'esprit*, Paris: Presses Universitaires de France.

De Munck, J. and Zimmerman, B., eds. (2008) *La liberté au prisme des capacités*, Paris: Éditions de l'EHESS.

Della Porta, D. (2005) Multiple belongings, tolerant identities, and the construction of 'another politics', in D. Della Porta and S. Tarrow, eds., *Transnational Protest and Global Activism*, Lanham: Rowman and Littlefield, 175–201.

Della Porta, D., Andretta, M., Mosca, L. and Reiter, H. (2006) *Globalization from Below*, Minneapolis: University of Minnesota Press.

Della Porta, D., Peterson, A. and Reiter, H. (2006) *Policing Transnational Protest*, London: Ashgate.

Della Porta, D. and Tarrow, S., eds. (2005) *Transnational Protest and Global Activism*, Lanham: Rowman and Littlefield.

Diani, M. and McAdam, D., eds. (2003) *Social Movements and Networks: Relational Approaches to Collective Action*, Oxford: Oxford University Press.

Díaz Polanco, H. and Sánchez, C. (2002) *México diverso*, Mexico: Siglo XXI.

Dierckxsens, W. (2001) Vers une alternative citoyenne, *Alternatives Sud*, 8(2), 127–40.

Doerr, N. (2008) Deliberative discussion, language, and efficiency in the WSF process, *Mobilization*, 13(4), 395–410.

Doerr, N. (2009) Language and democracy 'in movement': multilingualism and the case of the European Social Forum process, *Social Movement Studies*, 8(1), 149–65.

Dreano, B. (2004) In Paris, the global place is no longer Saint Germain des Prés: civil society and the French debate, in M. Glasius, D. Lewis and H. Seckinelgin, eds., *Exploring Civil Society: Political and Cultural Contexts*, London: Routledge, 93–101.

Dubet, F. (1994) *Sociologie de l'expérience*, Paris: Seuil.

Dubet, F. (1995) *Sociologie du sujet et sociologie de l'expérience*, in F. Dubet and M. Wieviorka, eds., *Penser le sujet: autour d'Alain Touraine*, Paris: Fayard, 103–22.

Dubet, F. (2003) *Le déclin de l'institution*, Paris: La Découverte.

Dubet, F. and Wieviorka, M., eds. (1995) *Penser le sujet: autour d'Alain Touraine*, Paris: Fayard.

Dumoulin, D. (2003) Local knowledge in the hands of transnational NGO networks: a Mexican viewpoint, *International Social Science Journal*, 178, 593–606.

Dupuis-Déri, F. (2004) Penser l'action directe des Black Blocs, *Politix*, 68, 79–109.

Dupuis-Déri, F. (2005) L'altermondialisme à l'ombre du drapeau noir: l'anarchie en héritage, in E. Agrikoliansky, O. Fillieule and N. Mayer, eds., *L'altermondialisme en France*, Paris, Flammarion, 199–231.

Durkheim, E. (2002) [1898] *L'individualisme et les intellectuels*, Paris: Mille et une nuits.

Epstein, B. (1991) *Political Protest and Cultural Revolution*, Berkeley: University of California Press.

Escobar, A. (1992) Culture, practice and politics: anthropology and the study of social movements, in *Critique of Anthropology*, New Delhi: Sage, 395–432.

EZLN (1994) *Documentos y comunicados 1 (01/01/1994–08/08/1994)*, Mexico: Era.

EZLN (1995) *Documentos y comunicados 2 (15/08/1994–29/09/1995)*, Mexico: Era.

Fall, A. S., Favreau, L. and Larose, G. (2004) *Altermondialisation, économie et coopération internationale*, Sainte-Foy: Presses de l'université du Québec.

Feffer, J., ed. (2002) *Living in Hope: People Challenging Globalization*, New York: Zed Books.

Fisher, D., Stanley, K., Berman, D. and Neff, G. (2005) How do organizations matter? Mobilization and support for participants at five globalization protests, *Social Problems*, 52, 102–23.

Fisher, W. and Ponniah, T. (2003) *Another World is Possible: Popular Alternatives to Globalization at the World Social Forum*, London: Zed Books.

Flores, T., ed. (2002) *De la culpa a la autogestión: un recorrido de trabajadores desocupados en La Matanza*, Buenos Aires: MTD Editora.

Forbrig, J., ed. (2005) *Revisiting youth political participation*, Strasbourg: Press of the Council of Europe.

Forrester, V. (1996) *L'horreur économique*, Paris: Fayard.

Foucault, M. (1984) *Le pouvoir, comment s'exerce-t-il?* in M. Foucault, *Un parcours philosophique*, Paris: Gallimard, 1984, 751–62.

Fougier, E. (2008) Où en est le mouvement altermondialiste? Réflexions sur l'essoufflement', *La vie des idées*, 3 April, www.laviedesidees.fr/Ou-en-est-le-mouvement.

Fraser, N. (1997) *Justice Interruptus*, New York: Verso.

Friedman, J. (1999) Indigenous struggles and the discreet charm of the bourgeoisie, *Journal of World-Systems Research*, 5(2), 391–411.

Friedman, J. (2003) Les vicissitudes du système mondial et l'apparition des mouvements sociaux, in M. Wieviorka, ed., *Un autre monde*, Paris: Balland, 107–26.

Fukuyama, F. (1992) *La fin de l'histoire et le dernier homme*, Paris: Flammarion.

Fundación Humbold (2002) *Memoria del III Foro mesoamericano, Frente al Plan Puebla Panamá: el movimiento mesoamericano por la integración popular*, Managua: Fundación Humbold.

Gadisseur, J. (1998) *Le crépuscule du capitalisme*, Proceedings of colloquium 'Du capitalisme au capitalisme', 13–14 March, Université Libre de Bruxelles.

Galland, O. and Roudet, B. eds. (2005) *Les jeunes européens et leurs valeurs*, Paris: La Découverte.

Gauthier, M. (2003) The inadequacy of concepts: the rise of youth interest for civic participation, *Journal of Youth Studies*, 6(3), 265–76.

George, S. (2004) *Another World Is Possible If*, London: Verso.

Giddens, A. (1990) *Consequences of Modernity*, Cambridge: Polity Press.

Giddens, A. (2000) *Runaway World: How Globalization is Reshaping Our Lives*, London: Routledge.

Gille, Z. (2001) Critical ethnography in the time of globalization: toward a new concept of site, *Cultural Studies – Critical Methodologies*, 1–3, 319–34.

Glasius, M., Lewis, D. and Seckinelgin, H., eds. (2004) *Exploring Civil Society: Political and Cultural Contexts*, London: Routledge.

Glasius, M. and Timms, J. (2006) The role of social forums in global civil society, in H. Anheier, M. Glasius and M. Kaldor (eds.), *Global Civil Society 2005/6*, London: Sage, 190–238.

Global Trade Watch (2006) *The World Trade Organisation – An Australian Guide*, Victoria: Global Trade Watch.

Gomez, M. (1998) *Mai 68 au jour le jour*, Paris: L'esprit frappeur.

Goodwin, J. and Jasper, J., eds. (2004) *Rethinking Social Movements*, Lanham: Rowman and Littlefield.

Goodwin, J., Jasper, J. and Polletta, F. (2001) *Passionate Politics: Emotions in Social Movements*, Chicago: University of Chicago Press.

Graeber, D. (2002) The new anarchists, *New Left Review*, 13, 61–73.

Gret, M. and Sintomer, Y. (2005) *The Porto Alegre Experiment: Learning Lessons for Better Democracy*, London: Zed Books.

Grinspun, R. and Kreklewich, R. (1994) Consolidating neoliberal reforms: 'free trade' as a conditioning framework, *Studies in Political Economy*, 43, 33–61.

Grubacic, A. (2003) Life after social forums: new radicalism and the question of attitudes towards social forums, *Znet*, 9 Feb. 2003, www.zmag.org/content/showarticle.cfm?ItemID=3010, accessed 1 June 2010.

Gutiérrez Narváez, R. (2006) Impactos del zapatismo en la escuela, *Liminar. Estudios Sociales y Humanísticos*, 4(1), 92–111.

Habermas, J. (1970) [1968] *Toward a Rational Society: Student Protest, Science, and Politics*, Boston: Beacon Press.

Habermas, J. (1984) [1981] *The Theory of Communicative Action*, Cambridge: Polity Press.

Habermas, J. (1989) *The Structural Transformation of the Public Sphere: An Inquiry into a Category of Bourgeois Society*, Cambridge: Polity Press.

Habermas, J. (1997) *Droit et démocratie*. Paris: Gallimard.

Hardt, M. and Negri, A. (2000) *Empire*, Cambridge, MA: Harvard University Press.

Hardt, M. and Negri, A. (2004) *Multitude: War and Democracy in the Age of Empire*, New York: Penguin.

Harvey, D. (2005) *A brief history of neoliberalism*, Oxford: Oxford University Press.

Hassoun, M. (2001) *Porto Alegre: voyage en alternative*, Paris: Syllepse.

Havel, V. (1985) The power of the powerless, in J. Keane, ed., *The Power of the Powerless: Citizens against the State in Central-Eastern Europe*, London: Hutchinson, 90–1.

Held, D. (1995) *Democracy and the Global Order*, Cambridge and Oxford: Polity Press / Blackwell.

Held, D. (2004) *The Global Covenant*, Cambridge: Polity Press.

Held, D. (2005) At the crossroads: the end of the Washington Consensus and the rise of global social democracy, *Globalizations*, 2(1), 95–113.

Held, D. (2007) Reframing global governance: apocalypse soon or reform!, in D. Held and A. McGrew, eds., *Globalization Theory*, Cambridge: Polity Press, 250–9.

Held, D. (2010) *Cosmopolitanism*, Cambridge: Polity Press.

Held, D. and Kaya, A. (2008) *Global Inequality*, Cambridge: Polity Press.

Held, D. and McGrew, A., eds. (2002) *The Global Transformations Reader*, Cambridge and Oxford: Polity Press / Blackwell.

Held, D. and McGrew, A. (2007) *Globalization/Anti-Globalization*, Cambridge: Polity Press.

Held, D., McGrew, A., Goldblatt, D. and Perrato, J. (1999) *Global Transformations: Politics, Economics and Culture*, Cambridge: Polity Press.

Hess, D. (2009) *Localist Movements in a Global Economy*, Cambridge, MA: The MIT Press.

Hirschman, A. (1970) *Exit, Voice, and Loyalty: Responses to Decline in Firms, Organizations, and States*. Cambridge, MA: Harvard University Press.

Hirschman, A. (1982) *Shifting Involvements: Private Interest and Public Action*. Princeton, NJ: Princeton University Press.

Hobsbawm, E. (1994) *The Age of Extremes: The Short Twentieth Century*, New York: Vintage Books.

Hocquengem, J. (2009) *Le rendez-vous de Vicam*, Paris: Rue des Cascades.

Hocquenghem, J. and Lapierre, G., eds. (2002) *Hommes de maïs, coeurs de braise: cultures indiennes en rébellion au Mexique*, Paris: L'insomniaque.

Hodkinson, S. (2003) Custard pies are off the menu, *Red Pepper*, March, 36–7.

Holloway, J. (2002) *Change the World Without Taking Power*, London: Pluto Press.

Holloway, J. (2003) Anche un bacio può essere un movimento anticapitalista, intervista a John Holloway raccolta da Marco Calabria, *Carta*, www.carta.org/campagne/partecipazione/forum+sociali/porto+alegre+2003/15635, accessed 1 June 2010.

Houtart, F. (2001) Des alternatives crédibles au capitalisme mondialisé, in *À la recherche d'alternatives*, Paris: L'Harmattan, 7–26.

Houtart, F. and Polet, F. (2001) [1999] *The Other Davos*, London: Zed Books.

Huntington, S. (1991) *Democratization in the Late Twentieth Century*, Oklahoma: University of Oklahoma Press.

Hurrelmann, K. and Albert, M., eds. (2002) *Jugend 2000: zwischen pragmatischem Idealismus und robustem Materialismus*, Frankfurt am Main: Fischer Taschenbuch.

Illich, I. (1973) *La convivialité*, Paris: Seuil.

IMF (2007) *Financial Globalization: The Impact on Trade, Policy, Labor, and Capital Flows*, Washington: IMF.

Inglehart, R. (1977) *The Silent Revolution*, Princeton: Princeton University Press.

Inglehart, R. (1997) *Modernization and Postmodernization*, Princeton: Princeton University Press.

Ion, J. (1997) *La fin des militants?* Paris: L'Atelier.

Jacquemain, M. (2003) *La raison névrotique*, Brussels: Labor.

Jaffrelot, C. (2005) *La démocratie par la caste*, Paris: Fayard.

Jasper, J. (2007a) Cultural approaches to the study of social movements, in B. Klandermans and C. Roggeband, eds., *Handbook of Social Movements across Disciplines*, New York: Springer, 59–109.

Jasper, J. (2007b) *Getting Your Way*, Chicago: University of Chicago Press.

Juris, J. (2004) Networked social movements: global movements for global justice, in M. Castells, ed., *The Network Society: A Cross-Cultural Perspective*, Cheltenham: Edward Elgar, 341–62.

Juris, J. (2005) Social forums and their margins: networking logics and the cultural politics of autonomous space, *Ephemera* 5(2), 253–72.

Juris, J. (2008a) *Networking Future*, Durham, NC: Duke University Press.

Juris, J. (2008b) Spaces of intentionality: race, class, and horizontality at the United States Social Forum, *Mobilization* 13(4), 353–72.

Juris, J., Caruso, G. and Mosca, L. (2008) Freeing software and opening space: Social Forums and the cultural politics of technology, *Societies Without Borders* 3, 96–117.

Juris, J. and Khasnebish, A. (forthcoming) *Movements: Activism and Ethnography*, Durham, NC: Duke University Press.

Juris, J. and Pleyers, G. (2009) Alter-activism: emerging cultures of participation among young global justice activists, *Journal of Youth Studies*, 12(1), 57–75.

Kaldor, M. (2003) *Global Civil Society Against War*, London: Polity Press.

Kaldor, M. (2007) *Human Security: Reflections on Globalization and Intervention*, Cambridge: Polity Press.

Kaldor, M., Anheier, H. and Glasius, M., eds. (2001–3) *Global Civil Society Yearbooks*, Oxford: Oxford University Press.

Kaldor, M., Anheier, H. and Glasius M. (2003) Global civil society in an age of regressive globalization: the state of global civil society in

2003, in M. Kaldor, H. Anheier and M. Glasius, *Global Civil Society 2003*, Oxford: Oxford University Press, 3–33.

Kaldor, M., Anheier, H., Glasius, M., Albrow, M., Seckinelgin, H. et al., eds. (2004–9) *Global Civil Society Yearbooks*, London: Sage.

Keck, M. and Sikkink, K. (1998) *Activists Beyond Borders*, Ithaca: Cornell University Press.

Khasnabish, A. (2008) *Zapatismo Beyond Borders: New Imaginations of Political Possibility*, Toronto: University of Toronto Press.

Khosrokhavar, F. (1996) Les nouvelles formes de mobilisation sociale, in A. Touraine, F. Dubet, D. Lapeyronnie, F. Khosrokhavar and M. Wieviorka, *Le grand refus*, Paris: Fayard, 195–246.

Kin Chi, L., ed. (2005) Le 'miracle chinois' vu de l'intérieur, *Alternatives* Sud, 12(5).

Kitschelt, H. (1995) Political opportunity structures and political protest: anti-nuclear movements in four democracies, in J. Dyvendak, M. Giugni, R. Koopmans and H. Kriesi, eds., *New Social Movements in Western Europe: A Comparative Analysis*, London: UCL Press.

Klandermans, B., Roefs, M. and Olivier, J. (1998) A movement takes office, in D. Meyer and S. Tarrow, eds., *The Social Movement Society*, Lanham: Rowman and Littlefield, 173–94.

Klein, N. (2002a) [2000] *No Logo*, 2nd edn, New York: Picador.

Klein, N. (2002b) *Fences and Windows: The Front Lines of the Globalization Debate*, Toronto: Vintage Canada.

Klein, N. (2007) *The Shock Doctrine: The Rise of Disaster Capitalism*, London: Penguin.

Klinenberg, E. (2007) *Fighting For Air: The Battle to Control America's Media*, New York: Metropolitan Books.

Konrad, G. (1984) [1982] *Anti-politics: An Essay*, London: Quartet Books.

Kriesi, H. (1993) Sviluppo organizzativo dei nuovi movimenti sociali e contesto politico, *Rivista italiana di scienza politica*, 23, 67–117.

Kriesi, H. (1996) The organizational structure of new social movements in a political context, in D. McAdam, J. McCarthy and M. Zald, eds., *Comparative Perspectives on Social Movements*, Cambridge: Cambridge University Press, 152–84.

Krugman, P. (1996) *Pop Internationalism*, Cambridge, MA: The MIT Press.

Kydland, F. and Prescott, E. (1977) Rules rather than discretion: the inconsistency of optimal plans, *Journal of Political Economics*, 85(3), 473–92.

Laclau, E. (2005) *On Populist Reason*, London: Verso.

Laïdi, Z. (1994) *Un monde privé de sens*, Paris: Fayard.

Lamoureux, D. (2004) Le féminisme et l'altermondialisme, *Recherches Féministes*, 17(2), 171–94.

Lappe, A. (2010) *Diet for a Hot Planet: The Climate Crisis at the End of Your Fork*, New York: Bloomsbury.

Latouche, S. (2002) À bas le développement durable! Vive la décroissance conviviale! *Silence*, 280, 8–13.

Laville, J. L., ed. (2007) *L'économie solidaire: une perspective internationale*, Paris: Hachette.

Le Bot, Y. (2009) *La grande révolte indienne*, Paris: R. Laffont.

Le Bot, Y. and Marcos, Subcomandante (1997) *Le rêve zapatiste*, Paris: Seuil.

Leonini, L. and Sassatelli, R., eds. (2008) *Il consumo critico: pratiche, discorsi, reti*, Rome: Laterza.

Loong-Yu, Au (2006) Chinese nationalism and the 'New Left', *Socialist Outlook*, www.isg-fi.org.uk/spip.php?article285, accessed 1 June 2010.

Lopez, L. (2009) Actores, movimientos y conflictos. ¿Es posible la acción colectiva en un contexto de fragmentación sociocultural? in F. Mestries, G. Pleyers and S. Zermeño, eds., *Movimientos sociales: de lo local a lo global*, Barcelona: Anthropos, 103–25.

López Bárcenas, F. (2005) *Legislación y derechoes indígenas en México*, Mexico, DF: CEDRSSA / Cámara de Diputados.

Lotringer, S. and Marazzi, C., eds. (2007) *Autonomia*, Los Angeles: Semiotext(e).

Louviaux, M. (2003) *D'un autre agir altermondialiste: l'analyse du Groupe d'Achat Commun de Barricade comme révélateur d'une pratique de contestation constructive*, Louvain-la-Neuve: UCL.

Lyotard, J. F. (1979) *La condition post-moderne*, Paris: Minuit.

Maclean, I., Montefiore, A. and Winch, P., eds. (1990) *The Political Responsibility of Intellectuals*, Cambridge: Cambridge University Press.

Marcos, Subcomandante (2007) [2003] *Calendrier des résistances*, Paris: Rue des Cascades.

Marcuse, H. (1981) [1964] *One Dimensional Man*, Boston: Beacon.

Marie, A. (1997) *L'Afrique des individus*, Paris: Kartala.

Martinez, E. (2000) Where was the color in Seattle? Looking for reasons why the Great Battle was so white, *Monthly Review*, 52(3), 141–8.

Massicotte, M. J. (2001) *Construyendo puentes en América del Norte: la emergencia de la Alianza Social Continental y sus redes transnacionales*, in R. Vargas Suárez, R. Gómez Arnau and J. Castro Rea, eds., *Las relaciones de México con Estados Unidos y Canadá*, Mexico: UNAM, 235–53.

Massicotte, M. J. (2004) Las organizaciones civiles y sociales mexicanas en las redes transnacionales, in J. Cadena Roa, ed.., *Las organizaciones civiles mexicanas hoy*, Mexico: UNAM, 347–86

Maye, D. and Kirwan, J. (2010) Alternative food networks, *Sociopedia*, ISA Online Encyclopedia.

McAdam, D. (1989) The biographical consequences of activism, *American Sociological Review*, 54, 744–60.

McAdam, D., Tarrow, S. and Tilly C. (2001) *Contentious Politics*, New York: Cambridge University Press.

McCarthy, J. D. and Zald, M. (1977) Resource mobilization and social movements: a partial theory, *American Journal of Sociology*, 82, 1212–41.

McDonald, K. (2002) From solidarity to fluidarity: social movements beyond 'collective identity' – the case of globalization conflicts, *Social Movements Studies*, 1(2), 109–28.

McDonald, K. (2006) *Global Movements*, Oxford: Blackwell.

McLaughlin, K., Osborne, S. and Ferlie, E., eds. (2002) *New Public Management: Current Trends and Future Prospects*, London: Routledge.

Mélenotte, S. (2009) Una experiencia zapatista: San Pedro Polhó, doce años después, in F. Mestries, G. Pleyers and S. Zermeño, eds., *Los movimientos sociales: de lo local a lo global*, Barcelona: Anthropos, 225–42.

Melucci, A. (1995) Individualisation et globalisation: au-delà de la modernité, in F. Dubet and M. Wieviorka, ed., *Penser le sujet: autour d'Alain Touraine*, Paris: Fayard, 433–48.

Melucci, A. (1996) *Challenging Codes*, Cambridge: Cambridge University Press.

Merklen, D. (2009) *Quartiers populaires, quartiers politiques*, Paris: La Dispute.

Merton, R. K. (1995) The Thomas Theorem and the Matthew Effect, *Social Forces*, 74(2), 379–424.

Mésini, B. (2003) *Anti/altermondialisation, des mondes en volition*, Aix: Pli Zetwal.

Mestrum, F. (2004) Le Forum social mondial: une alternative démocratique, in L. Delcourt, B. Duterme and F. Polet, ed., *Mondialisation des résistances: l'état des luttes 2004*, Paris: Syllepse, 205–20.

Michel, G. and Escárzaga, F., eds. (2001) *Sobre la marcha*, Mexico: UAM–Rizoma.

Michels, R. (1966) [1911] *Political Parties*, New York: Free Press.

Milani, C. (2009) Political ecology, environmental movements and transnational contention in Latin America, *Revista de Gestão Social e Ambiental*, 3, 141–59.

Milani, C. and de Freitas, C. (2007) O fórum social dos Estados Unidos em 2007: a manifestação alterglobalista no coração da hegemonia, *Portas*, 1, 43–66.

Millet, D. and Toussaint, E. (2005) *Who Owes Who? 50 Questions about World Debt*, New York: Zed Books.

Minc, A. (1997) *La mondialisation heureuse*, Paris: Plon.

Minc, A. (2003) *Epître à nos nouveaux maîtres*, Paris: Grasset.

Montagna, N. (2006) The de-commodification of urban space and the occupied social centres in Italy, *City*, 10(3), 295–304.

Montesquieu, C. (1979) [1748] *L'esprit des lois*, Paris: Flammarion.

MTD Solano, Colectivo Situaciones (2002) *La hipótesis 891: más allá de los piquetes*, Buenos Aires: De mano en mano.

Muñoz Ramirez, G. (2003) *20 y 10: el fuego y la palabra*, Mexico: Rebeldía y La Jornada.

Muxel, A. (2001) *L'expérience politique des jeunes*, Paris: Presses de Sciences Po.

Naughton, J (2001) Contested space: the internet and global civil society, in H. Anheier, M. Kaldor and M. Glasius, *Global Civil Society 2001*, London: Sage, 129–47.

Nava, M. (1992) *Changing Cultures: Feminism, Youth and Consumerism*, London: Sage.

Notes from nowhere (2003) *We Are Everywhere*, London: Verso.

Nuñes, R. (2005) Networks, open spaces, horizontality: instantiations, *Ephemera*, 5(2), 297–318.

Observatoire de la mondialisation (1998) *Lumière sur l'AMI: le test de Dracula*, Paris: L'esprit frappeur.

Olesen, T. (2005) *International Zapatismo*, London: Zed Books.

Olvera, J. (2003) *Sociedad civil, esfera pública y democratización en América Latina: México*, Mexico, DF: Fondo de Cultura Económica.

Ornelas, R (2007) *L'autonomie, axe de résistance zapatiste*, Paris: Rue des Cascades.

Osterweil, M. (2004) A cultural-political approach to reinventing the political, *International Social Science Journal*, 56(4), 495–506.

Osterweil, M. and Chesters, G. (2007) Global uprisings: toward a political of the artisan, in S. Shukaitis and G. Graeber, eds., *Constituent Imagination*, Oakland, CA: AK Press, 235–252.

Padilla, G. (2000) Droit fondamental indigène et droit constitutionnel, *Alternatives Sud*, 7(2), 213–30.

Park, M. (2009) Framing free trade agreements: the politics of nationalism in the anti-neoliberal globalization movement in South Korea, *Globalizations*, 6(4), 451–66.

Passet, R. (2001) *Éloge du mondialisme par un 'anti' présumé*, Paris: Fayard.

Passet, R. (2003) *L'émergence contemporaine de l'interrogation éthique en économie*, Paris: UNESCO.

Passet, R. (2006) Elections ATTAC: synthèse finale des rapports d'experts, http://hussonet.free.fr/rpasset.pdf, accessed 1 June 2010.

Patomäki, H. (2000) The Tobin Tax: a new phase in the politics of globalization? *Theory, Culture & Society*, 17(4), 77–91.

Patomäki, H. and Teivainen, T. (2005) *A Possible World: Democratic Transformation of Global Institutions*, London: Zed Books.

Pavarala, V. and Malik, K. (2007) *Other Voices: The Struggle for Community Radio in India* , New Delhi: Sage.

Petras, J. (2000) *La izquierda contraataca: conflicto de clases en América Latina en la era del neoliberalismo*, Madrid: Akal.

Petrella, R. (1996) *Écueils de la mondialisation*, Montreal: Fides.

Petrella, R. (2001) *The Water Manifesto*, New York: Zed Books.

Phelps-Brown, H. (1990) The counter-revolution of our time, *Industrial Relations*, 29(1), 1–14.

Picot, S. and Willert, M. (2002) Politik der Klick: Internet und Engagement Jugendicher, in K. Hurrelmann and M. Albert, eds., *Jugend 2002*, Frankfurt am Main: Fischer Taschenbuch Verlag, 221–68.

Pigeon, M., Hall, D., Lobina, E., Terhorst, P. and Lui, E. (2009) *Controlling the Agenda at WWF – The Multinationals' Network*, Brussels: Corporate Europe Observatory. www.waterjustice.org/uploads/attachments/wwf5-controlling-the-agenda-at-wwf.pdf, accessed 1 June 2010.

Pirotte, G. (2007) *La notion de société civile*, Paris: La Découverte.

Pleyers, G. (2003) Des black blocks aux alteractivistes: pôles et formes d'engagement des jeunes altermondialistes, *Lien Social et Politiques*, 51, 123–34.

Pleyers, G. (2004) Social Forums as an ideal model of convergence, *International Social Science Journal*, 56(182), 507–17.

Pleyers, G. (2005) *From disillusionment to a new culture of participation*, in J. Forbrig, ed., *Revisiting Youth Political Participation*. Strasbourg: Press of the Council of Europe, 133–44.

Pleyers, G. (2006) Sujet, expérience et expertise dans le mouvement altermondialiste, Ph.D. dissertation, Liège: ULg and Paris: EHESS.

Pleyers, G. (2007) *Forums sociaux mondiaux et défis de l'altermondialisme*, Louvain-la-Neuve: Academia.

Pleyers, G. (2009) Horizontalité et efficacité dans les réseaux altermondialistes, *Sociologie et Sociétés*, 41(2), 89–110.

Pleyers, G. (2010) El altermundismo en México, in I. Bizberg and F. Zapata, eds., *Movimientos sociales en el México al inicio del siglo XXI*, Mexico: El Colegio de México.

Pleyers, G., ed. (2011) *L'alter-consommation*, Paris: Desclée de Brouwer.

Pleyers, Gordy (2006) *L'endoctrinement affectif du citoyen: la politique à l'éclairage des sciences psychologiques*, Liège: Presses de l'Université de Liège.

Polanyi, K. (2001) [1944] *The Great Transformation*, Boston: Beacon Press.

Polet, F. (2008) *Clés de lecture de l'altermondialisme*, Charleroi: Couleurs Livre.

Polletta, F. (2002) *Freedom is an Endless Meeting*, Chicago: University of Chicago Press.

Polletta, F. (2005) How participatory democracy became White: culture and organizational choices, *Mobilization*, 10(2), 271–88.

Poncelet, M. (1994) *Une utopie post-tiersmondiste*, Paris: L'Harmattan.

Ponniah, T. (2005) Autonomy and political strategy: building the other superpower, *International Journal of Urban and Regional Research*, 29(2), 441–3.

Ponniah, T. (2006) The World Social Forum vision: radical democracy vs. neoliberal globalization, Ph.D. dissertation, Worcester, MA: Clarck University.

Putnam, R. (1993) *Making Democracy Work: Civic Traditions in Modern Italy*, Princeton, NJ: Princeton University Press

Putnam, R. (2000) *Bowling Alone: America's Declining Social Capital*, New York: Simon & Schuster.

Quaden, G. (1990) *Politique économique*, Brussels: Labor.

Randeria, S. (2007) The state of globalization: legal plurality, overlapping sovereignties and ambiguous alliances between civil society and the cunning state in India, *Theory, Culture & Society*, 24, 1–33.

Rebick, J. (2009) *Transforming Power*, Toronto: Penguin Books.

Rebughini, P. and Famiglietti, A. (2008) Un consumo diverso è possibile: la via dei centri sociali, in L. Leonini and R. Sassatelli, eds., *Il consumo critico*, Rome: Laterza, 85–112.

Reese, E., Chase-Dunn, C., Anantram, K. et al. (2008) Research note: surveys of World Social Forum participants show influence of place and base in the global public sphere, *Mobilization*, 13, 431–45.

Restier-Melleray, C. (1990) Experts et expertise, *Revue Française de Sciences Politiques*, 40(4), 540–85.

Rochín Virues, D. (2002) La huelga universitaria. ¿Una manifestación de las culturas juveniles de fin de milenio? in Nateras Domínguez, ed., *Jóvenes, cultura e identidades urbanas*, Mexico: Porrua, 327–45.

Roma, P. (2001) *Jaque a la globalización*, Barcelona: Grijalbo.

Rosanvallon, P. (2006) *La contre-démocratie*, Paris: Seuil.

Rowbotham, S. and Linkogle, S., eds. (2006) *Women Resist Globalization*, London: Zed Books.

Sapir, J. (2002) *Les Économistes contre la démocratie: pouvoir, mondialisation et démocratie*, Paris: Albin Michel.

Sassen, S. (2007) *Sociology of Globalization*, New York: Norton.

Sassen, S. (2008) *Territory, Authority, Rights*, Princeton, NJ: Princeton University Press.

Scholte, J. A. (2005) Globalization: A Critical Introduction, *2nd edition*, New York: Palgrave Macmillan.

Schumacher, U. (2003) *Lohn und Sinn: Individuelle Kombinationen von Erwerbsarbeit und freiwilligem Engagement*, Paris: Leske & Budrich.

Scott, J. (1998) *Seeing Like a State*, Yale: Yale University Press.

Sen, A. (1999) *Development as Freedom*, Oxford: Oxford University Press.

Sen, J. (2004) The long march to another world: reflections of a member of the WSF India Committee in 2002 on the first year of the WSF process in India, in J. Sen, A. Anand, A. Escobar and P. Waterman, eds., *World Social Forum Challenging Empires*, New Delhi: Viveka Foundation, 293–310.

Sen, J., Anand, A., Escobar, A. and Waterman, P., eds. (2004) *World Social Forum Challenging Empires*, New Delhi: Viveka Foundation.

Sen, J., Keraghel, C., eds. (2004) Explorations in open space: the World Social Forum and cultures of politics, *International Social Science Journal*, 56(182).

Sen, J. and Kumar, M., eds. (2007) *A Political Programme for the World Social Forum? Democracy, Substance and Debate in the Bamako Appeal and the Global Justice Movements*, New Delhi: CACIM and Durban: Centre for Civil Society.

Sennett, R. (1998) *The Corrosion of Character*, New York: Norton.

Sennett, R. (2006) *The Culture of the New Capitalism*, New Haven: Yale University Press.

Seyfang, G. (2009) *The New Economics of Sustainable Consumption*, London: Palgrave.

Shukaitis, S. and Graeber, G., eds. (2007) *Constituent Imagination*, Oakland, CA: AK Press.

Sikkink, Kathryn (2002) Restructuring world politics: the limits and asymmetries of soft power, in S. Khagram, J. Riker and K. Sikkin, eds., *Restructuring World Politics: Transnational Social Movements, Networks, and Norms*, Minneapolis University of Minnesota Press, 301–17.

Smith, J. (2008) *Social Movements for Global Democracy*, Baltimore: Johns Hopkins University Press.

Smith, J., Juris, J. and the Social Forum Research Collective (2008) We are the ones we have been waiting for, *Mobilization*, 13(4), 373–94.

Smith, J. and Wiest, D. (2005) The uneven geography of global civil society: national and global influences on transnational association, *Social Forces*, 84, 621–52.

Sousa Santos, B. (2004) The World Social Forum: towards a counter-hegemonic globalisation, in J. Sen, A. Anand, A. Escobar and P. Waterman, eds., *World Social Forum Challenging Empires*, New Delhi: Viveka Foundation, 146–56.

Sousa Santos, B. (2006) *The Rise of the Global Left: The World's Social Forum and Beyond*, London: Zed Books.

Sousa Santos, B. (2009) Looking ahead: taking the larger picture, interview by J. Sen, New Delhi: Cacim. www.openspaceforum.net/twiki/tiki-print_article.php?articleId=799, accessed 1 June 2010.

Spahn, P. (1996) The Tobin Tax and exchange rate stability, *Finance and Development*, 33(2), 24–7.

Srikant, P. (2009) *Tribal Movement in Orissa: A Struggle against Modernization?* Working Paper 215, Bangalore: ISEC.

Starr, A. (2004) How can anti-imperialism not be anti-racist? *Journal of World-Systems*, 10(1), 119–52.

Starr, P. (1979) The phantom community, in J. Case and R. Taylor, eds., *Co-ops, Communes and Collectives*, New York: Random House, 245–73.

Stiglitz, J. (2002) *Globalization and its Discontents*, New York: W. W. Norton.

Stiglitz, J. (2008) The end of neo-liberalism? www.project-syndicate.org/commentary/stiglitz101, accessed 1 June 2010.

Stiglitz, J. (2009a) *Recommendations by the Commission of Experts of the President of the General Assembly on Reforms of the International Monetary and Financial System*, New York: United Nations.

Stiglitz, J. (2009b) México no supo manejar la crisis, *El Universal* (Mexico), 19 November.

Stiglitz, J. and Charlton, A. (2006) *Fair Trade for All: How Trade Can Promote Development*, Oxford: Oxford University Press.

Stiglitz, J., Sen, A. and Fitoussi, J. P. (2009) *Report by the Commission on the Measurement of Economic Performance and Social Progress*, Paris: OECD.

Strange, S. (1998) *Mad Money*, Ann Arbor: University of Michigan Press.

Svampa, M. (2005) Risques d'isolement des piqueteros argentins, *Manière de Voir*, 84 (En lutte! État des résistances dans le monde), 16–17.

Svampa, M. and Pereyra, S. (2003) *Entre la ruta y el barrio: la experiencia de las organizaciones piqueteros*, Buenos Aires: Biblio.

Tamayo, S. (1999) Del movimiento urbano popular al movimiento ciudadano, *Estudios sociológicos*, 17(50), 499–518.

Tarrow, S. (1999) *Power in Movement: Social Movements and Contentious Politics*, Cambridge: Cambridge University Press.

Tarrow, S. (2005) *The New Transnational Activism*, Cambridge: Cambridge University Press.

Teivainen, T. (2002) *Enter Economism, Exit Politics: Experts, Economic Policy and Damage to Democracy*, London: Zed Books.

Teivainen, T. (2008) *Democracy in Movement: The World Social Forum as a Political Process*, London: Routledge.

Thomas, W. I. and Thomas, E. S. (1928) *The Child in America: In the Laboratory and In the Home*, New York: Knopf.

Thompson, E. (1963) *The Making of the English Working Class*, New York: Vintage Books.

Thompson, M. (2009) Democracy 2.0: the future of the Internet & civil society, CSGG lecture, LSE, 24 Feb.

Tilly, C. (1986) *La France conteste de 1600 à nos jours*, Paris: Fayard.

Tilly, C. (2003) *Stories, Identities, and Political Change*, Lanham: Rowman and Littlefield.

Tilly, C. (2004) *Social Movements 1768–2004*, Boulder, CO: Paradigm.

Tobin, J. (1974) *The New Economics One Decade Older*, Princeton, NJ: Princeton University Press.

Tobin, J. (1978) A proposal for international monetary reform, *Eastern Economic Journal*, 4, 153–9.

Tobin, J. (1997) Why we need sand in the market's gears, *Washington Post*, 21 Dec.

Tocqueville, A. (2000) [1835–40] *Democracy in America*, Chicago: University of Chicago Press.

Toscano, E. (2010) I'm my personal revolution: The purple movement in Italy, *Open Democracy*, 26 May.

Toscano, E. (2011) Entre radicalisme et créativité: les Centres Sociaux en Italie, in G. Pleyers, ed., *Alter-consommation*, Paris: Desclée de Brouwer.

Touraine, A. (1978) *La voix et le regard*, Paris: Seuil.

Touraine, A. (1984) *Le retour de l'acteur*, Paris: Fayard.

Touraine, A. (2000) [1997] *Can We Live Together?* Cambridge: Polity Press.

Touraine, A. (2001) [1999] *Beyond Neoliberalism*, Cambridge: Polity Press.

Touraine, A. (2002) From understanding society to discovering the subject, *Anthropological Theory*, 2(4), 387–98.

Touraine, A. (2007) [2005] *A New Paradigm to Understand Today's World*, Cambridge: Polity Press.

Touraine, A., Dubet, F., Wieviorka, M. and Strzelecki, J. (1983) *Solidarity: Poland 1980–1981*, Cambridge: Cambridge University Press.

Touraine, A., Hegeduz, S., Wieviorka, M. and Dubet, F. (1980) *La prophétie anti-nucléaire*, Paris: Seuil.

Touraine, A. and Khosrokhavar, F. (2000) *La recherche de soi: dialogue sur le sujet*, Paris: Fayard.

Toussaint, E. (2004) *Globalisation: Reality, Resistance and Alternatives*, Mumbai: Vika.

Toussaint, E. and Zacharie, A. (2000) *Le bateau ivre de la mondialisation*, Paris: Syllepse.

UNCTAD (2009) *The Global Economic Crisis: Systemic Failures and Multilateral Remedies*, New York and Geneva: United Nations.

UNDP (2002) *A Global Analysis of UNDP Support to Decentralization and Local Governance*, New York: UNDP.

UNDP (2006) *Human Development Report 2006*, New York: UNDP.

Varese, S. (1996) Parroquianismo y globalización: las etnicidades indígenas ante el tercer milenio, in S. Varese, ed., *Pueblos indios, soberanía y globalismo*, Quito: Abya-Yala, 15–30.

Wade, R. (2007) Should We Worry about Income Inequalities? in D. Held and A. Kaya, eds., *Global Inequality*, Cambridge: Polity Press, 103–31.

Wahl, P. (1997) Mythos und Realität der internationalen Zivilgesellschaft, in E. Altvater, A. Bruenengräber, M. Haake and H. Walk, eds., *Vernetzt und verstrickt*, Bochum: Westphalisches Dampfboot, 293–314.

Wainwright, H. (2005) Civil society, democracy and power, in H. Anheier, M. Gloasius and M. Kaldor, eds., *Global Civil Society 2004/5*, London: Sage, 94–119.

Wainwright, H. (2009) *Reclaim the State: Experiments in Popular Democracy*, Salt Lake City, UT: Seagull Books.

Wallach, J. (2001) *The Platonic Political Art: A Study of Critical Reason and Democracy*, University Park: Pennsylvania State University Press.

Wallerstein, I. (1999) *L'après libéralisme*, La tour d'Aigues: Aube.

Wallerstein, I. (2004) The ecology and the economy: what is rational? *Fernand Braudel Review*, 27(4), 273–83.

Waterman, P. and Timms, J. (2004) Trade union internationalism and civil society in the making, in H. Anheier, M. Glasius and M. Kaldor, eds., *Global Civil Society 2004–5*, London: Sage, 175–202.

Weber, M. (1963) [1919] *Le savant et le politique*, Paris: Plon.

Weber, M. (1995) [1922] *Économie et société*, Vol. I, Paris: Plon.

Weber, M. (2004) [1919] *The Vocation Lectures*, Indianapolis: Hacket.

Whitaker, C. (2004) The WSF as open space, in J. Sen, A. Anand, A. Escobar and P. Waterman, eds., *World Social Forum Challenging Empires*, New Delhi: Viveka Foundation, 111–22.

Whitaker, C. (2006) *Towards a New Politics: What Future for the World Social Forum?* New York: Zed Books.

Whitaker, C., de Sousa Santos, B. and Cassen, B. (2006) The World Social Forum: where do we stand and where are we going? in M.

Glasius, M. Kaldor and H. Anheier, eds., *Global Civil Society 2005/6*, London: Sage, 28–50.

Wieviorka, M., ed. (2003) *Un autre monde . . . contestations, dérives et surprises dans l'antimondialisation*, Paris: Balland.

Wieviorka, M. (2005) After new social movements, *Social Movement Studies*, 4(1), 1–19.

Wieviorka, M. (2009a) *Neuf leçons de sociologie*, Paris: Laffont.

Wieviorka, M. (2009b) *Violence: A New Approach*, London: Sage.

Willke, H. (1998) Soziologische Aufklärung der Demokratietheorie, in H. Brunkhorst, ed., *Demokratischer Experimentalismus*, Frankfurt: Suhrkamp, 13–32.

Williamson, J. (1990) *Latin American Adjustment: How Much Has Happened?* Washington: Institute for International Economics.

Wintrebert, R. (2007) *Attac, la politique autrement?* Paris: La Découverte.

World Bank (1997–2000) *Working Papers of the Social Capital Initiative*, Washington, DC: World Bank.

Wortis, H. and Rabinowitz, C., eds. (1972) *The Women's Movement*, New York: Halsted Press.

Wright, A. and Wolford, W. (2003) *To Inherit the Earth: The Landless Movement and the Struggle for a New Brazil*, Oackland, CA: FoodFirst.

Wright, S. (2008) Building networks of food sovereignty in South and Southeast Asia, paper presented at the International Studies Association 49th Annual Convention, San Francisco.

Wysham, D., Cavanagh, J. and Arruda, M., eds. (1994) *Beyond Bretton Woods: Alternatives to the Global Economic Order*, London: Pluto Press.

Youniss, J., Bales, S., Christmas-Best, V., Diversi, M., McLaughlin, M. and Silbereisen, R. (2002) Youth civic engagement in the twenty-first century, *Journal of Research on Adolescence*, 12(1), 121–48.

Zacharie, A. (2009) La troisième vie du FMI, *Le Monde Diplomatique*, May.

Zermeño, S. (1996) *La sociedad derrotada, el desorden mexicano en el fin de siglo*, Mexico City: Siglo XXI.

Zermeño, S. (2005) *La desmodernidad méxicana y las alternativas a la violencia y a la exclusión en nuestros días*, Mexico: Oceano.

Zermeño, S. (2010) *Reconstruir a México en el siglo XXI*, Mexico City: Oceano.

Zibechi, R. (2006) *Dispersar el oder: los movimientos como poderes antiestatales*, Buenos Aires: Libros de la Esquina.

Zumbrunnen, J. (2004) Elite domination and clever citizen: Aristophanes' Archanians and knights, *Political Theory*, 32(5), 656–77.

Index

Page numbers in bold indicate the main reference for the relevant heading